W9-ARQ-555

The Excellent Investment Advisor

The Excellent Investment Advisor

by Nick Murray

Also by Nick Murray

On Becoming A Great Wholesaler

Book design: Sisco&Evans, Ltd.

Printed in the United States of America

Library of Congress Catalog Card Number: 96-095073
ISBN 0-9655161-0-5

This book is dedicated
with love, and laughter, and
something very much like awe,
to my daughter

Karen Elizabeth Murray

Sister Golden Hair Surprise

"The only wealth in this world is children."

—**Michael Corleone,**
in Francis Ford Coppola's film,
The Godfather, Part III

Table of Contents

Luke Skywalker: All right.
I'll give it a try.

Yoda: No!
Try not.
Do.
Or do not.
There is no "try."

—from George Lucas's film,
Star Wars: The Empire Strikes Back

Two words

I. A Word About Terminology. The audience for this book is as wide as the retail financial services industry itself, and yet I had to name that audience something specific. "The excellent stockbroker/financial planner/insurance agent/bank investment representative/fee advisor" would have covered most (though still not all) of the bases...but it would have made (a) your eyes glaze over and (b) my writing hand fall off. So I settled on the term "investment advisor," not in the narrow SEC definition of a registered investment advisor, but in the broader context of everyone who gives professional advice to Americans on investments as the funding media for their financial hopes and dreams. The term was chosen simply for its inclusiveness and its economy.

II. A Word About Gender. If one is fortunate enough, as I am in this book, to be writing about a craft that is as often practiced by excellent women as by excellent men, one encounters a problem of language. The two most common ways of handling this problem are both unthinkable. I simply refuse to fall back on the mind-numbing he-or-she ("The excellent investment advisor must educate his or her clients so that..."). And political correctness is still no excuse for bad grammar, of the singular-noun-plural-pronoun variety ("When a person becomes an investment advisor, they must learn...").

My solution, I thought, was to go back and forth between genders, pretty much at random. But although you'll find The Excellent Investment Advisor described as "he" and "she" about equally often, somehow the journeyman (*sic*) advisor is always described as "he". I wonder if this isn't some insidious, unconscious sexism-in-reverse.

So let me make my position clear. The rise of women is, in my judgment, the single best thing that has happened in the financial services industry since I entered it, nearly 30 years ago. Women have made the business not merely better, but finer. On the odd chance that one infers any different attitude from this book, or from any other aspect of my work, I submit with the utmost respect that the fault is neither the book's nor mine.

Author's Preface

I began to write the book *Serious Money: The Art of Marketing Mutual Funds* on a plane home to New York from London, where my family had taken me for my 47th birthday: October 11, 1990.

That turned out to be a fairly resonant date in the history of American securities markets, for it was on October 11 that the stock market bottomed after its last 20% decline. The closing low for the Dow Jones Industrial Average that day was about 2365.

But I wasn't motivated to write the book by the state of the markets. Instead, I was observing a virtually tectonic shift in the way Americans chose to make their personal investments. From a nation of savers, we had, I believed, finally become a nation of investors. But whereas in the past investors had created their own portfolios by buying individual stocks and bonds, I was sure that the 1990s would be a new era: of managed money in general, and mutual funds in particular.

Mutual fund assets had gone from zero in 1924—the year of the founding of America's first mutual fund, Massachusetts Investors Trust—to a little over a trillion dollars (including money market funds) by year-end 1990. I was thoroughly convinced that the second trillion dollars of fund assets would come in during the next 10 years. That turned out to be spectacularly wrong: six years later, the balance was over $3 trillion. (And even that statistic fails to account for the hypergrowth of assets in "wrap" accounts, variable annuities and variable universal life insurance.)

And yet, on the eve of this explosion in America's desire for money management, there did not exist anywhere in print in 1990 a complete system for the sales and marketing of mutual funds. The growth of fund assets had been a function of what economists call "demand pull." The financial services industry wasn't really selling managed money to the investor (not least of all because it didn't know how); the investor was buying it from us. We were a bit like the general who demanded to know which way his troops had gone, so he could ride out to lead them. Indeed, a lot of the industry still thought of managed money as a fringe product.

The fundamental sales/marketing conundrum we faced was, I believed, that managed money was an intensely relationship-oriented approach to investing, whereas our industry's skills and style were still single-mindedly transaction-oriented. So I set out to write a genuinely complete system for communicating/counseling/selling managed money with the emphasis on mutual funds.

For reasons I still don't entirely understand, *Serious Money* quickly became the all-time best-selling book on the investment sales/marketing process. Over 100,000 copies were sold in less than five years, to brokerage firms, banks, insurance companies, fund management firms and financial planning groups throughout the English-speaking world. (Indeed, on a per capita basis, *Serious Money* is as popular in Canada, Australia and New Zealand as it is in the United States.) Along the way, it completely changed my life.

But, as the fifth anniversary of *Serious Money's* publication (August 1996) approached, it was clear to me that, however ahead of its time the book might have been in 1991, the industry's major themes and issues had begun to pass it by. For instance, the so-called load/no-load issue is practically the spine of *Serious Money*. Today, fees vs. commissions—indeed, the vast menu of pricing options—is the issue we seem to struggle with most. Moreover, some of the essential arguments in *Serious Money* (why managed money; what managed money can do for you) are now, thank heaven, moot. And no matter how conceptually right it may still be, a book the last major world event in which is

Desert Storm is simply, like its author, getting old. Finally, if I felt in 1990-91 that virtually no one was bullish enough, these days I can't escape a gnawing concern that most folks are a bit *too* bullish—or at least insufficiently conscious of the price of "performance." (People seem not to see that it isn't called the market *cycle* for nothing.)

Still, I had no desire simply to update *Serious Money*. The business has changed too much; the audience has changed too much. And, frankly, I've changed too much.

For one thing, *Serious Money* spent a lot of time helping you explain how all the different kinds of funds *work*. Five years on, I find our industry far too concerned with how investments (and portfolios thereof) *work*, and not nearly concerned enough with how real people *feel*. (Even as far back as *Serious Money*, I repeatedly said that feelings are to facts as 19 is to one. This message, I now believe, has gotten completely lost.)

Next, the cautionary comments of a moment ago notwithstanding, I've grown far less tolerant of debt investments, and correspondingly more zealous about equities. Again, *Serious Money* was premised in part on the idea that people understood bonds reasonably well and bond funds far less well, so it gave the latter a lot fairer hearing than I would today. With time, I've come to see that the fundamental 21st-century financial risk is not losing one's money but outliving it, which means equities are even more critical to financial survival than I thought they were five years ago. Moreover, *Serious Money* was written when the Berlin Wall was only a year gone, so the global capitalist revolution was still in its Lexington-and-Concord phase. Today, capitalism is the organizing principle of most of the human activity on the globe, and to be anything but a raging long-term bull on equities is to have missed the entire point of the last 10 years.

Finally, if the major initiative of *Serious Money* (in a world still entirely commission-based) was gathering assets, our increasingly fee-based world demands that a greater emphasis be placed on retaining and growing those assets, which is both a different psychology and a different skill set. ***Serious Money* was, in that sense, about getting money to move. This book is about getting it to stop moving.**

But for all the differences between *Serious Money* and the present volume, I hope you'll find the similarities—or at least the consistencies—far greater. For to me, *The Excellent Investment Advisor* pushes much deeper into the same territory first explored by *Serious Money*...and confirms that this territory is, indeed, the Promised Land.

Our amazing capacity to do good for the people who trust us (and for their heirs), our ability to integrate a tremendous variety of investments into a total financial plan, and our potential simultaneously to make a good living and a meaningful life...these are the essence of the wonderful profession we've chosen. They've only gotten better in the last five years. If you'll use this book consistently and well, they'll only get better still.

Foreword

The importance of what we do

"A great society is one whose men of business think greatly of their functions."

—Alfred North Whitehead

One day in the autumn of 1994, I was sitting in the speakers' "ready room" at the Hynes Convention Center in Boston, waiting to give the closing keynote speech at the annual convention of the International Association for Financial Planning.

I was (and still am) honored that the IAFP had invited me to fill this critically important slot, which had been occupied in previous years by such luminaries as former British prime minister Edward Heath and superstar money manager Mario Gabelli. Always at least semi-nervous before speaking [*if you're not, it means you don't care anymore*], I was, just at that moment, totally wired.

So when someone sent in a note to me, I tore it open anxiously. (Was it a reprieve? Could I somehow get out of having to make this speech?) It was a greeting card, with a handwritten message from a financial planner, telling me how much my work had meant to her—and to her clients—over the years, and how much she was looking forward to my talk. In my somewhat ragged nervous state, I started to choke up, as I finished reading the handwritten part, and turned to the card's printed message. It said, "*We make a living by what we get. We make a life by what we give.*"

For a moment, I was totally thunderstruck. "Wow," I thought, "that's...profound. It's...real, real *deep.* It's...it's...*it's absolutely, completely, spectacularly wrong! And that's the whole point of this glorious business!*"

When we do our job right, there's absolutely no friction between what we do for our clients and what we do for our families and ourselves. Indeed, the more good we do for people, the more assets they give us to manage, and the happier they are to refer us to their families, friends and colleagues. In turn, our income—as well as our deep satisfaction in our work, without which the income is ultimately empty—grows and grows. We make both a living *and* a life by virtue of the excellent advice we give. We achieve financial independence—and perhaps even multigenerational wealth—by providing those priceless endowments to our clients. We do well by doing good.

Moreover, the huge preponderance of the investing population cannot secure these endowments by dint of its own knowledge and efforts. Not one investor in a hundred, I'm convinced, can achieve lasting financial security unaided. Thus, what we do is not only critical to the future of the people we serve; *they can't do it without us.* (Whether they realize this or not is an entirely different matter. Most do; many—ceaselessly bombarded by "no-help" fund advertising and financial journalism—don't. You can lead an investor to water, but you can't make him think.)

This, then, is the wellspring from which the Excellent Investment Advisor draws virtually limitless reserves of strength:

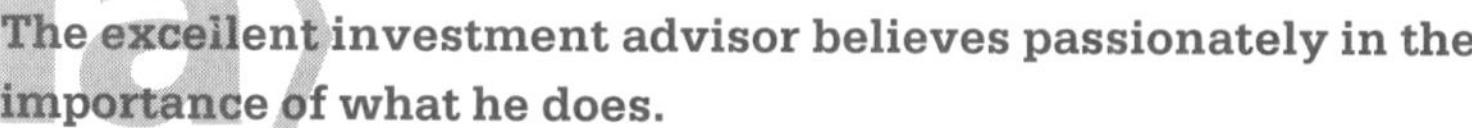

The excellent investment advisor believes passionately in the importance of what he does.

The Excellent Investment Advisor can, I believe, do more good for more people—and can then make that good endure far longer—than any physician who ever walked the earth.

When a person becomes ill, he goes to a doctor, who commences to fight a battle on the patient's behalf, using all of his powers and skills.

And perhaps, this time, he wins the battle. But he always loses the war. The physician fights a glorious holding action in the context of a war that he must ultimately lose: the war with death. A doctor's victories, then, are always temporary; his defeat is always final.

The war that the Excellent Investment Advisor wages—the war for lifetime financial independence—can be won, assuming the "patient's" cooperation, every single time. Moreover, that good can and should be made to transcend death. Today, we have the tools—or at least have ready access to the tools—for the endowment of multi-generational wealth. The fortune created by the Excellent Investment Advisor passes efficiently to future generations, and continues to accrete.

The memory of a parent's love, and the financial freedom inherited from that parent, need not be totally separate things. And if one's children and grandchildren are warmed by that love and nurtured by that wealth, is one not, in some very real sense, still alive?

The Excellent Investment Advisor believes in just that kind of immortality, and commits herself wholeheartedly (and confidently) to its attainment. Perhaps she can't prove that wealth created by her will provide medical school tuition to the person yet unborn who will rid the earth of leukemia. She can't prove that that wealth will buy someone the leisure to write the novel (or make the film) that will be to America in 2025 what *The Great Gatsby* was in 1925. But she knows that such good is not impossible. And it is just this—the limitless possibility for good—that fuels all her efforts.

Excellence, by definition, is exceedingly rare…and it feels wonderful. (Mediocrity, also by definition, is quite commonplace, and it feels awful.) There is, then, a high price to be paid for excellence—and it is a price that the Excellent Investment Advisor is happy to pay, because of the immense material and spiritual returns he receives on his investment.

Moreover, excellence feeds on itself (as does mediocrity; we are never standing still, but always either spiraling up or spiraling down). As our confidence in the quality of our work grows, we feel—and project—a deep conviction, when we sit with a prospective client, that we may just be able to alter the whole course of his family's history.

It is the intensity of that belief in ourselves and in our power to do good—not the accumulation of technical information that we know—which attracts and binds quality clients to us. **The Excellent Investment Advisor inspires people to believe in her to the extent that she believes in herself.**

(The journeyman investment advisor—with his numberless charts, graphs and scattergrams—unconsciously says, in effect, "I can't imagine you're going to believe in me, any more than I do, but maybe I can overwhelm you with all this intellectually irrefutable third-party technobabble." And then he genuinely doesn't understand why people find him such a turn-off. The journeyman always takes rejection personally—and is, I'm convinced, entirely correct in doing so.)

Knowledge, as we will have occasion to observe many times throughout this book, is of very finite usefulness to the Excellent Investment Advisor. He deals primarily with the hopes, dreams and fears of his clients. (Specifically, he works to make the hopes and dreams become reality, and to banish the fears forever.) Seeing that these are fundamentally emotional issues, the Excellent Investment Advisor perceives that they do not lend themselves to intellectual solutions.

Fear, in particular, is insusceptible to reason—and fear, not ignorance, is the primary cause of the failure of most investment plans. (In the end, which investments people buy isn't that important. The thing that matters most is what people do—or, with the proper advice, don't do—when those investments are down 25%-30%, which they will one day surely be.)

Thus, the greatest part of the Excellent Investment Advisor's capacity to do good is not in what he knows. And he does not primarily manage his clients' investments; he manages their emotions. His ability to modify his clients' behavior, rather than his exquisitely nuanced understanding of asset allocation, is what earns him treasure on earth and in heaven. The battle he fights is not one of knowledge vs. ignorance, but of faith vs. fear. And he operates not primarily from his store of knowledge, but from his belief system.

The Excellent Investment Advisor knows that her ability to do lasting good for her clients and their families is a pure, absolute function of their belief and trust in her. To the extent that you focus people's attention on the plans/portfolios you've designed for them, you diminish their sense of reliance on you. This is something the excellent advisor will simply never do, because neither her plans nor her portfolios are her ultimate product. Above all,

(eia)

The excellent investment advisor knows that her product is herself.

Thus, the excellent advisor would never dream of saying that his mutual fund portfolios will "outperform" those of some other advisor. In part, as we've just seen, this is because the critical variable isn't investment "performance" but investor behavior. And in part, it's because the excellent advisor is far too sane to make a statement he might immediately be asked to prove, and can't. But most of all, the excellent advisor would never mortgage his relationship with a client to a variable over which he has no control: "performance." Instead, he will say,

> "I can promise you that, throughout all of the years and even decades that we work together, you will never find another investment advisor who'll care more about you and your family, or who'll be more deeply committed to the realization of your financial goals.

I promise to invest your capital as carefully as I do my own, because I know that your hopes for your family's future are every bit as sacred to you as mine are to me.

I commit to tell you the plain, unvarnished truth all the time, especially when you may not want to hear it. When you ask me a question the answer to which I don't know, I promise always to say 'I don't know'—and then to move heaven and earth to get you the answer.

Finally, I will never, never, **never** tell you I can do something I can't, nor will I tell you I am going to do something, and then not do it.

You will surely encounter financial advisors 'smarter' than I am, and just as surely you'll run across advisors who are cheaper than I am. (Let me tell you, though, that you'll almost certainly never find someone who's **both** 'smarter' **and** cheaper.) But you will never in your life find an advisor you can trust more implicitly than you can trust me.

If we work together, in that spirit of mutual trust, there's nothing within reason that we can't accomplish. And perhaps the most important thing is: **you'll never have to worry anymore.**

You see, I insist that my clients plan, and then stick to the plan. Beyond that, I encourage them to hope, because I know that in investing, optimism is the only long-term realism.

But I absolutely forbid my clients to worry, because in a very real sense that's what you're hiring me to do. If you're going to pay for my investment counsel, and then worry about it, you haven't really accepted my advice, which in effect means you don't trust me. I can't handle your account on that basis; it wouldn't be fair to either of us.

Understand clearly that you are being asked to entrust your family's financial future to me. Not to a particular financial plan, not to an investment portfolio—to **me** (*optional*: and my firm). And I, for my part, am offering to accept that responsibility.

Do you feel that that's a basis on which we can proceed?"

Be assured of this: any prospect who can say "yes" to this approach is very probably a Client-For-Life (hereinafter referred to as a CFL). And, as we will see in a later chapter, it may only take 250 CFL family units—blissfully allowing you to do all of the good you're capable of doing for them—to make your professional life a source of the utmost happiness.

By the same token, someone who says "no" (or just, "Well, wait a minute; exactly which mutual funds do you want me to buy?"—which is the same as "no") is right. He's said he doesn't trust you, and isn't prepared to try to do so. In other words, he's said, "I refuse to let you wreak your limitless potential for good on me and my family." Let him go in peace. For many are called, but few are chosen.

You have more power to do good—and to do well by doing good—than virtually anyone you'll ever know. But that power exists only potentially, until you induce someone to set it aflame with the spark of trust.

"And the glow from that fire," as President Kennedy said, "can truly light the world."

1

The ghost of business future and the ghost of business past

"It ain't what a man don't know as makes him a fool, but what he does know as ain't so."

—**Josh Billings**

If you're just starting out in the financial services profession, you may be very daunted by the enormity of what you don't know yet. Don't be.

First of all, as we'll see, the things of paramount importance that you need to know are few, and relatively simple. Those things are easily understood, if not so easily practiced. And, in the end, ours is not a profession which rewards us for what we know. It rewards us for what we do, and for what we cause other people to do. (Indeed, after nearly 30 years in the business, I would say that, as a formula for success, doing is to knowing as four is to one.)

More to the point of this chapter, though, I invite the industry newcomer to delight in that status. Why? Because you never have to struggle with the burden of everything we veterans are having to unlearn.

The retail financial services industry changed more in the 1990s than it had since those fellows started trading government bonds under the buttonwood tree on Wall Street in 1792. In fact, there was no such thing as a "financial services industry" before 1990 or so. There were instead three heavily armed camps, each occupying a different sector of the war zone: banks, insurance companies and stockbrokers. (A fourth column, called financial planners, was fighting a guerilla action up in the hills.)

In essence, though, this was a phony war. The three major combatants had neither the weapons nor the desire to fight a decisive battle with each other. Banks took deposits and made loans; insurers insured life and health, and sold fixed annuities to the terminally chicken-hearted; stockbrokers sold stocks and bonds, and did a marginal business in a wimpy little product called mutual funds. And each combatant spent tens of millions of dollars every year telling the public that the other guys' products were carcinogens.

Looking back now, one can see that the seeds of the destruction of this uneasy truce were sown in the 1970s, with the advent of the industry's first truly revolutionary product since the mutual fund itself: the money market fund. Once the public could be induced to make the titanic act of faith that money market funds would never "break a buck" (i.e. reflect a net asset value of less than a dollar a share), the stampede was on. If you could get the same "safety" *de facto* from a money fund that you'd been getting *de jure* from an FDIC-insured passbook savings account—and at a higher yield—who wouldn't do it? Add check-writing privileges to that package, and you've eliminated the need for a lot of checking accounts (or at least a lot of checking account *balances*; same difference).

Next, the wild bull market in stocks and bonds that was born in 1982 began to have its effect on the life insurance industry. Life insurers had started to see the enormous potential for wrapping investments inside the guarantees and tax protection of an annuity contract in the '70s, via the success of the single-premium deferred annuity. But it wasn't until variable annuity sales took off—and then somebody had the bright idea of variable life insurance—that the life companies began to think the unthinkable: maybe the people who'd been saying "buy term and invest the difference" all those years were right. And, of course, life insurance agents found that their relationship-oriented sales skills were perfect for mutual funds.

Stockbrokers, meanwhile, had been gaining market share from both banks (through money funds) and life insurers (by licensing their reps to sell insurance/annuity products). Moreover, given the nature of this greatest of all bull markets, stockbrokers' essential marketing message ("Risk Is Good") had turned out to be right, just as banks' and whole-life insurers' essential message ("Risk Is Death") was seen to be wrong.

By the early 1990s, to paraphrase ol' Pogo Possum, we had met the enemy, and they was us. All three major combatants were in all the same businesses. And at that point, as uneasy allies, they turned together to face a new and implacable enemy: the "no-load" fund industry. For if the new allies all had the same game plan *vis-à-vis* each other ("You'd be better off paying me for all your financial needs rather than paying that other guy"), they now faced a foe who said, *"You'd be better off not paying* ***any*** *of 'em."*

As mutual funds became America's investment of choice, the financial services industry made a grave strategic error in letting the enemy dictate battle conditions. It even used the enemy's language ("load"/ "no-load"), rather than defining the issue for what it really was: help vs. no-help. Our industry thus placed itself in the ignominious position of having to counterattack a thesis that is not merely wrong but counterintuitive: namely, that most people are capable of establishing and maintaining a successful lifetime investment program without professional advice.

It didn't help that the enemy had co-opted the organs of the press, which never liked us much to begin with. The media are always thrilled to find themselves on the other side of an argument with investment professionals, and will therefore reduce that argument to a nine-second sound bite, in which you not only don't hear the other side of the story, you can't even remember that there was one. "Pay those fat-cat scoundrels when you can pick funds yourself that have the same or better results? Why would you ever do that?"

The Big Lie implicit in this seemingly irrefutable argument is, of course, the notion that fund results are synonymous with investor results. This canard was lent further credence by the rise of various mutual fund rating schemes, which—in the public mind, at least—quickly reached a *reductio ad absurdum:* in effect, "If you can count the number of stars, you too can select superior funds *and will therefore* enjoy superior results." (This is the Sesame Street school of fund selection, and is, I believe, the last thing its authors intended.)

For the second of perhaps two dozen times in this book, let me assert my firm belief that there is absolutely no relationship between *investment* performance and *investor* performance. The "no-help" argument implies (without actually stating) that they are synonymous. Investment professionals (and other sane observers) know they are well-nigh antithetical.

Unaided, most people invest through the rear-view mirror. They buy funds (or sectors, or countries) *after* an eye-popping rise, when most of the gains from the upward leg of a cycle are already in the past. "Mexico is the paradigm of an emerging capitalist democracy. Salinas is a combination of George Washington, Simon Bolivar and Lord Keynes. The Bolsa has gone from 1000 to 3000, and this no-load Mexico fund has five stars. I will buy this fund, and be rich and famous, and live forever."

In fairly short order, a perfectly normal cyclical setback will eventuate. And since volatility, like leverage, cuts both ways, the most spectacular rise will often be followed by the most horrific correction. ("Salinas's hand-picked successor has been shot dead. One Mexican state is in the hands of violent revolutionaries. The peso is turning into toilet paper, Salinas himself has gone to live in Europe, and his brother is under arrest for murder. The Bolsa's gone from 3000 to 1500. *Sell me out.*")

It is quite possible to become an immensely successful investor without ever having owned a fund with more than three stars. You just have to dollar-cost average into those funds every month of your working life. Then, when you retire, you do systematic withdrawal at a rate less than your type of fund's index return. (For example, you take 6% a year out of a big-cap stock fund, knowing that the S&P 500's historical return is 10½%. You get all the income you need, and your investment keeps growing in value for your children and theirs.)

Conversely, it is at least equally possible to become destitute investing only in five-star funds. You just buy 'em when everybody else does, late in a big bull market. Then you panic out when they go down 20% to 30%. Next, you watch the market rally to new highs, wait for another huge upsurge in bullishness among your peers...and plunge into a different five-star fund.

Another sure-fire formula for five-star disaster is to buy a top-performing fund in a particular sector (small-cap value, let's say) that just lies there like a beached whale for a year. Then, bored and enervated, you switch into a five-star performer in a hot sector that's up 50% in a year—healthcare, for instance, just before Congress suddenly votes a 20% cut in Medicare. (There may be an easier way to destroy yourself than buying last year's hottest sector, but I've never been able to discover what it is.)

I have no wish to drive this message into the ground like a tomato stake. I just want to make two points, early and often [*the way the Boston Irish used to vote*]. First, at the end of an investor's life, less than 5% of his total lifetime return will come from what his investments did versus other, similar investments. The other 95% will come from how the investor behaved. And the primary determinant of that behavior will be the quality of the advice he got, *or didn't get*. The second point is that it is entirely possible (and, late in a bull market, almost inevitable) for "performance" data to be both statistically accurate and a moral lie.

This brief digression into the history of the "load"/"no-load" wars brings us just about up to the present day—when the issue has, amazingly, become almost moot. (The key word in that sentence is, of course, "almost.") For suddenly, there is a plethora of programs that permit investment advisors to offer hordes of no-load funds and waived-load funds, and to add their own advisory fee thereto. These fees may be set at the pleasure of the advisor and his client, or mandated to some extent by the advisor's employer. It matters not; this is Endgame. The war's over. Everybody won.

The client can get the dispassionate professional advice he needs. The advisor can get fairly compensated, and that compensation can rise if and to the extent that the client's wealth grows. Not only is there no conflict of interest (there never was, where good advisors were involved), there's no real *potential* for conflict of interest. It's the millennium.

Again, if you just got into the business, this is all ancient history, and probably not very interesting history, either. You were [*professionally speaking*] born charging fees, and you have to be told that it wasn't always like this. You remind me of the time I took my son Mark, then about eight years old, to the Alamo. There we stood, in front of the display case containing Davy Crockett's rifle, Ol' Betsy. Above it hangs a painting of Davy at the penultimate moment, swinging Betsy like a club as Santa Ana's hordes close in.

I am, of course, all choked up. This is, after all, not just an American shrine but a piece of my childhood, when Disney's TV version of the Crockett legend seized the heart and mind of every boy who was Mark's age in the early 1950s...like me.

So it takes me a minute to notice that Mark is completely confused. I've forgotten that he wasn't raised on Fess Parker as Davy but on Stallone as Rambo, with automatic weapons that appear to fire about two thousand times before you have to slap in another banana clip. Then the lad speaks: "Why didn't he just keep shooting?"

Maybe you newcomers would like to skip ahead to the next chapter, or go get yourself a sandwich, or something, while I review, for us older folks, the full implications of how radically the business has changed.

I believe the future of the business is not merely different from, but diametrically opposed to, its past. There are six drop-dead critical areas in which this revolution most clearly manifests itself.

The Past	**The Future**
Commissions	Fees
Transactions	Relationships
Markets	People's Lives
Knowledge	Trust
Velocity of Assets	Longevity of Assets
Telephone	Face-To-Face

Before we begin analyzing these six aspects of the revolution, let me make a comment or two about an item you might have expected to see on the list, and don't: technology. Technology is a tool—a wonderful, potentially liberating tool in terms of saving you time, effort and energy—but ultimately just a tool. When the tool and its amazing capabilities become an end in themselves, rather than the electronic means to a human end, you're on your way out of the business.

What you and I do is not about machines, it's about people. It's not about facts, it's about feelings. And it's not about calculating the answers, it's about making sure you've got the questions framed right. The computer, then, can do an infinite variety of things that are of secondary importance, and nothing that is of primary importance.

The Excellent Investment Advisor could, if pressed, sketch out a high-quality lifetime investment program on the back of an envelope, using a No. 2 pencil. But he could never generate a computer printout that would prove to his clients that he truly cares about them. **And people do not begin to care what you know until they begin to know that you care.**

We return you now to our six-point past/future analysis, already in progress.

1 **Commissions/fees.** There used to be only one way people in our business could get paid: by generating commissions. We weren't paid anything for encouraging clients to own investments, but only for getting people to buy or sell investments.

There is a significant potential for conflict of interest in commissions. Please note that this is infinitely different from the statement, "There's conflict of interest in commissions." The latter sentence is manifestly untrue, as generations of ethical commission-based investment advisors have proven. But it is always the *potential* for conflict of interest about which people obsess. That's because it is the tiny minority of instances in which bad people do bad things which captures the headlines. Bad news is always good copy. And, since journalism isn't actually our friend, it is the bad apples who get all the publicity. The Attorney General of the US and the head of the Securities and Exchange Commission will do a joint press conference announcing the summary professional execution of 12, and I quote, "rogue brokers." But they will never stage a similar media event to read out the names and exploits of 12 Excellent Investment Advisors who've made their clients multigenerationally wealthy. Welcome to the world.

Never mind, by the way, that in a long-term, low-turnover portfolio strategy (which all the good ones are), commissions/"A" shares are the least costly way for the client to go. It is the potential conflict of interest which the public perceives as the critical issue. And in these matters, perception is the ultimate reality. So while we certainly have an obligation clearly to explain all of a client's options in the matter of our compensation, let's not be surprised if the client ends up saying, in effect, "I prefer to pay you 1% of my account's value every year for 30 years—which could sum to more than 100% of my initial investment—rather than pay you 5.5% today and maybe never again." There are such things as irrational good decisions, and this, I believe, is one of them.

The *sine qua non* of all successful advisor/client relationships is trust. Anything that threatens to tear the fabric of trust ("Is he really trying to do good for me and my family, or is he just trying to sell me something in order to make a commission?") is to be avoided, quite literally at any cost. Distrust, however small and insignificant it may be at first, always sets the client on the road to The Big Mistake. Since the Excellent Investment Advisor is forever asking the client to do counterintuitive things (e.g. double up on his dollar-cost averaging program when the Dow drops 30%), trust will forever be the critical issue. Without that trust, clients will do not what they need to but what they want to, which will, sooner than later, lead to The Big Mistake. And fees may, in the long run, be more expensive than commissions. But The Big Mistake is far more expensive than either...or both. The "best" compensation arrangement—indeed, the only sane one—is the one the client trusts.

And, in the end, there's no getting around the two great reasons that a fee-based approach is rocketing in popularity. First, it gets us as nearly alongside the client as we're ever going to be, in that our compensation rises and falls with the value of his investments. (Of course, our fee income also rises when he merely adds money to his account, regardless of how the account is doing. So there's a point past which even the identity-of-interest argument won't go.) Second, it allows us to get paid for telling the client to do nothing, when nothing is the right thing for him to do. And I must tell you, as a veteran of nearly 30 years of a commission-based business, that this is the real miracle. Our inability to be paid unless we caused the money to move was the key to the remaining five elements of Business Past, just as our ability to be paid for causing the money to stop moving is the key to the following five elements of Business Future.

2 **Transactions/relationships.** It's axiomatic that a commission-based world is transaction-oriented. Again, the emphasis is not on getting people to own investments, but to buy and sell them. This encourages us to seek advantages in one investment over another ("Let's sell growth stocks and buy cyclicals"), to trade ("It's October; let's buy natural gas stocks/futures for the winter run-up, and sell 'em in February at the top"), or to time markets ("This market's overdue for a correction; let's sell and try to buy 'em back cheaper"). Options and futures trading is the awful endgame of transaction orientation, in that it involves instruments that aren't investments at all.

Gathering assets, and deploying them pursuant to a long-term, goal-oriented strategy, are intensely relationship-oriented pursuits. The dreams, the goals, the proper portfolio balance—those are the watchwords of the new millennium, just as "Buy it now; it's hot" is a cry from the past.

That's why it's so sad to see relationship-oriented investments sold in transaction-oriented ways. Virtually all "no-help" funds are advertised in this kind of "It's been shooting the lights out for the last three years so buy it now because it's hot" way. This sets the investor up to fail when the next three years are, inevitably, not a bit like the last three. Nor, if the truth be told, are "help" funds insusceptible to this temptation. Not that long ago, I saw an ad for a "help" fund which actually said that the kind of stocks it owns historically get a pop in the three months through January. In other words, buy this cornerstone of an intelligent long-term fund portfolio *right now* because you'll get, in effect, a trade out of it.

Investments must never again be allowed to become an end in themselves, but must be seen as means to the end of achieving the Great Goals of Life for the client and his family. Thus, a particular investment—or even a whole portfolio of investments—ought not to be judged on any other basis than whether it's appropriate to the client's long-term strategy.

Make no mistake about it: in the future, success in this business will be a pure function of the openness, candor and mutual respect between the advisor and his client. This was always supposed to be a business of relationships, and for many it was. But now it's no longer an option: he who forges the best relationship—that is, engenders the most trust—will control the account...for a long, long time.

And let's not forget that all relationships involve an agreed-upon fair sharing of rights and responsibilities. "You wash and I'll dry" describes a relationship. "You wash and dry, and I'll watch the game" describes...something else. "You give me five-star, top-performing mutual funds and I'll give you my family's account" isn't a relationship. It's blackmail. In it, the client sets the agenda, and takes all the rights, while the advisor draws all the responsibility: "outperform" or get fired.

In a healthy relationship, the Excellent Financial Advisor asks for the following rights: full information as to all pertinent aspects of the family's finances, total stewardship of the family's entire investment portfolio, and the time and effort necessary to arrive at a complete understanding of investment goals. In turn, if he's granted those rights by the client, the excellent advisor assumes the responsibility for total trustworthiness, devotion to the client's best interests, and the creation and maintenance of an investment plan that will, within reasonable probabilities, achieve the client's lifetime goals.

Which brings us to the third of our Business Future/Business Past dichotomies.

3 **Markets/people's lives.** A commission-driven, transaction-oriented world is one in which, by definition, the primary focus is on markets, and what they're going to do next. A fee-based, relationship-oriented practice is focused on the real lives of real people, over decades if not generations. Thus, it doesn't matter what the markets are going to do next, but what they're ultimately going to do.

When the Dow Jones Industrial Average stands at 6000, the important issue isn't whether it's going to go to 5000 or 7000 next. The issue is whether it's ultimately going to get to 60,000. Since I know it is (although I don't know when), most of my planning/portfolio problems are solved. I'm free to work on the critical issues: how much are my clients going to need to retire on; how will their income grow to meet rising living costs through three decades of retirement; to what extent do they want to intervene financially in the lives of their children and grandchildren? When I know the answers to those questions, it's a virtual no-brainer to back into a portfolio strategy which will—assuming they're willing to invest enough money—get my clients where they need and want to go.

A market orientation is always and everywhere a short-to-intermediate term focus, which is entirely incompatible with a lifetime investment strategy. Square peg in a round hole, AC/DC, and all that. You not only can't realize The Great Goals of Life for people with a market focus; you probably can't remember what these goals are—and probably don't much care. And, in the end, what does the direction of the market's next 20% move have to do with the lives of a 60-year-old couple? Both of them may easily have a quarter century to live; one may live for three decades. And what of their dreams for their five-year-old granddaughter, who may just be finishing medical school 20 years hence?

A focus on the real lives of real people—which is the great luxury of the fee-based investment advisor—isn't just different from a market focus. It's the diametric opposite. So it isn't just that the excellent advisor doesn't try to make short-term calls on markets, nor on asset classes:

The excellent investment advisor has, as nearly as possible, no market outlook whatsoever.

This is perhaps the most countercultural hallmark of tomorrow's winners, as opposed to yesterday's. The excellent advisor tries to construct properly balanced portfolios that will achieve The Great Goals of Life for her clients over very long periods of time. She knows that a market outlook can only skew those portfolios in a certain specific direction, thus transmogrifying them from a plan into a bet. Since she loves plans and loathes bets, the excellent advisor cultivates a blissful ignorance of current market trends, in self-defense.

A great added benefit of having no market outlook is that it is also a wonderful defense against the inevitable depredations of clients seeking to tinker with the plan. Clients are constantly being bombarded by rumors, tips, communications from the spirit world, CNBC sound bites, and other ephemera. And they'll always call the advisor with the question, "What do you think of (fill in the blank)?" At such moments, the advisor's single-minded absence of a market viewpoint comes in mighty handy.

client: What do you think of gold?

excellent investment advisor: Makes lovely jewelry. In my experience, you can never go far wrong giving a gift of gold.

client: I meant, what do you think of gold as an investment?

eia: I think of it less as an investment than as a hedge. You see, gold is the ultimate international currency. When people are reasonably comfortable with paper currency (i.e. when their inflation expectations are relatively low), they invest in financial assets—stocks and bonds—that are denominated in currency. At such times, there's not much financial demand for gold, and its price is determined (I guess) by commercial supply and demand. But when people get very nervous about currencies—particularly about reserve currencies like the dollar and/or the yen—their fears of inflation are high, and they fly into gold. Some large investors always keep a percentage—say five percent of their portfolio—in gold, as fire insurance against a global currency meltdown. Since I don't generally buy into cataclysm theories of any sort, this one leaves me pretty cold. I respect the fact that stocks and bonds go down when inflation flares up, but I think there are smarter, income-producing ways to hedge against that: real estate and oil, to name two, both of which we've got in your portfolio. Does that answer your question?

client: What? No! I just saw a guy on CNBC who said that gold is going to $500 an ounce before year-end!

eia: That certainly would be a heck of a move. Did the fellow say why he was expecting that to happen?

client: What? I...well, he must have, but...I can't remember what he said!

eia: I see. [*Silence*]

client: Well, what do **you** think?

eia: About what, again?

client: About what gold's going to do between now and year-end!

eia: Gee, I really don't have the foggiest notion. But I shouldn't just say that about gold. Fact is, I have almost no idea of where the stock and bond markets will be at year-end, either.

client: [*Incoherent, spluttering noises*]

eia: On the other hand, given the absolutely lovely portfolio we're building for you, I have a very clear idea of what you and your wife are going to be living on a couple of decades from now, when you're in your eighties. I've even got a halfway decent handle on the legacies you'll be able to make to your children, grandchildren, and alma mater. Want to talk about that?

client: No, no, I...

eia: Wait; perhaps I've been insensitive. Were you just looking to have some fun trading something?

client: Well, shucks, I guess so...

eia: Do you have any mad money set aside for trading?

client: Heck, no. You and your damn plan are taking every spare dime I have.

eia: You mean the plan that's going to give you a long, worry-free retirement and still enable you to educate all your grandchildren?

client: [*Ruefully*] Yeah, that plan.

eia: Are we just about done on this?

client: Yes. And I can't tell you what a deeply religious experience this conversation has been for me.

eia: Hey, no problem. Call me up and ask me stuff I don't know whenever you feel like it. That's what I'm here for.

The shorter, "I'm-on-the-other-wire-let's-cut-right-to-the-chase" version of this colloquy is, of course:

client: What do you think of gold?

eia: What will it matter when you're 83 years old?

Even I, however, would admit that this is just a tad too confrontational and argumentative. But the principle is still sound: try always to answer market-oriented questions with people/goal-oriented questions of your own. (We'll practice this later, in the section on Q&A/Objections Handling.) Your client relationships will stay healthier, you and they will make more money, and you'll all live longer.

I'll be the first to admit that voiding your mind of a market outlook takes a tremendous amount of discipline, not least of all because the world around you keeps trying to give you a new outlook as soon as you've gotten rid of the last one. I regularly speak at industry conferences of all sorts, where I'm literally the only speaker in a densely packed day whose topic is not related to an interest rate, economic or market viewpoint, nor to which countries, sectors or stock groups are going to outperform the others. (Why is it, then, that people often take more notes during my presentation than they do all the rest of the day?) You just have to learn to tune that stuff out. Short- to intermediate-term, markets are unknowable; long-term, they're inevitable. And you can care deeply about markets, or you can care deeply about people. But I sincerely believe that nobody on earth can ever do both. And if, perchance, somebody can, I'm betting it isn't you.

4 **Knowledge/trust.** A commission-driven, transaction-based, market-focused practice runs, almost by definition, on the fuel of knowledge. ("I know what the earnings are going to be; I know what interest rates are going to do; I know who's shorting the stock; I know the CEO's mother's podiatrist; I know which raindrop is gonna get to the bottom of the window first.") It's an approach whose basic appeal is "Do business with me because I'm smarter than the other guy (or my research department can beat up his research department), and so I'm going to be righter than he is, and you'll make more money with me than with him." Kind of fatigues you just to read this, doesn't it?

As an industry, we tend to think that we've gotten further from this awful approach than we actually have. "Performance" selling of managed investments ("My mutual fund is up more/has more stars/has a lower standard deviation/lower beta/higher Sharpe ratio than the other guy's") is every bit as bad, if not worse. At least, in the bad old market-focused days, we never really pretended to be that interested in people's lives. Today we say we are, but then we go right back to talking about investments vs. other similar investments, rather than about investments as funding media for The Great Goals of Life.

The Excellent Investment Advisor is asking a family to place its entire financial future in his hands. This calls for a supreme act of trust by the investors, and that trust will be tested again and again over the years. I don't believe that any quantum of knowledge on the advisor's part can call forth that trust, not least of all because knowledge is intellectual, and trust is emotional, and never the twain shall meet.

We will have much more to say about the limits of knowledge in the next chapter. The point here is simply to contrast the knowledge-driven past with the trust-driven future. In the future, people will have to believe *that* you will make it all work out (trust) before they will be able to apprehend *how* you'll make it all work out (knowledge).

And the funny thing is, once they believe you'll take care of them, they may not even care how you propose to do it. But it will never work the other way around.

5 **Velocity of assets/longevity of assets.** In the past, there was no absolute relationship between your income and the amount of money you had under your stewardship. The critical issue was how often the money moved, i.e. the velocity of the assets. Portfolio turnover, not portfolio magnitude, was the driver of your income.

In the fee-based, relationship-oriented future, where your income will be a nearly pure function of the amount of money you have under management, the central issue will be the longevity of assets. Although much is made of asset *gathering* as the wave of the future, I think it's no more than a means to an end. It will not matter, for instance, how prodigiously you gather assets in a bull market, if you watch them melt away like snowballs in August the next time the markets back up 25% or so. Asset gathering, then, is no better or worse than the level of expectations you've fostered in the owners of those assets.

So while the commission/transaction/market-driven bad old days encouraged us to raise people's expectations ("Research says this stock could be up 50% this year! Jump in!"), asset longevity is more a function of guiding people's expectations down to historical norms:

> "The index return of large-cap stocks in America is about 10½% per year. Small-cap has done something like 12½%. And that's in a domestic economy that has a hard time growing at 3% overall. We can also include exposure to some of the emerging countries of Asia and Latin America, that are growing three and four times faster, albeit from a much lower—and more primitive—economic and political base. What I'm saying is that creating an equity portfolio with an underlying index return in a historical range of 11%–12% won't be too much of a stretch. If we can select managers who do better than their indexes over time—and I'm confident that we can—that adds something to the return. Finally, since you're going to be dollar-cost averaging, you'll end up outperforming your own managers. That's because you'll be buying an exaggeratedly large number of shares when prices are low, and correspondingly fewer shares when prices are high. Thus, you'll have a below-average cost, and therefore an above-average return.
>
> That's basically my three-part plan for building wealth for my family and those of my clients: harnessing the power of equities in a global capitalist revolution, trying to select superior managers, and letting the genius of dollar-cost averaging do its work. And every five years or so, when they have a Big Sale (or what amateurs call a Bear Market), you try to add as much money as you reasonably can.
>
> That's pretty much all it takes to make anyone reasonably wealthy. (The rest of this process is just the mechanics of portfolio selection.) If it takes a whole lot more than that, I'm just not sure it can get done. At any rate, I doubt I can do it for you. If I have to tell you you're surely going to do way better than that, I probably ought to take a pass, because it might not be true. And my "contract" with my clients says I can never tell them anything that isn't true.

> If you're comfortable with that approach, and you're willing to invest enough money consistently over the years to fund the plan we make together, I think your goals are readily achievable, and I'll take the responsibility for getting you where you need to go. If not, I don't think it'll work. Do you feel that that's a basis on which we can proceed?"

Longevity of assets is surely the key to the future, and is, I believe, primarily a function of reasonable expectations. In a commission/transaction/market-driven world, the emphasis may have been on trying to make a killing. But in a long-term plan for the creation and/or maintenance of real wealth, the essential thing is to make absolutely sure you don't get killed. Time and discipline (and not any number of stars) will take care of the rest.

And whenever you're tempted to relapse into your sinful old "performance"-selling ways, just remember this: peak "performance" *always* involves peak volatility. The latter is the price you pay for the former. They're two sides of the same coin. Peak volatility, more than any other single factor—and maybe more than all other factors combined—causes panic (i.e. loss of faith and trust). And panic will destroy any financial plan, as well as any financial planning relationship.

6 **The phone/face-to-face.** When your forte was knowledge of markets and investments, and you were paid to anticipate what was going to happen next, you had to stay close to the markets: to the ticker, the screen, the tape, the squawk box, and all those other sources of late-breaking news. (Perhaps you did not notice—because you didn't really get paid to notice—that the news is entirely different from, *and has no lasting effect on*, The Truth.) The emphasis was on being ahead of the markets, so you stationed yourself physically near the markets, and interacted with clients over the phone. This was only logical. The phone is still the most efficient medium for the generation of transactions, in that it lets one person communicate excitement and immediacy to another, in order to induce him to want to move his money.

Relationships, on the other hand, can only be created, nurtured and maintained face-to-face. No one is ever going to give you any serious money to invest without seeing you, much less entrust his family's entire financial future to you. Nor, once it's established, can a relationship be sustained by a voice at the other end of the phone. Sincerity, calm competence and a deep commitment to the client's success can always be *seen*; I'm not convinced, particularly in moments of great stress, that they can always be *heard.* And it's in stressful episodes that these values are most critical, because that's when the relationship is most at risk. Granted, you can't make 250 house calls—or any house calls, for that matter—on October 19, 1987. So it's important that you have a regular program of seeing all your clients.

Let me suggest that you get yourself a couple of magic markers—one green and one pink, let's say. [*Hey, it's my book. I'll pick any damn colors I want.*] For the next four working weeks, please draw a green bar through each time period when you are actually eyeball-to-eyeball with a client or prospect. Draw a pink bar through all the business-time clips in which you're not. At the end of the four weeks, just relate the amounts of pink and green time to each other. Obviously, the more pink time, the more you're still mired in Business Past, just as the more green time, the more positioned you are for Business Future. Generally speaking, if you've been in the business for more than a year, and this exercise yields a reading south of 30% green, assume you're in fairly big trouble. North of 60% green, I'd say you've got it knocked; you can't fail, and the only issue is how long it'll take you to reach your goals.

* * *

This chapter enunciates many of the planks in the platform on which the rest of the book will run for election. You can read on, if you like, but let me suggest that, if you can spare the time right now, you might be better advised to go back and read the whole chapter through, just once more.

In Summary

☞ Don't be too concerned with what you still have to learn. Future success may be largely a process of unlearning a lot of stuff that's no longer true.

☞ When life insurance agents make the greater part of their income from mutual funds and other variable products, bankers sell life insurance and annuities, and stockbrokers offer estate planning and home equity loans, you've entered...The Homogenized Zone. When everybody's products are the same as everybody else's, the only differentiable, value-added product is...you.

☞ Once and for all, it isn't "load"/"no-load." It's help/no-help. It doesn't matter what investments people buy; it only matters what folks do with those investments after they buy 'em. Which will be a pure and absolute function of the advice they get, *or don't get*. Once again, the critical issue is...you. Now please don't ever bring this issue up again. You see how much it upsets me.

☞ I have seen the future, and it is fees. Commissions may be cheaper in the long run (or they may not). But fees most closely align (though they do not perfectly align, because nothing can) the investor's economic interest and ours.

And fees finally allow us to be fairly compensated for advising the investor to do nothing, when nothing is the right thing for him to do.

☞ A commission-based business needed to cause transactions to happen; a fee-based business nurtures relationships. A fee-driven, planning-oriented, long-term arrangement is, above all, a personal/professional *relationship*. But we have not yet got to the Promised Land: resist the temptation to sell relationship-oriented products (i.e. all managed portfolios) in a transaction-oriented way. Investments can never be an end in themselves; they're a means to the end of The Great Goals of Life.

☞ All real relationships involve a fair sharing of rights and responsibilities. A situation in which one party has most of the rights and the other party most of the responsibilities isn't a relationship. It's an accident waiting to happen.

☞ Stop watching markets; watch people's lives. You can have exquisite control over clients' financial planning, and none at all over markets. So which are you going to bet your career on? Moreover, the direction of the next 20% market move is both unknowable and immaterial to the success of a lifetime investment program. It's the direction of the next 100% move that matters, and we know perfectly well which way that'll be, now don't we?

☞ The Excellent Investment Advisor has, as nearly as possible, no market outlook whatsoever. Saves an awful lot of wear and tear on everyone concerned. Besides, you don't want someone doing business with you because he agrees with your market outlook. (What if you're both wrong?) You want people to do business with you because they trust you implicitly.

☞ A commission-driven, transaction-based business ran on the fuel of knowledge. A relationship, almost by definition, runs on trust. And, in the end, knowledge of the future is impossible, but faith in the future can be limitless. When that faith is shaken, as it surely will be, knowledge won't hold it together. (The first thing you learn about fear is that it's insusceptible to reason.) Only your faith can rekindle the client's, and thereby save him.

☞ People don't care what you know until they know that you care. And they're not really interested in *how* it's going to be all right; they just need to believe *that* it's going to be all right. Knowledge they can get from charts, graphs and scattergrams. Belief they can only get from another believing human being. In this case...you.

☞ It used to be about getting the money to move; now it's about getting the money to sit still. The height of the expectations you give people will be inversely related to the length of time before the money leaves you. In other words, the more you guide expectations down to long-term historical norms, the happier people will be with the outcome, and the longer they'll stay with your plan…and with you.

☞ See the people. The phone was (and is) for transactions; people find relationships only in other people's eyes. "Telephone relationship," like "jumbo shrimp" and "water landing," is an oxymoron. *See the people.*

2

Places in the heart vs. places on some chart. . . . .

"Please excuse me for not wanting to talk about peace. I want to talk about my grandfather."

—**Noa Ben Artzi-Pelossof**, 18, granddaughter of Israeli Prime Minister Yitzhak Rabin, at his funeral, November 6, 1995

On that awful November Monday, along with tens of millions of other people around the world, I watched television coverage of the funeral services of Yitzhak Rabin.

Just as Richard Nixon, the ultimate cold warrior, was probably the only man who could have politically gotten away with thawing our country's relations with China, Rabin, perhaps Israel's greatest war hero, was the only person who could have pushed the Arab-Israeli peace process so far in so short a time. He knew he was risking his life to do so, and his life was now, terribly, forfeit.

The funeral was attended by the mighty of the earth: presidents, kings, prime ministers and other world leaders. And, one after another, they offered eloquent eulogies to their fallen colleague. They spoke, naturally, of the great issues: courage, leadership, sacrifice, the fate of nations, and the peace process.

And then that young girl, so small that she barely reached the podium's microphones, rose to speak. She began with the words above. But in the next instant she started speaking not about her grandfather but *to* him, as if, for all the world, there were no one else there. "*You always awake from a nightmare,*" she said, "*but since yesterday I was continually waking to a nightmare.*

> "The television never ceases to broadcast pictures of you, and you are so alive that I can almost touch you—but only almost, and I won't be able to anymore...
>
> I wanted you to know that every time I did anything, I saw you in front of me. Your appreciation and your love accompanied us every step down the road, and our lives were always shaped after your values. You, who never abandoned anything, are now abandoned. And here you are, my ever-present hero, cold, alone, and I cannot do anything to save you. You are missed so much.
>
> Others greater than I have eulogized you, but none of them ever had the pleasure I had to feel the caresses of your warm, soft hands, to merit your warm embrace that was reserved only for us, to see your half-smile that always told me so much, that same smile that is no longer, frozen in the grave with you...
>
> I am not able to finish this. Left with no alternative, I say goodbye to you, hero, and ask you to rest in peace, and think about us, and miss us, as down here we love you so very much. I imagine angels are accompanying you now and I ask them to take care of you, because you deserve their protection."

If you were able, that day, to listen to Ms. Ben Artzi-Pelossof all the way through without weeping, you are not only tougher than I am, you are tougher than I'll ever be. She spoke in Hebrew, which must have been the language she and her grandfather spoke to each other. So there had to be a simultaneous English translator on CNN, and near the end of her speech even he began to break up. And the young woman to whom this book is dedicated, who didn't see the speech on TV at all, cried just from reading the printed text in *The New York Times.*

No one in America today remembers Edward Everett, the great orator who gave the main speech—all two hours of it—at the dedication of the military cemetery at Gettysburg on November 19, 1863. That's because Lincoln's 272 luminous words on the same occasion put everything else that was said and done that day forever in the shade of history. Similarly, I believe that 100 years from now—when Israeli and Palestinian schoolchildren still memorize Ms. Ben Artzi-Pelossof's speech from their history books—no one will remember what else was said at Yitzhak Rabin's funeral. Indeed, no one will remember that anyone else spoke.

There are a couple of important lessons to be learned from all this. On a personal level, one lesson is not to assume that you are going to be able to tell the people you love exactly what they mean to you before one or the other of you goes to heaven. You may very well have that luxury, but you may not. Tell 'em now.

On a professional level, I found in that contrasting funeral oratory a disturbing paradigm for the direction the financial services industry has taken in the 1990s. Simply stated, we have become far more interested in academic and institutional methods of studying markets and investment portfolios than we are in the emotional responses of our clients to those markets and investments. We're more concerned with how people *should think* than with how they really *do feel.* We're investing more and more time and energy in studying places on some chart, rather than exploring places in the heart, where real people really live. This is never going to work, either for the investors or for us. For above all,

The excellent investment advisor knows that people don't make their investment decisions in their intellects. They make those decisions in their emotions, and then use their intellects to justify what they've decided.

Charts, scattergrams, asset allocation models and optimization software (whatever that is) speak volumes into the intellect, which operates primarily on the left side of the brain. The left brain (as you can see from the chart on the following page) loves to chew on logical, linear, sequential stuff. It not only wants but needs to believe that two and two always make four. The left brain will eagerly gobble up every bit of data you can feed it, and will then get hungry again half an hour later. There is only one problem: **The Boston Red Sox are going to win the World Series seven times before one investment decision ever gets made, anywhere in the world, on the left side of an individual investor's brain.** The intellectual, fact-based approach to investment sales/counseling is doomed by one very simple but incontrovertible fact: it will not matter how much wood you put in the fireplace, if there is no fire.

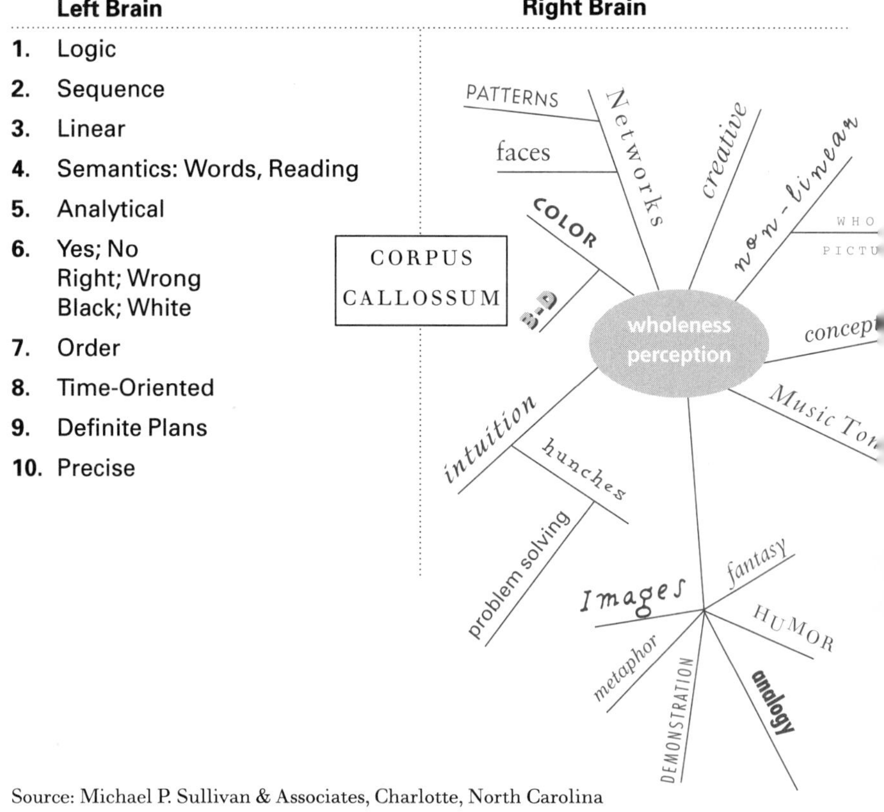

Source: Michael P. Sullivan & Associates, Charlotte, North Carolina

The fire is on the right side of the brain. Investment decisions are driven by the emotions of love, hope, faith and fear—in varying mixtures at different times (even within the same people). The right brain would never ask, "Does this column of figures add up?" Nor, even if the left brain had already checked the addition and signed off on it, would the right brain automatically infer a course of action from that fact. The right brain says, "That's fine, as far as it goes, but do I really feel I can trust the person who gave me this column of figures?" And if the answer is no—based on vibes, intuition, a hunch; call it what you will, it's purely right-brain—you're out of there. The right brain saw what you knew, but it didn't care, because (you guessed it) people don't care what you know until they know that you care.

The converse, delightfully, is also true. Suppose the left brain adds up your column of figures, and announces, "This dummy made a simple computational error; how can you ever rely on someone like that?" The right brain can still say, "Details. This is the advisor who our best friends, Bill and Esther, say has turned their whole financial lives around. And they're clearly doing better—or at least feeling better. You can feel it when you talk to them. No, this is life, it's not an arithmetic test. This person is right for us. *I can feel it.*"

If you are struggling with this analysis in any way, let me take you back to the beginning of the chapter. I suspect that you were somewhat moved by the story of Noa Ben Artzi-Pelossof, and that perhaps you misted up just a little when you read the excerpt from her eulogy. [*I know I did.*] And I imagine that you were at least slightly intrigued by the comparison I made between the mighty-of-the-earth/loving granddaughter dichotomy and the fact-based/feeling-driven difference in looking at our business. **Fair enough?**

ok, now let me assure you that *that entire mental process*—sympathy, sadness, and understanding of the analogy—*took place on the right side of your brain.* As I need hardly remind your left brain, there isn't a scintilla of logical, sequential, causal or even coincidental relationship between the people and events I described, and the business of advising investors. No direct connection whatever—except the one that the empathetic, intuitive, analogizing right brain instinctively *and correctly* perceived. Once again: in what we do, feelings are to facts as 19 is to one.

We have the entire rest of the book to work on the 19 really important parts of that formula. So we'll just use the balance of this chapter to describe—or perhaps I should say circumscribe—the very finite limits of the utility of knowledge. Please note that this is an inquiry into the *utility* of knowledge, and not into the nature or desirability of knowledge itself. I certainly have nothing against knowledge. Knowledge is...good. (It's not great; it's surely not bad. Above all, it's nowhere near half the battle. It's just ...good.) Knowledge is kind of like electricity: use it the right way, and it warms and lights people's lives. Use it the wrong way, and it kills them (and/or you). The issues are: how you're using it, and what you're using it for.

And so, direct from the home office in Chagrin Falls, Ohio, here are

The top 10 reasons why knowledge can never get you where you want to go

10 **Markets are fundamentally unknowable.** If markets and/or investments lent themselves to rational analysis in any significantly predictive way, somebody (or, more properly, somebody's computer) would have perfected that analysis long since, and would have taken away all the chips of everybody else at the table. This has not happened. And if it hasn't happened by now—with every computer nerd in the world washing through his computer every recorded trade since the Assyrians swapped wheat to the Babylonians for bronze—it ain't gonna happen. The secret is: there is no secret. Two and two make four just often enough to lull you into a false sense of security. Then, the very next day, they make five. And at one or another critical juncture in your investing career, they make fish. Or, in the words of the great Zen master Charles Dillon Stengel, *"Good pitching always beats good hitting. And vice versa."*

9 **No matter how prodigious your store of knowledge is, somebody out there is—and maybe a lot of somebodies out there are—"smarter" than you are.** And if you have trained your clients to think that knowledge is the magic elixir, then as they encounter people with more knowledge than you have, you will lose all your accounts. The Excellent Investment Advisor is too...smart for that. He says, *"You will always meet people 'smarter' than I. You will never meet anyone who is more deeply committed to your family's financial success."*

8 **The more you know, the less of what you know you can communicate to normal people.** That's the conundrum: as your store of knowledge compounds, the *percentage* of what you know that you can usefully—or even comprehensibly—tell folks approaches, and then arrives at, the vanishing point. By the time you get anywhere near this

$$\widetilde{R}_i = [b_{i1}\widetilde{F}_1 + b_{i2}\widetilde{F}_2 + \ldots + b_{in}\widetilde{F}_n] + \widetilde{e}_i \quad *$$

it's all over but the crying. Put the chairs up on the tables, and the last one who leaves please turn out the lights. The party's over. You are now so smart that no one on earth (except some other math wizard, who's not a prospect because he does his own investing via the Internet) can understand you.

*The key equation utilized in factor analysis.

7 **Knowledge is Vietnam.** It's a quagmire. You can only slog deeper and deeper into it; you can never turn around and walk back out. You never get "enough" knowledge, because the complexities of markets, investments, products and services are proliferating and changing more and more rapidly. As soon as you know something new, there are nine other, even newer things to learn. It's like: a guy is standing 40 feet from a wall. He walks halfway to the wall, and stops. Then he walks half the remaining distance to the wall, and stops again. He keeps doing this. Question: How many times does he move before he gets to the wall? Answer: He never gets to the wall, because he's always covering only half the remaining distance. That, folks, is a parable for the quest for "enough knowledge." Hope you enjoyed it.

6 **Knowledge ultimately becomes indifferentiable as to its real usefulness. You lose the ability to distinguish between "need to know" and "nice to know."** There is a lifetime supply of moral wisdom and ethical guidance to be found in the Old and New Testaments, the Torah, the Koran, and the Bhagavad Gita. And I can decide that, ideally, I want to assimilate those lessons as a preparation for living my life. (A) I'll never get a life, because I'll be studying this material 'til I die, and (B) I can actualize a huge portion of that wisdom and guidance, if I believe and practice these 11 words:

Do unto others as you would have others do unto you.

The more you know, the less important each individual thing you know is. Try, if possible, to know fewer, more important things.

5 **The fundamental reason people seek advice is not that they don't know, it's that they don't want to know.** I don't know how to repair my car, but it goes far beyond that: I have a deep and abiding commitment never to learn how to repair my car. Or any car. So when I'm standing in a service station on a summer Friday, I do not want the mechanic to explain to me the subtle interplay of my starter, my battery, my carburetor and

my transmission. I want to know only one thing: "*When can I drive my car to the beach?*" Similarly, it isn't just that most people don't know what modern portfolio theory is. I believe they consciously, actively do not want to know what it is. That's why they come to you. They're asking, "When can I drive my car to the beach *and stay there for the rest of my life* without having to worry about running out of money?"

4 **No matter how much you know, you still can't prove what's going to happen in the future.** And the more you try to prove what's going to happen, the more you put yourself in an obviously false position. The further you climb out on the limb of "proof," the easier it is for your naturally skeptical prospect to saw if off. Once again: no one can, with any precision, give his clients knowledge of the future. But we can—and we must—give them faith in the future. The battle (nay, the holy Crusade) we fight is not one of knowledge vs. ignorance, but of faith vs. fear.

3 **How much "smarter" than your prospects and clients can you become before you start offending them?** People don't like to be talked down to. They hate jargon. And (most of the time) they fear markets and investments, which they don't really understand, and are keenly aware of not understanding. There is, therefore, a point at which you and your knowledge (and that damned laptop you whip out every time they see you, with its incomprehensible "optimization software") are actually driving a wedge between you and the clients. And your technobabble may be daunting and frightening them even further as they glimpse the enormity of what they don't understand. This is the law of unforeseen consequences at its perverse worst: knowledge as the ultimate turn-off.

2 **To the extent that your approach is knowledge-based, you're actively discouraging people from trusting you.** At the very least, the knowledge-driven journeyman advisor is saying, "You don't have to trust me; I can demonstrate all this statistically." At worst, he's saying, in effect, "I *forbid* you to trust me because I can *prove* all this to you *and I insist that you understand the proof.*" Then one year the market will be down 31% amid various reports of the end of economic life on the planet as we have known it. The journeyman will proudly point out that his exquisitely asset-allocated portfolio is only down 26.8%. And he'll be genuinely surprised when the clients say, "Sell us out and send us our check, you blackguard. More than a quarter of our retirement nest egg is *lost!* We should have known: we never trusted you to begin with!" People simply do not entrust their financial lives to advisors they "understand." *They place their financial lives in the hands of advisors they trust.*

And the number 1 reason that knowledge can never, *ever* get you where you want to go:

It doesn't matter how much you know if you are too paralyzed by anxiety to go out and ask people to do business with you! What difference does it make if you're your firm's leading expert on high-yield bonds, but are so shattered by "rejection" that you can't pick up the phone? What does it avail you to have mastered asset allocation if you can't get people to make a decision? What value do you provide if you know which five countries' equity markets will be the next decade's top performers, but you can't induce people to trust you? Once and for all: in this business, doing is to knowing as four is to one. *Our profession rewards us not at all for what we know, but for what we do, and for what we are able to convince other people to do.*

So far, then, this chapter has been a voyage of negative discovery. Like Captain Cook, on his epic journey of 1772–75 to find the fabled Great Southern Continent, we have sought that which was believed to exist, and proved that it doesn't.

For instance, we've established that the thing investors want most for us to tell them—what's going to happen next—is unknowable. But, happily, we've also demonstrated that, in a plan for lifetime wealth-building, what happens next won't matter. The only thing that matters is what ultimately happens, and we feel we've got a pretty decent handle on that. We can't, for instance, tell clients with any certainty which way the next 1000-point move in the Dow will be, but we can tell them with total conviction which way the next 6000-point move will be, and that's obviously much more important.

We can't tell people whether it will be better to be in stocks or bonds over the next 12 months, but we can assure them that it will probably be about twice as good for them to be in stocks rather than bonds over their investing lifetimes. We can't tell people whether small-cap or big-cap stocks will outperform over the next block of time, but we can assure them that small-cap will have a significantly higher return (historically, 20% or so) in the long run. Moreover, since small-cap is inherently more volatile than big-cap (hence the premium return; it's only logical), a dollar-cost averager will do even better in small as opposed to large stocks. (See the discussion of dollar-cost averaging in Chapter 12.)

Thus, the Excellent Investment Advisor takes a planning-oriented, lifetime (if not multigenerational) approach not just because it's best for the clients but because it vastly increases the number of outcomes he can predict with reasonable assurance. A long-term focus, then, isn't something the excellent advisor has to be defensive about. Far from it. It's the long term about which the excellent advisor feels most confident. And confidence—not knowledge—is the one thing that most reliably sparks the flame of trust in a prospective client.

By professing a blissful ignorance about the unknowable (what's going to happen next), the excellent advisor shows in lovely contrast the serenity of his belief in the ultimate outcome. His studied incomprehension of everything that doesn't matter proves immensely attractive to genuinely serious investors—and maddening to crazies. In a very real sense, then, the right kind of ignorance becomes an extraordinarily effective prospecting tool.

potential client for life: Do you think mainland China will take over Taiwan?

excellent investment advisor: Not my field, really. The mysterious East, and all that. I do think that a portion of every serious investor's assets should be in Asia, and in the developing countries of the Pacific Rim. The growth out there is clearly going to be phenomenal. But I think we need to hire money managers on the ground in those areas—through mutual funds, or whatever—to keep tabs on the geopolitics, and run that part of your portfolio.

pcfl: Do you think that a unified European currency will ever go through?

eia: Your guess is every bit as good as mine. Better, probably. It's so hard to separate the economics from the politics…or to separate either of those things from emotional issues like nationalism. I'm the wrong person to ask. However, we do have extraordinarily effective managers based in Europe who get paid a lot of money to worry about that stuff. The larger issue is: would your family's long-term financial goals be served by having some exposure to the European markets? And I can't know that unless and until we get to the point of sitting down and making a plan…

pcfl: Well, uh…what do you think interest rates are going to do?

eia: [*Laughing at himself*] Oh my gosh, interest rates! As ignorant as I am about China, I'd rather make **six** predictions about China before I'd make even one about interest rates! Seriously, I never have the slightest idea what interest rates are going to do next. Of course, Warren Buffett and Peter Lynch always say the same thing.

pcfl: Then…I guess I don't understand what it is that you do.

eia: I work with a certain number of families like yours to establish very specific financial goals for the attainment of wealth—as you define wealth, which could be anything from a retirement with no compromise in lifestyle, to the education of all your grandchildren…or whatever. That's the part that you decide. Then, together, we make a financial plan for the realization of those goals. Finally, I devise a specific portfolio strategy that's appropriate for the execution of our plan. So, to review, it's (1) goals, (2) plan, (3) strategy.

In broad outline, my strategy is always to create portfolios of professionally managed accounts with two basic characteristics: (1) The blended long-term return of the portfolio would historically have gotten you where you need to go, with room to spare. Of course, past performance is no guarantee of future results. (2) My portfolios are constructed in such a way as to spread and balance the historical risks and volatility of the different kinds of investing we're doing. We can go into as much detail about that as you like, when and if we get to that point. Suffice it to say that we want to get you where you want to go, but we'd rather you didn't get there via roller coaster.

In effect, if you're the President of the United States, and you want to go to war for financial independence/a worry-free retirement/multigenerational wealth, I'm the Chairman of the Joint Chiefs of Staff. You tell me what our war aims are, and I'll create and execute a strategy for winning the war. The portfolio managers we hire are the different branches of the service—Army, Navy, Air Force and Marines—and they do the actual fighting. Once in a while, we may have to relieve a general, and replace him with another general. But basically, the strategy remains the same as long as your goals do, and we let the commanders in the field make the tactical decisions.

[*EIA then rolls into his "commitment" recitation, from the Foreword to this book.*] Does that seem like a basis on which we can proceed?

I'd encourage you now to go back and read the statement that the Excellent Investment Advisor just made, starting from "I work with a certain number of families" and including the "commitment" recitation. *Please read it out loud;* in fact, if it isn't too much trouble, tape it, and then play it back so you can listen to yourself saying it. And just ask yourself: if I were sitting in the prospect's chair, how would that speech make me feel?

I think the answer to that question is fairly obvious. A real prospect—somebody with a real career, and a family he cares about, and not a lot of time to watch CNBC—will say, "This advisor sat there professing total ignorance about all the specific questions I asked, and told me as subtly and politely as he could that none of them mattered. Then, calmly and without a trace of hyperbole, he said—at least I think he said—that, with him on the case, all of my investment worries would be over. I want to believe this. I'm going to keep asking questions, but…*I want to believe this.*"

On the other hand, an adrenaline junkie/market maniac type will go sub-orbital (not just ballistic) when he hears this, and start screaming (try to hear Gilbert Gottfried's voice as you read):

adrenaline junkie: What!? What are you talking about? Family? My wife left me! What do you mean, you don't know about Taiwan! What about the market? How many stars do your funds have? What's your fee? Don't you know anything?

eia: [*Sadly*] I know just about everything that matters, and virtually nothing that you seem to want to know. [*Silence*]

aj: What? What is that supposed to mean? What's your performance? How much of a discount do you give? My old broker…

eia: Probably committed suicide by falling on his Cross pen. Listen, for heaven's sake, get some therapy. Screaming, hostile and over-trading is no way to go through life, son. Now, if you'll excuse me…

aj: Wait! I like you! What do you think of biotech??

eia: Take two, and don't call me in the morning. Or ever.

Here you see ignorance (whether real or pretended) as a tool for qualifying prospects—and, just as important, for disqualifying them. By not answering the prospect's factual inquiries, even if he actually had an opinion on Taiwan or Europe, the excellent advisor was able to channel the conversation into his area of specialty—long-range wealth-building. As it usually does, this approach proved intriguing to the real prospect, and caused the crazy to de-select himself.

We'll have much more to say about the prospects you want and don't want in the next chapter. For now, please see that the only thing that would prevent you from taking this direct, straightforward, I-make-the-difference approach is your own anxiety (i.e. your fear that you do not, in fact, make the difference). And even I would admit that no script I give you is going to work unless you believe the script. My answer: read the rest of this book, then read the whole book again, and then just keep acting out the script until you *do* believe it. "We are what we repeatedly do," Aristotle said. "Excellence then is not an act, but a habit."

And, after all, what's the alternative? Are you going to put on knowledge as a mask for your insecurity? Are you going to try to hide a diminished sense of professional self-worth behind the toxic illusion that two and two always make four? Surely you realize that this can never work. People will ultimately see you not for what you know but for what you are. "What is done for effect," said Emerson, "is seen to be done for effect, and what is done for love is felt to be done for love."

The Excellent Investment Advisor works, then, not from her store of knowledge but from her belief system. She knows that our profession—which, simply stated, is convincing people that what they need to do with their money is the opposite of what they want to do with it—requires passionate belief rather than encyclopedic knowledge. If all you have is knowledge, all you'll end up doing is arguing with people. And, in the absence of your ability to prove the future, all arguments about investing—like all arguments about religion and politics—are unwinnable.

So you need something much more powerful than the ability to convince people intellectually. If you're going to be really successful, you have to develop the power to inspire belief—*especially when the factual evidence runs counter to the belief.* Forgive me, but any journeyman can convince people to stand up and pledge allegiance to the flag of equities when the stock market's up 150% in six years without so much as a 10% correction on a closing basis (as it did after the October '90 lows). But only the Excellent Investment Advisor can get a family to commit its financial future to equities in the midst of a 25%–30% generalized decline. And that—right where the rubber meets the road—is the difference between communicating knowledge and inspiring belief.

You can't be all things to all people, nor even most things to most people. But you can be an unwavering beacon of light and truth to some number of people who have made an act of faith in your guidance. And the ability to induce people to make that act of faith in you is the essence of all real, lasting success. *No one ever became an Excellent Investment Advisor until he learned to rise above the facts.* And I can sum up everything of paramount importance I've ever learned, during nearly 30 years in our profession, in just six words:

When I believe, I am believed.

Note that I did not say, "When I understand, I am understood." Because not only is that not true, the *opposite* is true (see Reason Number Eight, above).

So no matter where you are on the great learning curve that is your career, I would urge you—right here and now—to declare a 90-day moratorium on further increases in knowledge of any kind. *Just say no to more knowledge.* For 90 days, learn no facts, ratios, statistics, betas, standard deviations, Sharpe ratios, or earnings estimates. No new products, portfolios, managers, sectors or styles. Instead, invest in a child's school copybook—probably set you back about a buck—and every single day for those 90 days, write one short paragraph (or even one sentence) about *what you believe.* Label your book "A Journal of My Belief System."

The idea here is, in the words of the Carly Simon song, to turn down the noise in your mind. (What she really meant was "turn down the noise in your left brain," but she probably couldn't get anything to rhyme with that.) Give your unconscious a consistent, unhurried 90 days to search that stupendous four-billion-circuited computer that is your brain, in order to produce—in no particular order—the sum of your beliefs.

Don't try to write any big, long essay on any one day. (On the other hand, if a big, long essay freely appears, let it come.) In fact, don't *try* to do anything at all. [*Remember Yoda.*] All my experience is that meaningful change can only come over a minimum of 90 days, and that it is very hard for people of our personality type (about which more later) to do *anything* consistently for 90 days. Which is really too bad, because I've found that one can literally accomplish anything by dividing it into 90 one-day clips. (I did not, for instance, write this book *as such.* I'm not a writer, I'm an investment advisor, and I would find it too daunting and intimidating to have to write a whole book *as such.* But I can fairly easily discipline myself to write five pages of manuscript each and every day for 90 days. And that's what I did.)

And don't be put off by the phrase "belief *system.*" You'll systematize it when it's all done, at the end of 90 days. In the meantime, let it come in as random and unstructured a way as it wants to come. Don't try to control the process in any way. (Your unconscious is much, much smarter than you are; let it work the way it wants to work.)

One day, you may find yourself writing, totally out of the blue, "I believe in China. I believe it is going to be the largest single thermonuclear explosion of capitalism ever recorded on the planet. I also believe it will be the scariest ride of my life, because the social and political upheaval inherent in China's conversion to true free-market capitalism is going to be just terrible. But for people who can stay the course, even a 5% portfolio exposure to China may, I believe, be a lifestyle-changer in the long run."

The very next day, you may write, "I don't care what anybody says, I believe in corporate bonds in retirement accounts. You get to compound relatively high and ordinarily taxable returns on a tax-deferred basis. Slow and steady wins the race; this is folks' most serious—and probably most scared—money. I just don't believe that the incremental return of stocks is worth the risk of panic." Granted, these two perceptions haven't got anything to do with each other, except that they are vital—and very interesting—pieces of the puzzle of your perhaps hitherto undiscovered belief system. *All your greatest potential strength comes from the power of your beliefs.* We just have to bring those beliefs to the surface, where we can see them, and then get them organized.

Even on days when you think you've run dry, you have to write something, even if it's only one sentence. Let me assure you—as someone who is constantly amazed to find myself writing things I didn't know I knew—that your unconscious is always trying to tell you something, *if you'll let it.* Just keep saying, "I believe...," and wait for something to pop into your mind, even if it seems to have nothing whatever to do with the business. At the end of the 90 days, you may find that there are important messages hidden in some of that random stuff.

I was writing this on an airplane, and I had to sit there for several minutes, trying to think of something that would illustrate this to you. Suddenly I wrote, "I believe...that the Blues Brothers *were* on a mission from God!" Remember Belushi and Aykroyd, being chased by every cop in the state of Illinois, running up a jillion flights of stairs to the Cook County assessor's office so they could pay the back taxes on the Catholic orphanage where they were raised? Well, how come all those cops—and everybody else who was after them all through the movie—didn't catch 'em? I know what your left brain says: because it's a movie, dummy. But, sitting there on that plane, my right brain said: because, as Elwood Blues (Aykroyd) keeps telling everybody, all through the flick, "We're on a mission from God." (Except that Elwood pronounces it—him being from Chicago and all—"Gad.")

And in the next instant, I saw that, while this sentence appears to be utterly random—just something I'd write so as not to break my 90-day journal contract—there's an unconscious message in it, sure as shootin'.

It should be clear to you, even at this early stage in the book, that I believe there's a spiritual dimension to our profession, when we do it right. That dimension is implicit in our virtually limitless capacity to do good for the families who come to believe in us. While I don't believe that wealth can give anyone true peace, I know that peace is nearly impossible when people are harried by financial worry. So, in my capacity to create wealth, I feel I bring people the opportunity to find true peace. If that's not spiritual, I don't know what is. And thus, sure enough...I'm on a mission from Gad.

So, just for 90 days, please write a little something—anything—in your journal of beliefs, all the while maintaining a calm, passive resistance to the encroachment of all incremental knowledge. Indeed, as you clear your conscious mind every day before writing in your journal, you may wish to repeat to yourself a line from a Buddhist text called the *Sutra of Forty-Two Chapters.* The Buddha said:

> *"If you endeavor to embrace the Way through much learning, the Way will not be understood. If you observe the Way with simplicity of heart, great indeed is this Way."*

Your belief system will be your sword and your shield in the Crusade of faith vs. fear. But only when you consciously know what that belief system is. I promise you that, when you see those 90 journal entries—seemingly so random and unconnected—you'll very quickly be able to edit them down into a powerful statement of your core beliefs. And that statement will be the platform on which you will run for election to the status of Excellent Investment Advisor.

Perhaps if I just list here some of *my* core beliefs about investing, it will give you a track to run on as you begin your journal. (This will also serve as a confession of my biases. And since, of necessity, this book is shot through with my biases—some of which you may very legitimately disagree with—forewarned is forearmed.) Please remember, though, that since investing is just a part of what we do—investments are only a means to an end—this is deliberately only a partial list of my core beliefs.

1 **I believe that the fundamental investment risk is not losing one's money, but outliving it.** Risk has changed, because life has changed. People are looking at upwards of 30 years of retirement, and in 30 years consumer prices triple. So the risk isn't loss of principal, it's the extinction of your purchasing power while you're still alive.

2 **I believe, therefore, that the only safety lies in the accretion of purchasing power.** If risk is the inexorable grinding down of purchasing power over time, safety can only be the building up of purchasing power. I define accretion of purchasing power as a positive return from my investments, net of inflation and taxes. Investments which provide such a return are, by my definition, safe. Those that do not are not. By this definition, common stocks are by far the safest financial instrument in the long run.

3 **I believe that the great long-term risk of stocks is not owning them.** On July 8, 1932, the intra-day low of the Dow Jones Industrial Average was 40. On October 14, 1996, the Dow closed over 6000. The intervening period was the worst in human history: Depression, WWII, Cold War. However anecdotally, I infer from these data three things. The right time to buy stocks is now (as long as you have the money); the right time to sell them is never (unless you need the money); the great risk is not owning them.

4 **I believe that everything you need to know about the movement of stock prices can be summed up in eight words: the downs are temporary; the ups are permanent.** [*This is actually the English translation of the Ibbotson chart.*] I never mistake fluctuation for loss. Stock prices *go* down all the time—25% or so on an average of every five years (albeit not lately)—but since they never *stay* down, it turns out not to matter. Markets fluctuate, but do not create losses. Only people can create permanent loss by mistaking a temporary decline for a permanent decline, and panicking out. No panic, no sell. No sell, no lose. The enemy of investment success is not ignorance, it's fear. So it's my faith, not my knowledge, that saves the investor's financial life.

5 **I process the experience which most people describe as a "bear market" in two different words: big sale.** Since all declines are temporary, I regard all major generalized equity price declines as an opportunity to stock up on some more truly safe investments before the sale ends.

6 **I don't believe in individual stocks, I believe in managed portfolios of stocks.** I can break a pencil; I cannot break 50 pencils tied together. That's *diversification.* Thus: one stock can go to zero. Stocks as an asset class can't go to zero. There is also the issue of *professional management.* When I entered the business in 1967, NYSE volume was 80% individual and 20% institutional. Today, it's around 80/20 the other way. I like the story of David and Goliath as much as anybody does, but the key to that story is that there was only one Goliath. When you're still David, but almost everybody else in the game is Goliath, you're going down. You can't beat 'em. Join 'em.

7 **I believe that dollar-cost averaging will make the dumbest person in the world wealthy. Hey, look at me: it already has.** The more "knowledge" you have, the more you try to outsmart the market, and the worse you do. The more you see the market as long-term inevitable/

short-term unknowable, the more you're inclined to just dollar-cost average, and the better you do. Dollar-cost averaging rewards ignorance with wealth.

8 **I ♡ volatility.** Volatility can't hurt me, because I'm immune to panic. And it can help me, in a couple of ways. First, in an efficient market, higher volatility means (and is the price of) higher returns. Second, higher volatility when I'm dollar-cost averaging means even higher returns. Higher returns are good. Trust me on this.

9 **I'm not afraid of being in the next 25% downtick. I'm afraid of missing the next 100% uptick.** And I've noticed that I have no ability whatever to time the markets. Still, I have found a way to machine the risk of missing the next 100% uptick down to zero. It's called staying fully invested all the bloody time. Works for me.

10 **I believe that, prior to retirement, people should own as close to 100% equities as they can emotionally stand. Then, after retirement, I believe they should own as close to 100% equities as they can emotionally stand.** "Suitability" is a very big issue, but it's an emotional issue, not a financial one. The emotional pull of bonds in retirement is very strong—and I'm the guy who said that feelings are to facts as 19 is to one—but systematic withdrawal from stock funds makes more financial sense. Forget about income vs. principal for a moment, and think in terms of total return. Would you rather have 6% a year from a portfolio of 6% bonds? Or would you rather take 6% a year from stock funds (1½% dividends and 4½% principal, let's say) whose index return is north of 10%? The latter way, your income has room to grow, and your principal has *lots* of room to grow. My belief is that, even in retirement, bonds are a non-starter. See, I *told* you you weren't necessarily going to agree with all this stuff.

OK, go ahead, say it: "Why, you're one of those Equity Zealots!" Yes, I am. I don't think debt investments are evil; I certainly don't think bond fund holders are bad people. (I *do* think that advisors who call bonds "safe" and stocks "risky" should be burned at the stake; see Belief Number Two, above.) But my business has to be run off my belief system—that's where all my strength comes from—and so I can't help people who want to invest mostly in debt securities. I can't help people who want to buy individual stocks—don't believe in 'em (see Belief Number Six). I can't help people who want to go in and out of the markets (see Belief Number Nine); it's impossible for individuals to do this well, and it misses the point (see Beliefs Number Three and Four). Finally, I can't help people who want to retreat to the "safety" (!) of bonds in retirement (see Belief Number 10). *I know who my prospects are by knowing very clearly who they are not.* (And we'll have much more to say about *that* in the next chapter.) My belief system—not my store of knowledge—focuses me on people for whom I can do the most good, and thus on people who can do the most psychic and financial good for me.

* * *

We began this very long inquiry into the limits of knowledge with a righteous, right-brain true story. Let us close with a right-brain parable: My best pal, Indiana Jones, has (unbeknownst to him) contracted a rare disease on one of his expeditions to a tropical jungle. He'll be dead in a year, unless he takes a serum made from the venom of a particularly vicious species of snake.

So, with my buddy's best interests uppermost in my mind and heart, I go out and collect a whole bunch of these snakes and take 'em over to Indy's house in a burlap bag. I toss the writhing, hissing bag of snakes on Indy's kitchen table and start explaining the situation to him.

In the middle of my very first sentence, I hear the kitchen door slam, and when I look up, Indiana is long gone. How could I have forgotten: *he hates snakes!*

The threat of slow death months and months from now was nowhere near frightening enough to keep him in the same room with those snakes. And given what I clearly know about his irrational fears, I should have anticipated that.

I just as easily could have stopped off at a laboratory, had the guys in the white coats extract the venom from the snakes' fangs, and let them cook up the serum. Then I could have given it to Indy, mixed in with his favorite soft drink.

But no, not me. I had to prove what a hero I am. I had to force Indy to sit through a presentation of my Herculean effort in obtaining the bag of snakes. The result: instant and total failure. Indy still doesn't see what a neat thing I did for him...and he's still dying.

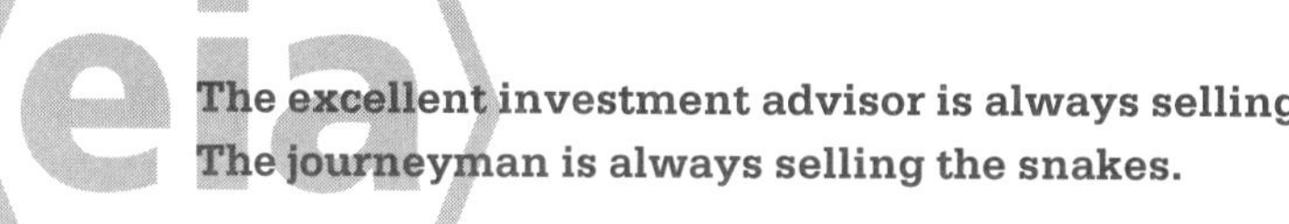

The excellent investment advisor is always selling the serum. The journeyman is always selling the snakes.

In Summary

- The Excellent Investment Advisor knows that people don't make their investment decisions in their intellects. They make those decisions in their emotions, and then gin up intellectual "justifications."

- Thus the left brain can process an infinite amount of information. But the right brain is the decision-maker. And the right brain doesn't reason; it *feels.*

- Knowledge is OK, as far as it goes. But it can never get you where you need to go.

  —Markets are fundamentally unknowable.

  —There's always somebody with more knowledge than you.

  —The more you know, the less of what you know is comprehensible to normal people.

  —Knowledge is Vietnam. You never get "enough," and there's always more to be learned. That's a formula for quagmire.

  —The more you know, the less important each thing you know is. Try to know fewer but more important things.

  —People don't want knowledge. They want someone they trust to tell them what to do.

  —No amount of knowledge can prove the future.

  —Too much knowledge may offend prospects, daunt them with the weight of everything they don't know, or both.

—A knowledge-based approach actively discourages trust.

—Above all, knowledge is useless if you're too paralyzed to prospect. This business rewards not what we know, but what we do, and cause others to do.

☞ The right kind of ignorance (genuine or feigned) can help you steer conversations away from what doesn't matter, and toward what does, without getting you stuck to the tar baby of argument. That sort of "ignorance" attracts serious people and automatically de-selects crazies.

☞ The Excellent Investment Advisor's six-word credo: "When I believe, I am believed."

☞ Start a 90-day, one-short-paragraph/sentence-a-day "Journal of My Belief System." (During those 90 days, try not to learn anything by way of left-brain information.) When it's done, you'll know what you believe, which is to say: who you are. And all your potential strength comes not from what you know, but from who you are.

☞ I'm an Equity Zealot. That's my mission. That's who I am. I mention this only as a way of calling the ultimate question (which only you can answer): *Who are you?*

☞ I know who my prospects are by eliminating (through the filter of my belief system) the others.

☞ Are you selling the serum or the snakes?

3

From belief system to business plan

"The vision of things to be done may come a long time before the way of doing them becomes clear, but woe to him who distrusts the vision."

—**Jenkin Lloyd Jones**

The emphasis in the last chapter on developing your belief system was intended, in part, to put you in touch with the enormity of what you never need to know.

For instance, having chosen the Way of the Equity Zealot, I am excused from having to know anything at all about bonds. But wouldn't I take a $7 million bond account? Probably not. If one were referred to me, I might work out some sort of fee-sharing arrangement with a colleague who's a bond maven. But I would never deceive the client into thinking that I was managing the account. And I don't rule out the possibility that I would turn the account down, if I thought that the investor was seriously disserving his heirs by keeping all his money in bonds, and I couldn't get him to move some of it into equities.

The other reason that consciously codifying your belief system is so important is that it gives you a tremendous head start on setting your own professional agenda. When you've clearly delineated your belief system, you've essentially answered (at least from the standpoint of your profession) the question, "Who am I?" And your sense of professional self becomes, in turn, the basis for your vision of the kind of business you wish to build.

In the example of my own belief system, I feel that it is not merely *a* way to achieve financial independence/multigenerational wealth, but that it is The Way. Still, devotees of asset allocation may quite reasonably suggest that theirs is a better way, in that it can get clients most of the returns of equities with less risk. An equity zealot's answer is threefold:

> **1.** Why settle for most of the returns of equities, when you can have them all?
>
> **2.** You've mistaken risk for volatility. Volatility is the gyration of prices, which has no lasting effect. Risk is located between the investor's ears: it's that he'll panic and turn the volatility into loss. My clients won't, because I tell them not to, and they trust me.
>
> **3.** Since, in an efficient market, higher volatility always translates into higher returns, I'm not interested in anything that's primarily designed to reduce volatility—especially when I'm dollar-cost averaging.”

If people trust me, they'll be at least as stoical about volatility as I am. [*At best, they'll be as delighted by it as I am.*] If they don't trust me, they're going to panic out (of the equity portion, at least) of the most subtly nuanced asset allocation model, when the percentage hit gets big enough and the six o'clock news gets bad enough. So we equity zealots tend to see asset allocation as a mechanical way of trying to substitute for the trust that isn't there. Since, in all the excellent advisor's client relationships, the trust is *always* there…we just don't see the point.

This certainly does not make asset allocation objectively “wrong.” *It just makes it unattractive to someone with my belief system.* And if I turn traitor to my belief system, whence will come my strength? I can't accept the account of a 55-year-old couple who read in some magazine that your equity exposure should be your age subtracted from 100, and who therefore want to be no more than 45% in equities. (An infinite number of monkeys, typing on an infinite number of computer keyboards, would eventually type out all the articles in all the past issues of *Money* magazine. And they may already have.)

That nice couple won't make it all the way through retirement on 45% equities. (On the odd chance that they do, they'll have nothing to leave their children and grandchildren.) And I can't accept an account that's doomed to failure. The excuse, "Well, that's what the clients wanted to do," just doesn't work for me. Because I know that the essence of excellence is getting people to do what they need to do, in the full realization that that's almost always the opposite of what they want to do.

Compromising my belief system would feel shabby and dirty to me; it would chip away at my self-esteem, and start me on a downward spiral. I can't afford that. All my strength comes from my belief system; the price of maintaining and accreting that strength is that I can't sell out my belief system for 30 pieces of silver, even (and especially) when a prospect wants me to.

The Roman emperor and Stoic philosopher Marcus Aurelius wrote, "Man must be arched and buttressed from within, else the temple will crumble to dust." In that same vein,

⟨eia⟩

The excellent investment advisor knows that you have to be who you are, and you have to sell what you believe in.

Now, if you've been in the business for only a year or so, let's say, you may conclude as follows:

> "Here is what I believe. I believe I'm so green that I still don't know my, uh, armpit from third base. I believe it would be lunacy for me to take a crypto-religious vow of blind faith in equities—or in anything else—this early in the game. I believe I would no more turn down a $7 million bond account than I would swallow a dozen live goldfish.

I believe that if some poor 55-year-old couple only wanted to start with 45% equities, I'd take the account so fast it would make your head spin. Then, after they'd gotten to know me and trust me, I'd gently raise the question again in a year or so.

I believe that there's so much diversity of product in my firm, and so much technical support available to me in so many different areas, that I can well afford to hold myself out to the world as a generalist. I tend also to believe that a diversified book of business, without overconcentration in equities or any one area, is safest for me in the long run. And I can always decide to specialize later in my career, when I know enough to make an informed decision.

I believe that this book I'm reading right now has some interesting points to make, but that zealotry of any stripe gives me the creeps, and that, in particular, this guy's seat back and tray table are definitely not in their full upright and locked position.”

Well and good, say I. This is actually a fairly complete, and potentially very effective, belief system (although I probably could have lived without the comments at the end). For in this statement, the fledgling advisor adopts a number of valuable beliefs:

(a) He concludes that there is wisdom in the safety of a diversified book of business. [*There is.*]

(b) He decides that there is still a place for the generalist, but instinctively realizes that he needn't become an expert in everything...or anything. Instead, he'll marshal the technical personnel his firm employs, as the need arises. [*Right again.*]

(c) He realizes that he is temperamentally suited to taking even flawed accounts and trying to change them gradually, once he's gotten inside and built up a reservoir of trust. [*Bless him.*]

(d) Above all, with respect to choosing an area of specialization, he decides that it would be best for him not to decide right now. And

> the decision not to decide can always be a valid business decision, in that it dispels uncertainty and second-guessing, which are time-wasters and energy-depleters. [*Amen.*]

All in all, for somebody who might have thought he didn't even have a belief system, this new advisor has found a very solid basis on which to set his professional agenda. And, of course, *his belief system is better for him than mine would be, simply because it's his own.* Now all he has to do is to build a business plan on the firm foundation of that belief system. Indeed, that's all anybody has to do.

All the excellent investment advisors I've ever known **(a)** had a very clearly defined, written business plan, **(b)** believed implicitly and unshakably in that plan, **(c)** were impervious to external circumstances, so that they didn't alter the plan every time the wind changed direction, and **(d)** continued to work their plan steadfastly, *no matter how long it took,* until the plan inevitably succeeded. The excellent investment advisor *acts;* the journeyman is acted upon (by people, markets, and "circumstances," whatever those are). And it is much easier to act if you are carrying out a plan in which you have complete faith.

That business plan is, in turn, the intermediate step between your belief system and your ultimate goals for yourself. So if you clearly have a vision of the nature of the good you can do for people, you must now proceed to put, in effect, a specific price tag on the creation of all that good. And from that goal, you can back into a plan.

Consider the statement, "I can do an incalculable amount of good for a very great number of people, and earn an excellent living thereby." Do not let the stirring nobility of this pronouncement take your eye, even for a moment, off the fact that it is, in essence, smoke. First, it says that one *can* do a lot good; it gives no indication that one has made an irrevocable decision to do so. And there can be no success without the steel of irrevocable decision for a spine. Next, the statement gives no indication of how many people one can do meaningful good for; without this, almost no strategic planning is possible. Finally, it sets no goal in terms of compensation for the good that one proposes to do. And in the absence of a definition of success, success is impossible. In sum, the whole statement isn't a plan. It isn't even a goal. It's a daydream.

So let me outline a process of goal-setting and business planning, based on my own belief system, and on my experience of what a reasonably diligent person can accomplish. Once again, please realize that this is offered only as an example, in the hope and expectation that you'll adapt it to your own needs. It's not a prescription, in that sense; it's a track to run on. But if I had to start—or simply decided to start—all over again tomorrow, here's how I'd lay it out.

1 **Set a long-term goal for the income you ultimately require.** Let's say that I need, and have made a commitment to deserve, an income before taxes of half a million dollars a year. The first thing I need to do is make a budget for the amount of money my practice will have to gross—and what deductions and expenditures I'll need to make against that gross—in order to net a half million dollars before taxes.

Just to pick a conservative number off a bus, let's say I find that my net income will run about 40% of the gross fees and/or commissions my practice generates. That means I'll need to achieve gross revenues of $1,250,000.

2 **Next, establish a goal for assets under management which would yield your target gross income.** In an overwhelmingly—if not exclusively—equity-based practice, I can't see a whole lot of difficulty generating fee and/or commission income equal to 1% of my assets under management. (Indeed, no commissions and a fee of 1% a year is where I suspect the business is ultimately going to settle out.) So I need to get to $125 million in assets under management.

3 **Decide on your target-market average account size and the number of those accounts you need.** Being basically a family guy, whose greatest professional satisfaction is endowing other families with multigenerational wealth, my target account is one involving the assets of two, three and sometimes even four generations within a family. (More about the theory and practice of what I call Multigenerational Marketing later on in this book.) Among all those folks, it's not that hard to find—or to see that the family can soon accumulate—$500,000 in investable assets. So, for the rest of my life, all I have to do is recruit 250 of those families.

Alternatively, you *could* go after (among other permutations) 500 accounts with average investable assets of $250,000. This may look a lot easier, and in the beginning it is. But after a while, you'll start to see the very significant diseconomies of scale involved. As any experienced advisor will tell you, it is neither twice as hard nor twice as time-consuming to handle 500 smaller accounts as it is to handle 250 larger ones. The degree of difficulty in the bigger number is, at the very least, three times, and may get as high as five times, especially at tax time and in down markets. (And if you run into a down market *at* tax time: Nelly, bar the door.) You gotta do what you gotta do, but I recommend going after fewer, bigger accounts. You'll live longer, you'll have more fun, and you'll get better referrals.

4 **Establish a specific time frame for the realization of your asset/account goal.** "Someday I'll have 250 accounts of $500,000 each" is smoke. Put a fuse on it, because that's the only way you can get a handle on the level of daily activity you'll have to perform in order to get where you want to go. (And regular daily activity, as we'll see in the next chapter, is all that really matters.)

I believe that anybody who will work at this single-mindedly can get to the goal in three years, assuming

(a) six months to fill up the prospect pipeline, and to go on enough appointments that you make all your mistakes and get comfortable with the process.

(b) Then, for two and a half years, two appointments a day, 10 a week. Assuming you're qualifying people at all well (by telling them before the interview that you're most effective in counseling families with $500,000 of investable assets), you'll open no fewer than two accounts a week. (And don't be surprised if it's three, or even four. Then, later on, the referrals will start to come, and your closing ratio will arrive at, and even surpass, 50%.)

That's about all there is to it. Figure that there are around 50 million Americans—roughly 20% of the population—in households with at least $85,000 in annual income. For you consistently to earn half a million dollars a year (i.e. to be in the top one-half of one percent of all earners in America), you just have to win the hearts and minds of 250 of these households. *You may not particularly like the work of prospecting, but you've got to love those odds.*

Admittedly, the business-building program outlined above is partially premised on a standing start: the single-minded and totally focused hunt for 250 elephants in three years assumes you have the great luxury of just starting out (or starting over). But what if you are one of those benighted souls who already have 286 accounts with average assets of $69,280? Chances are those people are taking up all of your time, and more. (A book of business like that lets you know how it would feel to be pecked to death by ducks.)

Clearly, you have some important decisions to make. One is whether you really have a burning desire for excellence in the first place. Because, on the evidence of your current book, you apparently don't. Or, if you do, you have not made the irrevocable decision to seize it. Remember that the path to excellence is always the same, no matter where one is in one's career:

(1) An all-consuming desire for its achievement.

(2) The irrevocable decision to achieve it.

(3) The creation of a written plan for its achievement in a specific period of time.

(4) Execution of the plan regardless of external circumstances.

Everything after that is just methodology—or, if you will, tactics. "Ought we to make our great landing in Normandy or at Calais?" is a question at least nine levels down from "Is our war aim anything less than the extirpation of Nazism from the earth?" Similarly, "Should I prospect corporate executives or individual entrepreneurs?" isn't a remotely strategic question. It's high-level tactical, but no more.

So if you are one of those people whose days seem very full, but who aren't happy with what they're full of, in a sense you really *do* have to start over.

This is why I think that your "Journal of My Belief System" is critically important. So much so that, if you are more than three years in the business, you have my permission to write that journal over the next 30 days, if you think that 90 is just too much foreplay. Do not, however, try to do it in fewer than 30 days. Our personality type is subject to huge upsurges in short-lived enthusiasms, followed by self-recriminating depression when we can't follow through. The journal may be the very first step in weaning you off that destructive cycle (the clinical, technical term for which is up-in-the-clouds-down-in-the-dumps). **Don't rush it.**

When your belief system is edited down from the totality of entries in your journal, you can sit down with your account book in one hand and your core beliefs in the other. Then, go through each account in your book, and ask, "Is this person getting me closer to, or farther away from, the realization of excellence based on my true belief system?" You see, the essence of mediocrity in our business is taking the accounts you can get rather than seeking out the accounts you really want. (As in all things, the road to hell is the path of least resistance.) And, in just a moment, we'll clearly outline the characteristics of who you want and who you don't.

The immediate challenge is to clear away enough of the wreckage so that you have an unobstructed path to the creation of a new business plan, as least for part of your working day. The minimum it will take to make meaningful prospecting strides is, I believe, three hours per day. Stated another way, this is three-eighths of your time, assuming an eight-hour day. But meaningful change can never be effected other than by changing behavior every single day. (That's the only way your unconscious will ever get the message that you're really serious.) So let's call it for what it is: you need to clear three hours in every business day.

Those three hours will need to have two very important characteristics. First, they have to be the same three hours every day. Second, you can't do anything but prospect during those three hours. You even have to train your clients that you can't take calls, or call people back, during those times. To let the rest of your day creep back into those three hours is an avoidance behavior.

There are any number of permutations of ways to find your three hours. Let me suggest just one:

(1) *Arrive at the office every day one hour earlier than you do now.* That's one of the three clear hours you need, right there. What you do in that hour is not that important yet (Normandy or Calais?). Maybe it will be one of your prospecting hours. Maybe it'll be an hour in which you do a lot of the paperwork you now use as an avoidance behavior by strewing it all through your day, so you don't have to prospect. It matters not. We've found one of the three hours we need, and we only have to find two more in the following eight, or 25% of your current day.

(2) *Give away the bottom 25% of your accounts.* One way or another, these people are costing you at least 25% of your time now (even if that time is concentrated around April 15, when they all need to know the cost basis for their 268.91 shares of Gronsky Whatever-Was-Red-Hot-Three-Years-Ago Fund). Alternatively, they're small accounts who *don't* take up much time—which means you have no relationship and do no business. By keeping them, you are waiting to win the lottery, rather than going out and working for wealth. Only losers do that. Keeping those accounts drains your self-esteem and your energy by signaling your unconscious that you think you're a loser. So even if you're not talking to those people much, your diminished self-esteem is robbing you of the courage to prospect. Same difference. I say again: you will find, directly or indirectly, the other two hours you need every day by bagging the bottom 25% of your book.

(3) *Fire your single most corrosive PITA account.* PITA, as I'm sure I need hardly tell you, stands for Pain In The, uh, Neck. If you've been in the business for a while, chances are you have one fairly large (if not *very* large) account, who does a big percentage of your business, and causes you an even bigger percentage of your grief and pain. "Needing" this account—which is synonymous with believing you deserve the pain—is the clearest possible signal you can send your unconscious that, deep down, you think you're a loser. *Fire him* (or her). You'll rationalize not doing so by saying you need the business. But let me spell out the message your soul is trying to send you: *You need the self-esteem* that only firing your biggest PITA can restore to you. (Because, make no mistake: you had that self-esteem once, but sold it for 30—or 30,000, or however many—pieces of silver.)

But hey, wait, haven't you already found the three hours you need by taking those first two steps? Yes, but this third step ensures that you have the self-esteem (and the motivation) to *keep* those three hours, and to pour into them every ounce of ferocious determination you can muster. As you value your career—as you truly desire excellence—*fire your biggest PITA now.* If it will take some financial sacrifice—and it almost certainly will, if only for a while—go home and explain things to your family. I'm betting that you'll be amazed by the economies they volunteer, and the love and support they offer. That will give you even more pure fuel for what you have to do.

You can play around all you want with permutations of the first and second steps of this program. (For instance, how about coming in at the same time you do now, but giving away the bottom three-eighths of your book?) *The third step is simply indispensable.* Of course, instead of steps one and two, you could just reconcile your account book with your re-codified belief system, and start giving away everybody who'll really never fit the profile. Radical surgery? Sure, but it'll probably free up no fewer than five hours a day, and shorten your pilgrimage to excellence by a year...if not more. You decide. But once you've made the decision, hold on to it for dear life, and put it into practice every single day. You're not getting any younger, and you may never have a better opportunity to achieve excellence than you do by starting right here and now.

The way you prospect to the point of being able to have two appointments a day with the right kind of people is the subject of the next chapter. Please see that we are reasoning backward, from your ultimate goal, to a business plan for selecting the people who will get you to your goal, to how to prospect for those people.

We have established who your prospective clients are in quantitative terms, i.e. what they earn and how much they have to invest. We come now to the other issue, the one that is both subtler and far more important: not just how much money they have, but *what they're like.*

As difficult as this may be for you to believe, clients have to deserve you. If you are the person I think you are—deeply committed to the craft of wealth-building, diligent, ethical, knowledgeable and professional—you ought to have clients who respect you, and those qualities in you. You're the person who is going to manage the realization of 250 families' hopes and dreams, and also the one who's going to banish their fears. There are certain kinds of people who will be most apt to recognize and value your great capacities. Even more important, there are clearly certain types of people who will not esteem you, no matter what you say and do.

Steve Moeller is my fellow columnist at *Dow Jones Investment Advisor* magazine. He's the president of American Business Visions, a Tustin, California, consulting firm that helps financial advisors identify and obtain wealthy clients (the firm's toll-free phone number is 800-678-1701). Steve has worked up demographic (objective facts) and psychographic (interests, opinions and attitudes) profiles of the clients the Excellent Investment Advisor wants—and those she does not. Steve feels that 80% of a typical investment advisor's day is wasted talking to poorly qualified people. So he and I believe that his profiles can be immensely effective in forcing you to focus on the right types of people, and to avoid the troglodytes.

Steve's ideal client profiles are divided into working "accumulators" and financially independent "preservers." His "accumulators" have the following demographic characteristics:

▶They're extremely busy with their careers or businesses and don't have time to manage their money themselves.

▶They're young enough to accept your advice but old enough to really benefit from it (40–70 years old).

▶They have bright financial futures and will be making ongoing contributions—both personally and for their employees—to their accounts with you.

▶They have $50,000 or more to invest each year.

▶They have a responsibility to invest "prudently."

▶They have lots of social and business contacts to refer you to.

▶They're likely to inherit a substantial sum (and will be willing to refer you to their parents).

The psychographics of Steve's "accumulators" are:

▶They understand investment markets and are highly motivated to work with a professional advisor.

▶They're oriented toward capital preservation.

▶They take a long-term view of performance.

▶They're in a business/professional field that you're interested in.

▶They were referred to you by a happy client.

▶They trust you, and consider you an expert in your field.

▶They're open-minded and willing to learn new things.

▶They're honest with you, and fully disclose their assets, values, goals and concerns.

▶They're decisive.

▶They value your service, advice and professional relationship—and are willing to compensate you fairly.

▶They want advice, not just information.

Steve's "preservers," on the other hand, don't usually expect to make further investments. "But they start with a large pool of capital," he says, "and they want you to help them keep what they have and minimize the impact of taxes and inflation."

The ideal "preserver," Steve and I agree, has $500,000 or more invested, "enough to support their lifestyle from dividends. They can leave capital gains to build their asset bases. And they have lots of other things they'd rather do than manage their money. They believe that's a job for a trained professional—you."

Steve counsels us to avoid those who:

[Demographics]

▶have a little money, just enough to entice you to work with them;

▶because they don't have much capital, "need" to consistently earn above-market returns to support their standard of living;

▶are so young they know it all—or so old they can't make decisions;

▶are investment hobbyists and have plenty of time to "play with their money;"

▶have few social or business contacts they could refer to you;

▶are past their career peak and don't expect to make additional contributions to their investments;

[Psychographics]

▶are performance- rather than relationship-oriented;

▶don't understand investments or the markets;

▶focus on short-term results;

▶demand a high level of service and seem to enjoy the attention;

▶are in a field that doesn't interest you;

▶have a lot of time on their hands, and don't mind wasting yours;

▶are overly analytical and constantly compare your recommendations and performance to their alternatives;

▶worry about their money and need constant reinforcement;

▶get confused easily, and call you constantly for help reading statements and confirmations;

▶are extremely frugal and whine about your fees;

▶want information rather than advice.

This is simply the best, most economical profile of who the Excellent Investment Advisor wants—and doesn't want—that I've ever seen, or ever expect to see. If you take three minutes to re-read it every morning of your three-years-to-$125-million-under-management quest, I believe you'll save yourself literally months of wasted energy and time.

For instance, you may now be inclined to spend an hour with a frightened older person, trying to calm his fears about rolling an $80,000 CD—a very large percentage of his invested capital—into a bond fund.

You feel good about doing this, because **(a)** the prospect would, indeed, be financially better off, **(b)** you genuinely are trying to win his trust rather than teach him the nuances of the yield curve, and **(c)** it's a decent-sized ticket.

But suddenly it's an hour later, and the prospect keeps talking about friends of his who "lost money" (!) in a bond fund in 1994, and what about the national debt, and how there's no sales charge on CDs. In the bad old transaction-oriented, commission-driven days, you might—with the best heart in the world—have kept trying to wear this old fellow down. But with your eye fixed firmly on excellence as you've defined it, and with Moeller's alarm system now at DEFCON-3, suddenly you see the truth: this is the prospect I've got, *but it's not the prospect I want and need!*

Suppose this guy actually *does* buy the bond fund? *Then* where am I? I know the phone is going to ring every time the long bond backs up 20 basis points. I know the guy will be on the other end of the phone, saying, "I lost (*sic*) 14 cents a share yesterday!" I know that, even if the bond fund goes up (because rates go down), this guy can only refer me to...other people like him! Who won't want to do anything because... "interest rates are too low right now!" This way lies madness! I'll end up face down on the conference room floor...*pecked to death by ducks!* Aarrrghh!

Putting yourself in front of the right sort of people is almost the entirety of what you have to do in order to achieve excellence. (Doing is to knowing as four is to one, remember?) And a critical component of getting in front of the right people is staying out of the faces of the wrong people. Twenty-odd years ago, when my daughters were still very young, I heard a famous child psychologist postulate the Law of The Soggy Potato Chip. He said that a child, not having access to fresh potato chips, will eat soggy potato chips, if that's all he can get. And if he can't get real affection and healthy boundaries from his parents, he'll whine and nag and break stuff in order to get exhausted, frustrated feedback from them. Because a child lives for parental feedback.

In the quest for excellence, which can—if we allow it to—become very frustrating at times, we are always in danger of falling victim to the Law of The Soggy Potato Chip. With no good prospect in sight, we may seize on the marginal prospect we've got, just because he's the one we've got. That's the way journeymen become journeymen. It's the tar baby. It's the ultimate downward spiral.

You get out of this business exactly what you put into it. Indeed, let's put that up in **capitals**, because it is one of the Excellent Investment Advisor's core beliefs:

⟨eia⟩

The excellent investment advisor knows that you take out of this business exactly as much value as you put into it.

(Or, to quote Richie Havens's twist on Lennon/McCartney, "In the end, the love you save will be equal to the love you gave.") To disbelieve this—to feel that your finest efforts can be wasted, and may not ever be rewarded—is to despair. And despair is the invisible monkey on the back of every journeyman. Just as faith in the long-term efficacy of her good work (which is the same as saying: faith in herself) is the beacon that guides the excellent advisor on. We are, after all, trying to induce people to have faith in us. And the first requirement of that process is faith in ourselves.

So, before going on to the next chapter—which is probably the pivot point of the whole book—I invite you to take yourself down to the local bookstore, and treat yourself to an inexpensive copy of Emerson's *Essays*. Sit down someplace very comfortable, when you know you won't be disturbed, and read the essay "Compensation." For just as every spacecraft can rise just so high into the atmosphere, but then needs a booster rocket to blast it out of the earth's downward pull and on to its space mission, "Compensation" may be just the thing to put your quest for excellence into orbit.

"If you serve an ungrateful master, serve him the more," says the sage of Concord. *"Put God in your debt. Every stroke shall be repaid. The longer the payment is withholden, the better for you; for compound interest on compound interest is the rate and usage of this exchequer."*

Now, what will it be? Calais...or Normandy? For the issue is not: will we good people win the war? The only questions are when, where... and how.

In Summary

- Your belief system doesn't just tell you how much you don't have to know. It answers the professional question, "Who am I?" Which is critical because...you're selling yourself.

- Even the decision not to decide can be a valid business decision. If you want to be a generalist for a while, make a conscious decision to be an excellent generalist. Just don't dither about it.

- The business plan most likely to yield you long-term excellence is the one rooted most deeply in your core belief system. Thence comes all your strength.

- All excellent advisors—not some, not most; *all*—

  (a) have a clear, written business plan,

  (b) believe implicitly and unshakably in that plan,

  (c) are impervious to external "circumstances," and

  (d) continue steadfastly to work that plan until, inevitably, it succeeds.

- The procedure is: codify your belief system. Define professional excellence in financial terms. Then create a business plan that bridges those two decisions.

☞ One way of creating a plan:

(a) Set an income goal.

(b) Figure out what asset base will yield that goal with no strain.

(c) Decide on an ideal account size, and divide that number into (b) to see how many accounts you need. Err on the side of larger accounts.

(d) Set an irrevocable time frame for the achievement of (c).

(e) Your target households may number upwards of 50 million people. On a very, very bad day, you may need 500 of those households. You gotta love those odds.

☞ The critical elements are: burning desire; irrevocable decision; written, date-specific plan; execution of the plan. Everything else is methodology. Don't get hung up on the methodology.

☞ Experienced advisors will need to create and/or clear three prospecting hours every day. They have to be the same three hours, and you can't do anything else, including taking incoming phone calls, during those three hours. Prospect, or just sit there. Everything else is an avoidance behavior.

☞ At the very least, experienced advisors should lop off the bottom 25% of their book. It's dead weight, and it's draining your time, energy and self-esteem—which are three ways of saying the same thing.

☞ At best, experienced advisors should disengage from all those accounts who don't fit the profile of the people who are going to get you where you need to go...and whom you really can't help. Scarier, sure. And it'll cost some business—maybe a lot of business—in the short run. Think of the foregone revenue as an investment in shortening the path to excellence.

☞ In any event, fire your biggest PITA account. You can't journey to excellence carrying a human scorpion on your back. Corrosive people are inimical to your self-esteem...without which excellence is impossible.

☞ Even more important than how much money they have is *what your prospects are like.* Use Steve Moeller's demographic/psychographic profiles to keep you focused on who you want, and to help you avoid who you don't want.

☞ Don't think you're going to win the lottery. Don't touch the tar baby; you'll get stuck to it. And above all, beware the Law of The Soggy Potato Chip: never mistake the prospect you have for the prospect you want.

☞ In the end, the love you save *will* be equal to the love you gave. You take out of this business exactly as much value as you put into it.

4

Mastering the art of painless prospecting........

"Let us not grow tired of doing good, for in due time we shall reap our harvest, if we do not give up."

—**St. Paul,** Letter to the Galatians (6:9)

• • • • • • •

Most things in life that are simple are also easy. And most things that are complex are also relatively hard. Building a first-class investment advisory business is one of those rare enterprises which are at the same time simple...and very hard.

This book's main theme is the immense capacity that people in our profession have to do good—and to do well by doing good, because when we do this business the right way, our interests and those of our clients are in virtually perfect harmony. The awareness of our power to do good, and our determination to use that power to change people's lives, together give us access to a vast reservoir of psychic energy—the kind that is released only by a labor of love. And most days in this business, you need every last scintilla of energy you can get.

In the Foreword to this book, I said—and now say again—that the Excellent Investment Advisor can do more good for more people, and can make that good last longer, than any doctor who ever lived. There's just one problem. Almost everyone you will ever prospect in your life either

(a) doesn't recognize that you're the doctor,

(b) doesn't know he's sick,

(c) knows he's sick, but doesn't really want to get better, or

(d) thinks there's a cheaper way to get better then by hiring you.

The critical word in that analysis—indeed, the one glorious word that's the key to all success in this business—is *almost. Almost* everyone you prospect may not have been given the grace to see you as the end of all his family's wealth-building problems. *But a very small minority will.* And those relatively few people are the key to all of your professional—and much of your personal—happiness.

The obvious solution to this problem is, of course, simply to prospect the enlightened minority—the few who'll get it. Unfortunately, you can't know who they are, other than by process of elimination. So you also have to prospect the many who won't get it. For many are called, but few are chosen. You have to hear "no" a lot of times before you can hear "yes." That's just how it works. That's the job you signed up for. That's the deal you elected to make.

And what a deal it is, when you think about it. First of all, you are not subject to an externally imposed income limit. Since no one can, at any time, prevent you from doing more good, no one can prevent you from increasing your income. If you've been in the business for a while, and are experiencing an income limit, be assured that it is one which you've unconsciously imposed on yourself. There is no salary scale in what we do. If you're earning $80,000, and the person in the next office is earning $240,000, the difference is entirely attributable to decisions that you both—albeit unconsciously—have made. And I feel no more sorry for you than for your colleague. Granted, you have some major issues to resolve. But that poor guy, if he would only get out of his own way, could—with the same or less effort—be earning half a million dollars. (And, deep down, he knows it.) Indeed, in all aspects of his career,

The excellent investment advisor is subject only to self-imposed limitations.

The excellent advisor also has no real boss. Nobody can tell you, in any real sense, what to do. You make your own hours, set your own work pace, decide what kinds of investments you want to work on, and what kinds of clients you want to work with. Moreover, the excellent advisor can never be unemployed—not least of all because, no matter what firm's name is on the door, she's fundamentally self-employed. A professional with a good, clean, growing business will never be fired, and will in fact be actively recruited by other firms seeking that rarity which is her excellence. In an age of massive corporate layoffs, this is no small thing.

Finally, our profession permits and even encourages us to go on learning and growing for as long as we like—long after most people's careers have topped out, or even ended altogether.

And all you have to do, in order to obtain a life filled with these extraordinary benefits, is to accept a job in which there's no salary, *and in which almost everybody to whom you offer your services says "no."* That's The Great Trade-Off. And "no" is the key to all happiness, for "no"—regardless of how it may feel sometimes—is never quite unanimous. Once in a while, amid a great chorus of "no," a single golden "yes" always rings out. But the physical law that governs our professional universe mandates that you have to personally encounter a certain incidence of "no" in order to hear the one golden "yes."

The realization that there *is* such a universal law—that the relationship of "no" to "yes" is not random, but constant and therefore knowable—is the making of the excellent advisor. Whereas for the journeyman, who either does not know the law or has lost faith in it, prospecting is a gauntlet of relentless, remorseless "rejection." The difference between success and failure in this business, then, is not the incidence of "no" (i.e. the raw number of times one hears it), but purely in *the advisor's emotional response to "no."*

The journeyman responds to "no" as if it were a soul-corroding acid, and unconsciously erects a huge system of defenses and avoidances against it. He does not see—or, more properly, can no longer bear to look at—the fact that everything that keeps away "no" is also a perfect insulation against "yes." The excellent advisor sees prospecting for what it truly is: heaven's own original numbers game, in which a certain incidence of "no" is the only possible means to one statistically inevitable "yes." Thus, for the excellent advisor, "rejection" is the ultimate fuel. (In fact, as we'll see in just a little while, to the winners in our business, "rejection" isn't even "rejection," but something different—and much better.)

We all start out, with respect to prospecting, a little like the rat in the psychology experiment. Maybe you remember this little guy from the lab part of a behavioral psychology course you took in college. As class began in September, you were shown this very rotund rat in a cage with a button at one end. And the people in the white coats told you that, all summer long, the rat had been conditioned to know that every time he hit that button, he got a food pellet.

So here you saw the Orson Welles of rats, lolling around in a cage strewn with food pellets—because now the rat would hit the button even when he wasn't hungry, for the sheer fun of getting a free pellet.

Once the lab professor had explained the methodology to you, the real experiment began. The button was re-wired so that, instead of getting a food pellet when he hit it, the rat got an electric shock. Well, the first time he did it, the rat got zapped all the way across his cage. He picked himself up, looked around, and went right back to the button. Zap! Rat shakes his head just a moment longer, hits the button a third time. Zap! Rat stops to think about what's going on, but since rats can't think, he just shrugs and goes over to the button for a snack. Zap!

Slowly, you observe that the time lapses between the rat's forays over to the button are getting longer and longer. He's getting hungrier all the time, though, so he keeps going back…and he keeps getting zapped. By the end of the experiment, the rat is cowering in the corner of the cage farthest away from the button. He's slowly starving to death...but he'd rather starve than get zapped by that damned button again!

There is, I believe, something of that hapless rat in all of us. We come into the business all fired up with visions of the limitless income we can earn, if we'll just go out and show our firm's nifty products and services to the waiting world. Yes, it'll be a sales job, because an awful lot of people will say no to us at first. But we've been trained to respond "correctly" to every objection, so surely all sales resistance will melt away under the warmth of our powerful statistical arguments. We won't close everybody, but...we'll do pretty darn well.

So we skitter across our cage, and smack that button called the telephone. Zap! "I'm not interested." Zap! "I already have a broker." Zap! "I don't have any money." Zap! "I only buy no-load funds." Zap! Zap! Zap! Until, one fine day, we find ourselves sitting on the far corner of the cage, and saying, in effect, "I may not be making enough money, but I'll be damned if I'm going to hit that button and get zapped again." Except we never admit this to ourselves consciously. The rejection-shocked rat has taken over the controls of our unconscious, and is sending up cheap rationalizations to the conscious mind, which is desperate for any excuse not to have to hit the button:

▶ "You can't start prospecting now. You have to read *The Wall Street Journal* cover to cover, including the Bolivian trade figures and the ballet reviews. You never know when a prospect might ask you about this stuff."

▶ "You can't start prospecting now. You have to study the latest changes in your firm's asset allocation model. Hey, you never know: maybe if you show people 52% stocks/39% bonds/9% cash, instead of last week's 49%/43%/8%, all their sales resistance will vanish."

▶ "You can't start prospecting now. *You have to load all your prospect files into your computer.*"

As the psychological pain of not having the guts to get zapped again rises, the rationalizations for not prospecting become more and more bizarre. Shame, guilt and anxiety build up to toxic levels, poisoning the well of your self-esteem even more. The awful downward spiral takes another turn, as the interval between trips to the button lengthens even further…

Stop. Wake up. You've been having a bad dream. You're not the rat in the psychology experiment at all.

Instead, you're a person who's just walked through the door of a magical room. There's nothing in the room but a kind of elegant slot machine, with a comfortable chair in front of it. The machine takes quarters. And here is what I want you to know about it: every one thousand times you put in a quarter and pull the handle, this wondrous device pays you $1,000.

It will certainly take significant amounts of time, patience and energy to feed in a quarter and pull that handle a thousand times, won't it? Why, you may never be able to do it faster than, say, once every 10 seconds. That means you can only do it six times a minute, so you'll need close to three hours of uninterrupted work to get the machine to pay off once. With time out for lunch and reading *The Wall Street Journal* cover to cover [*which suddenly doesn't seem so critical, does it?*], no way you can make that machine pay off more than…twice a day.

Doesn't bother you much, does it? Why, you might even decide to get in an hour earlier, skim the *Journal* even before you enter the magic room, and have a cup of soup and a sandwich brought into the room at midday, so you won't have to stop pulling the handle. And, at that rate, you might just be able to get the machine to pay off three times before you go home, exhausted but happy.

Well, with deep apologies for having analogized what we do to any form of gambling: welcome to the business. It's the elegant machine in the magical room. And programmed into the machine is a cosmic law: every N number of times you pull the handle, you get a prospect.

Is this analogy flawed? Only in its details. No, you can't talk to somebody new every 10 seconds. But by the same token, it takes an awful lot less than a thousand people to yield you one new prospect. Never mind the mechanics; focus on the great, cosmic law. And realize that, whatever its flaws, this analogy is infinitely closer to reality than that of the rat in the psychology experiment. For in that story, the rat gets zapped *every single time*, until he despairs and dies. In the fable of the elegant machine, *almost* every try doesn't pay off. And therein lies the supreme secret of our business: **the golden "almost"!**

Even if it takes three hours (or whatever) of remorseless, relentless "no," we who have the knowledge of (and faith in) the golden "almost" are undaunted. Because we know that, on the average of once every three hours (or whatever) we hear that one statistically inevitable "yes." And so the "no's" don't bother us that much. Who pays attention to the 999 pulls that don't pay off? We're just passing the time, doing what we know we have to do to get to the thousand dollars every thousandth pull. Some of us have to go into our own pockets for the thousand quarters we need to put into the machine. Some of us even get staked to those quarters by our employer. (Although he then claims a larger portion of our earnings.) No matter: wherever the input comes from, the point is that the output is sure to be there, once in some number of tries.

The formula that governs all our prospecting efforts is

$$P = \frac{1}{N}$$

That is, you get a prospect once for every N number of new people you approach and suggest that they utilize your services. This is the great cosmic law that explains literally everything in our professional lives, just as Einstein's simple, elegant $e = mc^2$ explains the workings of the physical universe.

When you come to the end of your career, and go to the Great Home Office in the Sky, you'll take along your lifetime production report. At the end of the last page of that run, all the way over on the right hand side, will be one number. Literally and figuratively, it will be the bottom line: total lifetime production.

That number will have been determined, over the entire span of your career, by one variable and one only. It will not be who you called; it will not be what you said. It will not be how smart you were, or which investments you recommended, or what "the market" did. The sole determinant of your lifetime production is simply this: *how many people you talked to about hiring you to be their investment advisor.* Because every time you had that conversation with N number of people, you got a prospect.

This has nothing to do (at least not directly) with your persuasiveness, your strength of character, or your personal charm. It is not a function of what we usually think of as "sales skills." How many times have you heard someone say, or even heard yourself say, "You put me in front of a prospect, and I'll open the account; no problem." Or, "Once I get an account, I develop a relationship that lasts until one of us dies; I simply never lose accounts." By and large, we have great confidence in our selling/account management skills. But we seem to have tremendous difficulty getting ourselves in front of enough qualified new prospective clients.

This should suggest to you that selling/account management (which is a very high art form) and prospecting (an exact, pitiless science) require completely different sets of skills. That notion, I think, runs counter to the training most of us have had, which held that prospecting/selling/account handling were all points along the same continuum.

When you get face-to-face with a prospective client, I recommend that you turn loose all your emotional energy, in order to let the other person feel and respond to the depth of your belief. On the other hand, I think it's a mistake to throw your emotional energy into a process where four out of five (or nine out of 10, or even 19 out of 20) people you talk to will brush you off.

Prospecting is a science. It's a process of trial and error where you find out what works (i.e. who is a prospect) by experimenting with a fairly large number of things that turn out not to work (i.e. the great chorus of "no"). The exact relationship between the number of things that work and the number of things that don't is stated as

$$P = \frac{1}{N}$$

In the fable of the elegant machine in the magical room, the machine paid multiples of your investment every 1000 times you tried it. This process can also be reduced to a formula:

$$P = \frac{1}{1000}$$

where P is the payoff of $1000. The formula, then, simply states what we already know, which is that payoff occurs one one-thousandth of the time, or on one try in a thousand. The formula for painless prospecting

$$P = \frac{1}{N}$$

simply states that, by the same inexorable force of numbers, payoff—obtaining a qualified prospect—occurs once in N number of tries. The only difference is that we don't yet know what number N is. But I hope you can see that once we *do* know what number N is, all your problems are solved, *providing you believe in the basic formula.* Because if you don't believe in the power of $\frac{1}{N}$ you must think the process of success is utterly random. Or, far worse, you think it's governed by forces you can't understand and that are outside your control. "I could succeed if I had enough *motivation,*" I hear people say. Well, gee, how do you measure "motivation," exactly? (pints? cubic feet?) And if you can't measure it, how do you know when you've got "enough"? Is "motivation" a liquid? A gas? A mysterious force emanating from crystals, or from the planet Gronsky? (You were sufficiently motivated to take a job with no salary, so you could live entirely by your own wits and have no limit on your earnings. Isn't that motivation enough?)

Let's proceed on the assumption that you believe you do, in fact, get one prospect for every N number of new contacts you make. I submit that once you know what N is—once you know how many quarters/pulls it takes to force the machine to pay off—all the anxiety goes out of prospecting. And, when you're no longer anxious, you no longer have an emotional reaction to "no." Instead, you see "no" as the distasteful but necessary means to the statistically inevitable end of "yes"—once in every N tries. In other words, the only thing in this world you ever have to do to get a prospect is to listen to N-minus-one (N−1) poor souls say "no."

Listening to people say "no" is the process that journeymen call "rejection." "Rejection" is very painful to the journeyman, and soon he stops exposing himself to it (or reduces it to a bearable minimum) by limiting (or, in extreme cases, ending) his prospecting activity. This has the unforeseen but inevitable consequence of limiting (or, in extreme cases, ending) his career. That seems like a very high price to pay, in order to avoid something that has no power to hurt you in the first place.

For when a person says "no" to you, there is not an iota of pain in that event *other than the pain you create, and inflict on yourself.* Indeed, after nearly 30 years in the business, I'm convinced that "rejection" has no chemical properties of its own, until it is mixed with our emotions regarding it. The journeyman blends it with his own fear, shame, guilt and self-doubt...and distills an unbearably corrosive acid that sears his very soul. But you must see that the pain is not caused by the "rejection," but by the way the journeyman decided (albeit unconsciously) to experience "rejection."

Philosophers have known this indispensable truth all through the ages. From ancient Rome, we have the writings of an emperor (Marcus Aurelius) and a slave (Epictetus), speaking to the same point. Marcus Aurelius says, "Things as such do not touch the soul in the least: they have no avenue to the soul, nor can they turn or move it. It alone turns and moves itself, and it makes what is submitted to it resemble the judgments of which it deems itself deserving." And Epictetus says, "Men are not disturbed by things, but by the views which they take of things." Almost a thousand years later—and almost a thousand years ago—St. Bernard of Clairvaux (1091–1153) said it best for me:

> *"Nothing can work me damage except myself. The harm I sustain I carry about me, and never am a real sufferer but by my own fault."*

Does the excellent investment advisor experience any less "rejection" than the journeyman? On the contrary; if you believe in the inexorability of $\frac{1}{N}$ (which is like saying: if you believe in gravity), you have to know that the excellent advisor has gotten rejected much more—because he has so many more clients. How, then, do they differ? Only in the way they process the experience of "rejection." The journeyman turns it into acid;

The excellent investment advisor experiences "rejection" as fuel.

Once again: "rejection" has no chemical properties. The excellent advisor blends it with her faith in herself and in her belief system, and with her faith that she will get a prospect every N-minus-one times she gets "rejected"—and the "rejection" becomes the psychic equivalent of rocket fuel. For she knows, through the marvelous operation of the cosmic law $P = \frac{1}{N}$:

The more I get "rejected," the more prospects I get.
The more prospects I get, the more accounts I open.
The more accounts I open, the more money I manage.
The more money I manage, the more money I earn.

In fact, if it will help you to sharpen and clarify that unbreakable chain of causality, you may wish simply to write down its only possible beginning and its only possible outcome:

The more I get "rejected"...the more money I earn.

But you can never intervene in the middle of this process, and start from there. Granted, it begins to be fun at the point where "The more prospects I get, the more accounts I open." But how does one get the prospects? Only from getting "rejected" (N−1) times per prospect.

This is the eternal truth that the journeyman unconsciously rejects. He tries to find ways to get to "yes" without hearing the cosmically necessary incidence of "no." He seems to believe—because he needs so desperately to believe—that there is some magic formula of words, phrases, zip codes and/or "target markets" that will raise his incidence of "yes" while lowering the number of times he hears "no." The journeyman/rat thinks, finally, that what you say can, in and of itself, change the number of people to whom you have to say it. But it can't, and the sooner you accept that painful but ultimately liberating fact, the sooner you can step off the journeyman's treadmill to oblivion, and onto the glory road.

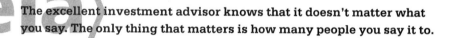

The excellent investment advisor knows that it doesn't matter what you say. The only thing that matters is how many people you say it to.

The journeyman's search for a prospecting method which will enable him to evade the inexorable $\frac{1}{N}$ is like the quest for the right crowbar with which to alter the course of a river. This tool does not exist, for the simple reason that a river has no fulcrum. There's no place along the river where you can go, put the crowbar under it, and lever a change in the river's path.

And yet the excellent advisor knows a way—indeed, the only Way—to change the course of the river that is his career. All he has to do is pick one spot along the river, go there every day, and begin dropping stones in the water. Each morning he goes to that same spot, and drops stones in the river until nightfall. All day, every day. No one stone will have any impact. Indeed, for a very long time, his efforts may appear to be futile. But the cumulative effect of the dam of stones the believer is creating will, one day, change the course of that river. It's inevitable. And it's only a matter of time, and of his unwillingness to give up.

For what does the believer have? Only these things:

(1) perfect faith that he can alter the river's course;

(2) an irrevocable decision to alter it;

(3) a plan by which to make his decision a reality, and

(4) the steadfast determination to keep working that plan, *no matter how long it takes,* until the plan inevitably succeeds.

For, when all is said and done,

The excellent investment advisor knows that success is the inevitable consequence of the failure to fail.

My prospecting role model is Thomas A. Edison, the man who invented the Twentieth Century. Edison had only about three months of formal schooling in his life, and was, from adolescence on, all but deaf. Yet he was intuitively possessed of the single greatest truth of science: that anything which is possible is also inevitable. All that's required is a relentless process of experimentation—of persistent and at times seemingly endless trial and error—to make the possibility a reality.

Edison became convinced at some point that incandescent electrical illumination was possible...and therefore inevitable. He saw it as a technical problem: what material, or alloy of materials, could stand enough electrical resistance that it would glow brightly, but would not quickly burn up?

It is recorded that Edison conducted no fewer than 10,000 separate, distinct "failed" experiments over the space of two years, in an effort to find the right material. (It must have helped that he literally could not hear everyone around him saying it wasn't going to work.) Yet he appears never really to have doubted the outcome. And, of course, in the end he was right.

There is much we can learn from "The Wizard of Menlo Park." The first thing is unshakable faith in the outcome. (If your goal is possible, then it is inevitable.) Second is that, once again, the critical issue isn't what you know (was there ever a scientist with less education than Edison?) but what you do. And the last great lesson is threefold:

(a) that you can experience innumerable "failures," but

(b) you can never *be* a failure unless

(c) you stop experimenting (prospecting) before you arrive at the inevitable successful conclusion. *All success proceeds from the failure to fail.*

Edison didn't know how many materials he'd have to experiment with until he succeeded. Nor did he get emotionally involved in the outcome of any one experiment. He simply accepted experimentation for what it is: the scientific method of arriving at inevitable success by process of elimination.

Similarly, I don't know how many of the 50 million people in households with income over $85,000 I'll have to talk to, in order to find my 250 Clients-For-Life with average investable assets of half a million dollars. Nor do I care. I have a hunch that I'll find my 250th CFL before I've had to contact the entire 50 million. But if I have to get in touch with them all, that's what I'll do. And then I'll start through the whole list again, if that's what it takes. In other words, I don't care at all how big my N turns out to be (i.e. how many people I have to contact in order to get one prospect.) As long as I believe that P does, indeed, equal $\frac{1}{N}$ and as soon as I know what my personal N is, I've got this business licked. If I do high quality work, and simply show that work to enough people, I can accomplish whatever I want to in our profession.

Every time I hear "no," I am, by process of elimination, one step closer to a prospective CFL. I have successfully identified one more material that will not support incandescent electrical illumination. In that sense, even my "failures" are successes: I now know another person whom I never have to call again! Damn, I *love* this job!

I'll have to admit, though, that it took me a long time to realize this. You see, I was trained (as I'm betting you were) to regard a call in which somebody said "yes"—I'll buy 1000 shares, or you can call me when you have an idea, or whatever—as a "good" prospecting call. And when someone said "no"—where did you get my name; you felons are all alike; I hope you freeze to death in the dark and your cat dies with you—that was to be regarded as a "bad" prospecting call. So it was not until I understood, and *emotionally accepted*, the cosmic law $P = \frac{1}{N}$ that I could see the truth:

The excellent investment advisor knows that all prospecting calls are good prospecting calls and that the only "bad" prospecting call is the one you don't make.

Faith in the inevitable outcome of the numbers game frees the excellent advisor to put his emotional energy into improving the quality of his work. Belief in the quality of his work, in turn, only increases his imperviousness to "rejection." (What? You have a chance to hire me to endow your family with multigenerational wealth, and you're saying "no"? Let me out of here! These people are *nuts!*)

The excellent advisor ultimately comes to believe that he has no power at all to affect the outcome of any one prospecting encounter. At the end of the day, he has no clear idea of why the people who said yes to him did so, nor any idea why the people who said no said no. So he completely removes his emotions from prospecting—because what's the point of investing your emotions in something you not only can't control, but can't even predict? And, paradoxically, the excellent advisor's resultant calm proves very attractive to good prospects, and his results get better, *just because he stopped trying to force the outcome.* Prospects hear a steady, poised, serene professional, full of quiet confidence in his ability to create wealth, and with no need to jump up and down, screaming and hyperbolizing about it. Smart people, rich people, and especially smart rich people really like that.

The journeyman is so obsessed with outcomes ("I gotta get my numbers up, I *gotta* get my numbers up") that he has no energy left to invest in the quality of his work. Hence, his work is usually mediocre, and occasionally quite dreadful—charts, graphs and scattergrams flying all over the bewildered prospect's office, and the journeyman sweating profusely and babbling about higher returns (than what?) with less risk (than whom?). Personally, the journeyman is thus a complete turn-off, because his anxiety gives prospects such bad vibes. So of course he doesn't make his numbers...which makes him even more frenzied about outcomes. Which makes him look, sound and act even more desperate. This may seem like a vicious cycle, but it's actually a downward spiral.

The excellent investment advisor invests all her emotional energy in the process of prospecting, not in the outcome.

The outcome is a foregone (favorable) conclusion, so why worry about it? (To the journeyman, who has no faith in the outcome, prospecting feels like running the gauntlet: how many of these people will whack me with their tomahawks before I lose consciousness?)

Everybody has slumps. Everybody bats 0-for-August sometimes. The difference is that the journeyman internalizes it ("I've lost it; maybe I'll never get it back"). But the excellent advisor says, "Well, given my lifetime batting average (i.e. my N), it's obvious that I'm gonna hit .628 in September, provided that I just keep swinging the bat. So let me not waste a lot of time thinking about it. Remember what Yogi Berra said: 'How can you think and hit at the same time?' And, hey, if I'm having trouble finding prospects, so is everybody else. And most of them will take it personal, and end up curled in the fetal position under their desks, moaning piteously and looking at the phone like it's a live grenade that just rolled into their foxhole. Hey, I know what I'll do. *I'll call everybody the journeyman is too scared to call!* God, I *love* this job!"

"Rejection" is, finally, the ultimate validation that you are doing exactly what you need to do to be successful in this profession. ("The more I get rejected...the more money I earn.") On another—and not insignificant—level, "rejection" is a tremendous validation of what you are selling, and of the way you are going about your business. Far more people are interested in plunking $10,000 in a red-hot mutual fund on any given day than are desirous of sitting down to discuss a lifetime financial plan. (That's why all those transaction-oriented, commission-driven dinosaurs in our industry aren't dead yet.)

So you will probably get far less "rejection" if you prospect in the old transaction-oriented way, with a hot fund in hot markets, and with CDs and municipal bonds in down markets. In other words, when you prospect with what people want to buy, your N may be relatively low. But then, in a few months, people will discover that they bought the wrong thing at the wrong time, and they'll blame you. (Confucius said, "The superior man understands what is right; the inferior man understands what will sell.")

Or you can prospect in the new, healthier, relationship-oriented way. You'll get "rejected" more—your N will be higher, and maybe a lot higher. But you'll get far better quality prospects:

> "Mr. Jones, I'm *(name),* an investment advisor with *(firm). (Or:* "...an independent investment advisor and the head of my own firm.") My business is the long-term, prudent accumulation of wealth for my own family and the families of about 250 of our neighbors. I find that I can do the most good for people with *(your preferred account size)* in investable assets. I have room in my practice now to take on another family, and I'm calling/approaching you as a substantial person who may find what I do very helpful. It only takes about 20 minutes for me to outline my beliefs and capabilities, so I wondered if I could buy you a cup of coffee one morning before we both get real busy, and see if there's a fit. How about next Tuesday morning, or does Thursday work better for you?"

Now, no matter how high my N is with that approach (i.e. no matter how many times I have to hear "no" in order to hear one "yes"), I can tell you that my ultimate closing ratio will be very high, and that I'll be opening extremely good-quality accounts. Because, in effect, I've already presented my whole approach (with the obvious exception of my passion for equities; people need to *see* my belief in order to accept that). And, by agreeing to see me, a prospect has indicated that my approach makes sense to him. He's also confirmed, if only by not demurring from my target account size, that he's financially in the ballpark. There isn't much more you could reasonably ask someone to do, on a first contact in which what you said to the prospect took 50 seconds.

In the next chapter, we'll go through the process of establishing what your personal N is. For now, I hope that all the myths you've ever heard about prospecting have been dispelled, and that you're left with nothing but the determination to play heaven's own numbers game to its inevitably successful conclusion.

John Wayne's last movie, *The Shootist*, is about an old gunfighter dying of cancer. (It is all the more poignant because, during the filming, Wayne was himself dying of cancer.) An adoring teenage boy, who's read of all of Wayne's character's legendary gunfights, rhapsodizes about how fast on the draw he must have been in his prime. Wayne answers that being a great gunfighter isn't about how fast you are. "It's being *willing*," he says.

Well, now you know how prospecting really works—which is to say, you know how the business really works. I just have one question:

Are you willing?

In Summary

- Almost everybody you ever prospect will decline to do business with you. The glorious, golden word in that sentence is "almost." For many are called, but few are chosen.

- There is no limit to the amount of good you can do in our profession, so there's no limit on your earning ability. All limits in this business are self-imposed.

- The good that you do, and your earnings for doing it, will be an absolute function of the number of times you hear people say "no."

- Every N number of times you hear "no," you hear one "yes." Stated algebraically, $P = \frac{1}{N}$. We play heaven's own original numbers game.

- Prospecting is an exact, pitiless science. Selling/account management is a very high art form. Each requires an entirely different set of skills.

- "Rejection" has no power to harm you, other than the power you decide to give it. Journeymen experience "rejection" as a corrosive acid. The excellent advisor experiences it as fuel.

☞ The more you get rejected, the more prospects you get, the more accounts you open, the more money you manage, the more money you earn. Simplified to its lowest common denominator: the more you get rejected...the more money you earn.

☞ There is no short cut. There's no way around N. It doesn't matter what you say, it only matters how many people you say it to.

☞ Enough stones will eventually change the course of any river. Success is the inevitable consequence of the failure to fail.

☞ Like Edison, you can experience innumerable "failures." But you can never *be* a failure...unless you stop prospecting.

☞ They're all good prospecting calls. The only bad prospecting call is the one you don't make.

☞ When you don't care about the outcome of a particular prospecting call, your insouciance comes across as confidence. And your closing ratio goes up, precisely because you stopped trying so hard to force the outcome. Invest your emotional energy in the input; the outcome will take care of itself.

☞ "Rejection" is the ultimate validation that you're doing the right thing, and that you're selling the right things in the right way. Woe betide you when most people want what you're selling.

☞ You can lower your N any time you want by selling in the bad old transaction-oriented way. That's not what you want. You want a higher N, fewer but better prospects, and a higher closing ratio.

☞ Are you *willing?*

5

The seven steps to discovering your personal **N**

"Do the thing, and you'll have the power."

—**Ralph Waldo Emerson**

• • • • • • •

Unlike any of the variables in Einstein's $e = mc^2$, each individual investment advisor's N is as personal and unique as he or she is.

We saw at the end of the last chapter that you can effectively raise or lower your own N (i.e. deliberately increase or decrease the number of people you need to talk to in order to get one prospect) by the kind of approach you make.

A product-driven, transaction-oriented approach ("tax-free; AA-rated by both services; 4.8% coupon priced at 101 to yield 4.78%; maturing in 2016; non-callable until 2009; debt service covered three times by the tolls on the Gronsky River Bridge; I've got 20 bonds left; do you want 'em?") will give you a relatively low N...if that's what you really want, which I sure don't think it is. A planning-oriented, relationship-based approach ("I want to talk to you about creating a retirement income that you cannot outlive, about building a legacy of wealth for your children, and about endowing the education of your grandchildren") will raise your N considerably...as it raises the quality of your prospects.

The message here is not just that N varies with the advisor and with the prospecting style. It is that *prospecting is a process over which the excellent advisor can exercise a considerable amount of control.* The journeyman's desperation and elevated anxiety levels stem from the fact that he thinks prospecting is a process that is random, and that controls him. In sum, the excellent advisor is the author of his prospecting style; the journeyman is the victim of his.

When you have a lot of confidence in the way that you're prospecting—when your style is deeply rooted in your belief system, and in your vision of the kind of professional you really want to be—you look better, sound better and have more energy. Your anxiety levels fall...along with your N. In that sense, your N can never be entirely driven by who you prospect and/or what you say. Your N is ultimately a function of *who you are*, which is just another reason why you have to put in the time and effort to codify your belief system.

Setting your own agenda—acting rather than reacting—always accretes your energy, no matter how hard you're working. Surely you have had a day, sometime in your life, when you were "in the zone"—when you couldn't seem to put a foot wrong, and joyfully poured all your energy into everything you did. At the end of the day, you may have been surprised to discover that you were more than ready to go another eight hours. Somehow, you ended the day with a greater reservoir of energy than you started it with. Setting your own agenda—laboring at what you love and believe in, for the sheer joy of doing it well—always does that. It always accretes your energy.

Reacting, on the other hand, is a terrible energy depleter—no matter how "correct" your reactions are. If you've been in our business for any length of time—particularly in the six years after October 11, 1990—you've had days where a dozen people (or more) gave you some variation of the "market's too high" objection. Chances are you were prepared, with closely reasoned, carefully documented and statistically complete responses. And almost nobody bought your argument.

In part, as we'll see in the section of this book on Q&A/Objections Handling, this was because you were trying to get your arms around smoke. "The market's too high," like all other stated objections, isn't a prospect's real objection. But beyond that, I think you found that even though your responses to the objection were brilliant and irrefutable, the act of repeating those responses drained all your energy, so that at the end of the day you felt like a limp rag. That's the reality of reacting: it always depletes your energy.

Incidentally, if the suspense is killing you, let me just zip through three sample responses to "the market's too high," all of which are energy-accreters because, instead of answering the "objection," they re-set the agenda:

I. What will it matter when you're 83 years old?

II. If you think it's too high today, you should have seen it the day I was born.

prospect: Huh?

me: I was born on October 11, 1943. The Dow closed at 136.61, having much more than tripled in the last 11 years. You knew by then that we were going to win the war. And that it was only the war that had finally pulled us out of the Depression. So you knew when the war was over, and all the military spending stopped, and 11 million uniformed men came home to no jobs, we'd go back into the Depression. Thus, the market was way "too high" that day. It's way "too high" today. It's always way "too high" **if you're looking backward.** Great investors don't look back, they look ahead. Please look ahead with me, to the balance of your life, and of your children's lives…

III. What are you investing for?

prospect: Huh?

eia: The money you're not investing today because "the market's too high." What's it for?

prospect: My granddaughter's college and master's degree, if she wants.

eia: College and a master's take a total of six years. What year is the midpoint of that period?

prospect: Well, she's four now. Figure the midpoint—junior year in college—is when she's about 20. So...16 years from now.

eia: Do you have any idea where the Dow was 16 years ago?

prospect: Well, uh...1981...no, where?

eia: Say 900 on the Dow.

prospect: Did you say 900?

eia: Ballpark. And every day in 1981, a different person said the market was too high. All of those people have granddaughters who are in college today on student loans. And some of those bright, beautiful girls are starting to think that graduate school is out of the question, because the money just isn't there. Do you want to bet your granddaughter's master's degree on the notion that you can time the market?

prospect: Why...no. I don't.

eia: Thank you.

Do these responses always work? Of course not; nothing does. (But these work a lot more often than some tortured statistical analysis of the market's historical price/earnings ratio.) They are offered as examples of *re-setting the agenda* in terms of long-term life perspective rather than short-term market guesswork. And when you regain the agenda, you always start to feel great again, so you have more energy to talk to more people. And talking to more people is, as we have observed, the beginning and the end of all real success in this business.

Please don't misunderstand the point of setting/re-setting your own agenda. It isn't primarily to make fewer people say "no" and more people say "yes." It is simply to give you the self-approval that, in turn, releases the energy to keep you putting quarters in the slot and pulling the handle of the elegant machine in the magical room. You have no power to affect outcomes (other than through the glorious operation of $\frac{1}{N}$), so outcomes are the wrong thing in which to invest your emotions. You have, on the other hand, potentially total control over inputs. So that's where you want to be putting your constantly accreting, agenda-setting energy. Thus,

⟨eia⟩

The excellent investment advisor knows he has little or no ability to change prospects' behavior, and almost limitless ability to change his own behavior. Therefore, he invests all his energy in changing his behavior.

All chronic production issues, as the sales psychologist Aaron Hemsley has been saying for years, are behavior issues. If and to the extent that there is a gap between my actual achievements and my targets/goals, that shortfall is attributable to my failure to behave appropriately. Specifically, the underperformance stems directly from my not approaching enough people and offering them my services. I'm not getting "rejected" enough. So I'm not getting enough prospects, I'm not opening enough accounts, I'm not getting enough money to manage, and I'm not earning enough. Fortunately, since this is a problem entirely of my own making, *it is totally within my power to fix.* All I have to do is change my behavior, and return to appropriate levels of prospecting activity.

When I achieve my production goals, I will certainly want to take full credit for having done so. I won't ascribe my success to "good luck," an excellent branch manager, or a hot market. By the same token, then, I can't reasonably attribute my failure to reach my goals to anything but my own (as yet) inadequate prospecting activity. "Bad luck," a branch manager whose knuckles scrape the ground when he walks, and/or a rotten market are not valid excuses. Nothing is a valid excuse. The Excellent Investment Advisor's credo is quite simple:

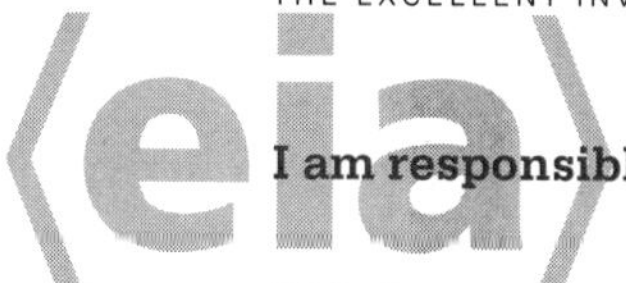

I am responsible.

Life happens to losers; winners happen to life. The excellent advisor knows that what becomes of him in the end will be what he caused it to be—or failed to cause it to be. A code of total personal responsibility is the first prerequisite to success. After that, this business is no more or less than a battle with your own anxiety.

Your own anxiety—usually manifesting itself in the form of a hypersensitivity to "rejection"—is basically the only real impediment to success in our profession. Everything else—time, the genius of capitalism, the inexorable upward bias of markets—is on your side. So all you ever really have to do is to de-sensitize yourself to "rejection," so that you can experience it as fuel rather than as acid.

As we've seen, the ultimate antidote to prospecting anxiety is simply the knowledge of what your N is—of how many times you have to pull the handle of the elegant machine before you get the statistically inevitable payoff.

If you are relatively new in the business, and are therefore conditioned to a fairly high level of prospecting activity, this is quite simple. For 90 days, just record every prospecting contact you make. Although this record can include as much information as you care to note (e.g. what the prospect said, how you responded, even a one-word description of how you felt), it need not be anything more than a hash-mark on your desk calendar for each person you speak to. Separately, make one hash-mark for every prospect you get. At the end of 90 days, divide the number of contacts you made by the total number of prospects you got, and there's your N.

Thus, all you really need in order to determine your N is a statistically meaningful number of prospecting contacts. The only problem arises if and when you have already been in the business for a good long time—and your rejection-shocked rat/unconscious has you sitting in the far corner of your cage, unwilling to go anywhere near that infernal button. (A variation on this theme is the production plateau. Plateaus occur when advisors reach an equilibrium state of pain: they do just enough business to manage their personal financial obligations, but not so much that it would require a new round of serious prospecting. So you see that, in its essence, a plateau always results from an unconsciously negotiated cease-fire between the rat and one's creditors.)

The way most people respond to these problems is to cast about desperately for a magic formula. They look for some miracle that will spring them from their production trap without the cruel necessity of real prospecting. So, for instance, they'll spend $500 on some charlatan's all-day "motivational" seminar, after which they make 1300 cold calls on Monday, 600 on Tuesday, three on Wednesday...and Thursday and Friday they're out sick with a mysterious stomach ailment. The following Monday, it's back to business—or the absence thereof—as usual. Rather than a response to the problem, feverish, "motivation"-driven prospecting activity is merely another way of denying that one has a problem.

Other delusional time-wasters include the search for the perfect prospecting list (presumably the one with a lot of "yes" and not a lot of "no" in it) or for the very-nearly-six-star mutual fund, which is so hot it will cause all sales resistance to melt away. The latter is, of course, transactional selling at its very worst, since any style/sector/country that's been *that* hot for *that* long is cyclically about to go right over a cliff. (But at least, while one is diligently searching for the Magic Elixir Fund, one doesn't have to call anybody. This is the prospecting equivalent of "I'll start my diet tomorrow.")

Finally, the most elaborate form of serial denial I've observed is the target-market pipe dream. In this classic, the advisor identifies a very specific and narrowly focused target market. That discovery is followed by a veritable whirlwind of activity: getting lists of people in that market, joining the relevant professional organizations, drafting and getting approval for new prospecting letters specific to the target market, and re-programming one's computer (whatever that means). Finally, the journeyman is ready to start contacting actual human beings...and soon discovers a fatal flaw in the plan: most people—no more or less than in any other market, just most people—say "no." This is good for a couple of months of total paralysis. And then, of course, the poor soul gets *another* idea for a target market...

These are some of the activity frenzies that the shame-based, self-recriminatory journeyman is prone to. And they can never work. One gets into the habit of prospecting inactivity very slowly, and one can only change his habits very slowly. There is no wealth-without-risk, there is no 30-pounds-in-30-days-without-dieting weight loss plan—and there is certainly no major, lasting, but overnight alteration in prospecting behavior. So the first thing you have to do—and I know this is asking a lot—is to relax. The transition from the journeyman's prospecting behavior to that of the excellent advisor is a process, not an event. It doesn't come in cans, like Popeye's spinach. I say again: relax. In a very real way, this recovery process can only start when you climb down off your own back.

In order to establish beyond a doubt what your own personal N is, we'll follow a program that combines two types of effort:

(a) a genuinely dispassionate Edisonian scientific experiment, and

(b) a sort of exercise regimen, in which you'll train yourself to increase your tolerance for "rejection" very gradually over time.

As Edison would have been the first to remind you, if it is possible to discover your N, then it is inevitable that you will do so; just continue to experiment, keeping your ego and emotions well out of the process. And, after all, Edison had to discover something no one had ever found before: incandescent electrical illumination. You're just being asked to find your N, which many successful people before you have already done. So, assuming you've had more than three months of schooling and can hear reasonably well, your job seems pretty straightforward—at least compared to Edison's.

But, just as you can't leap up from 10 sedentary years as a couch potato and run five miles after bench-pressing your weight, you can't suddenly and sustainably generate the large statistical sample of prospecting contacts necessary to determine your N. (The rat won't just go ballistic, he'll go sub-orbital. And he'll find a way to hurt you, just to stop you from zapping him. Remember how the journeyman got mysteriously sick within a week after his "motivational" experience?)

So let's proceed to construct our scientific experiment/"rejection"-aerobics training program.

Step one:

Resolve to record all your prospecting activity. The first thing you have to do in any scientific experiment is to take notes, right? You have to record the progress of the experiment. Oddly enough, that's probably the first thing we *stopped* doing when our prospecting behavior began tail-spinning toward the deck.

Remember how we all kept call sheets when we were first starting out? When did we stop doing that? And why, for heaven's sake?

I'll tell you why. Because, as the daily onslaught of rejection slowly took us down, white spaces began to appear at the bottom of our call sheets. And they inched further up the page until they all but overwhelmed it. And when we could no longer bear to look at all that empty, white space...we just stopped keeping call sheets altogether. Hell, we were veterans by now, anyway. Call sheets were for rookies. (As if, every day, we weren't unconsciously still carving those white spaces into our souls with a dull knife.)

So the road back starts with recording your activity—which is to say, it starts with being *willing* consciously to face, and to accept personal responsibility for, your prospecting inactivity. (You can't overcome any problem unless/until you (a) admit that you have a problem and (b) stand ready to face the problem.) Are you *willing?* Then start by writing everything down.

Step two:

Collect "baseline data" on your current ability to prospect. The reason you don't jump up after years on the couch and try to run five miles is that you'll kill yourself. So you just go out the first day and do a nice, easy jog for as long as you can, until you're winded. You measure how far (or for how many minutes) you were able to jog…and that becomes your baseline. The next day, you just try to jog that far (or for that long), *but no less.* When you've done your baseline jog consistently for a week, you can start to think about going a little farther/longer in the second week. But then, when you've turned it up a notch, you want to just stay at that slightly higher level—but no less—for, say, another whole week. You train, but you don't strain. You're looking to significantly increase your capacities—slowly, surely, sustainably and safely—over a long period of time.

It is—or ought to be—exactly the same after a long period of diminished, sporadic or even nonexistent prospecting activity. You don't really know what your baseline capacities are. (You don't, in other words, know how many zaps the rat can handle before he suggests that you go to lunch with another advisor, read *The Wall Street Journal* cover-to-cover, or stop everything to look for Mrs. Gefarbnick's missing dividend check.) And there's really only one way to find out. That's to do the prospecting equivalent of jogging 'til you're winded, and recording your baseline. You're looking for that nice, easy, comfortable level of prospecting activity that you can do every day—but no less—and stop just before the rat spazzes out on you.

So we'll start with my version of a series of techniques that Aaron Hemsley taught me in 1983, and which I mark as a turning point in my career. (Hemsley, the Archdruid of behavior modification, has continued to do extremely valuable and original work, and I commend him to all who desire excellence. To find out what he's up to these days, you can call him at 714-832-6109.)

To establish your current baseline level of prospecting capacity, just sit back for a week and observe your own behavior, in as detached and scientific a way as you possibly can. (There's absolutely no room in this process for negative self-talk, of the "woulda/shoulda/coulda" variety. If Edison had started saying to himself, after the 9,862nd fried filament experiment, "Maybe I shoulda stayed in school just a scosh longer," you might be reading this book by gaslight.)

During this first week of self-observation, all you need do is to commit one act of prospecting behavior *whenever you feel like it.* (You're not "supposed" to be able to run five miles on the first day. You're "supposed" to just do what you can, so you can find out what that is.) Then, simply make one hash-mark on a piece of paper—the first of five pieces of paper for that week.

Yes, I know what you're saying: what exactly is "an act of prospecting behavior"? To me, it's any genuine attempt to start a conversation with another human being. (Mailers, then, are the ultimate act of non-prospecting. They're an activity frenzy, designed to consume huge amounts of time and energy with no possibility of ever starting a conversation with anyone but a coupon-clipper.)

Our terribly self-judgmental belief system says we've only performed a real prospecting behavior when we've actually spoken to the prospect himself. I don't buy that at all; it's way too harsh. (Everybody alive is, in some form or fashion, his own worst enemy, but people of your and my personality type really raise this to the level of an art form.) Remember, we can only control what we can control: *inputs, not outcomes.*

Let's say I've got a lead that my manager gave me: somebody who wrote in for one of our publications. Good stationery, firm handwriting, smart address: everything that would keep me from calling the person. Because, after all, how often do you get a great-looking lead like that? Man, I *can't* call this guy, because if I don't call him, he can't say "no," and if he doesn't say "no," I can't get "rejected"...and I've still got a terrific lead.

But now, it's the Monday of my baseline-data-collecting week, so what the heck, I'll give him a call. Dial the phone; get the administrative assistant. She says, "He's on a business trip to Guam. Call back next

Tuesday." Inputs, not outcomes, kiddo: give yourself a big ol' hash-mark, say I to myself. You done good.

As I'm going over this modest behavioral triumph in my mind, I suddenly remember another lead I've got tucked away somewhere. (Because if I don't call him, he can't say "no," and if he doesn't say "no" yadada yadada yadada...) Decide, just for the sake of science, to give *him* a little ringy-dingy. Get his assistant, who reads me a prepared statement: (a) Mr. Big does not take calls from "salesmen," and (b) he devoutly hopes that I, and every one of my kind, may starve to death in the dark. Gonna give myself an extra-large hash-mark for that one!

Are you starting to get the hang of this? It is your behavior we're investigating, here, and if you do the right thing, *regardless of the outcome,* you get the hash-mark. Baseline data, that's all we're looking for: nobody's asking you to do more than you're good and ready to do.

OK, so we've decided that each and every genuine attempt you make to start a conversation—in person or on the phone—is a hash-mark-worthy prospecting behavior. And incidentally, when I call that first guy back next Tuesday, and the assistant says, "He went on to Borneo; call back next St. Swithin's Day," you better believe I get another hash-mark. See, I can't control where the guy is. I can only control my prospecting behavior. I performed the behavior that inevitably leads to success: I called on the phone, or knocked on the door, or walked up to the guy at our sons' soccer game, or whatever. I did exactly what I'm supposed to do, and I get rewarded with a hash-mark.

You may still insist that "it's only a hash-mark if I talk to the guy." Well, that's very noble of you, in a puritanical, self-flagellating sort of way. But I guaran-damn-tee you that, when you've gone through an entire morning of constantly dialing the phone, listening to he's-in-Sarawak-he's-in-a-meeting-he-doesn't-take-calls-from-pond-scum-like-you, and you haven't got a hash-mark to your name by lunch time, you're going to put that phone through a wall and go off this program. **Guaranteed.**

Once again, just for this first week, don't try to commit a prospecting behavior when you "should." (You'll feel and sound strained, which reinforces the bad vibes on both sides of the conversation.) Do a prospecting behavior only when you feel really good about doing a prospecting behavior. Prospecting is *supposed* to feel good. And when it does, you'll sound good, look good, think clearly and speak well—as opposed to moaning and mumbling like someone who's running the gauntlet, and this call is the 49th tomahawk blow of the day. Give yourself a hash-mark for each prospecting behavior.

Do this for one whole week. Keep your emotions out of it; we're scientists collecting baseline data, here, and emotion can only get in the way by contaminating the data with woulda/coulda/shoulda. ("How could I have only done three prospecting behaviors in a day? I *shoulda* done at least 10. Oh, what a rogue and peasant slave am I! If only my hearing were better; if only I'd stayed in school for *four* months...")

Don't even think about counting prospects yet. (A) You may not have gotten any. (B) If you did, consider it a statistical fluke and/or beginner's luck. You still have far too small a statistical sample to have any idea what your N is. (C) It's exactly that old results-oriented scorekeeping system ("yes" is a good call; "no" is a bad call; "He's in Borneo" is no call at all) that corroded your soul—and drove the rat completely crazy—in the first place. The appropriate behaviors—the hash-marks in and of themselves—are the winning experiences you're looking for.

This phase of the experiment ends when you add up the number of hash-marks you got in the first week of data collection, and divide that number by the five days you've worked. This tells you the average number of prospecting behaviors per day that you *may* be sustainably capable of. It gives you, in other words, the first potentially meaningful idea you've had in quite a while of your true baseline level of prospecting.

Step three:

Test your preliminary baseline prospecting level by repeating it every day for 10 business days. Take that number of average behaviors per day—which we're hypothesizing may be your baseline—and try to do that exact number each day for two weeks. This may seem perfectly straightforward, but please note two important caveats:

(1) There may be days, during these next two weeks of the experiment, when you feel a great surge of energy, and want to commit more prospecting behaviors than your baseline level. You have permission to do so, but cautiously. Be on the alert: this may be just another attack of "up-in-the-clouds-down-in-the-dumps." No matter how many more behaviors you can do on a given day, *you can never do less than your baseline on the other days.*

(2) Your baseline is a minimum daily requirement. If it's five a day, it's five *each* day, not three on Monday, seven on Tuesday, none on Wednesday, five on Thursday and 10 on Friday. Drop the word "average" completely out of your scientific vocabulary. We're trying to alter your habit-force, and the key is consistency, no matter how low that consistently sustainable level of effort may be at the outset.

If you find that you can't sustain the first week's level of baseline activity each and every day for 10 more days, that's OK. (Assume the rat slipped a dose of "shoulda" in your coffee during the first week, so the number came out unsustainably high.) Simply drop back by one behavior per day, and try *that* for 10 days. If that doesn't take, drop back one more behavior for 10 more days. Keep doing this until you get down to that bedrock baseline number which you can do for 10 days straight. When you perform the same minimum number of behaviors for 10 straight days, be sure to reward yourself with a specific, pleasurable, memorable treat. You're on your way.

Step four:

Add to your baseline one additional prospecting behavior; see if you can sustain the increased effort for 10 more days. Once you've got 10 days of consistent minimum behavior under your belt, try to add just one prospecting behavior per day, and see if you can sustain *that* level for the next 10 days. If you can, add one more behavior, and do the new minimum level for 10 additional days. Keep adding only one behavior at a time, and never until you've logged 10 days at the level below. The point is to raise the hum of activity in your unconscious so slowly that the rat gets used to it, and can sleep soundly through it. You never want to jack the noise level up a lot suddenly, because we don't want the rat to wake up in a panic, go berserk, and start running around chewing through your telephone wires.

At some point you will inevitably hit a level of activity that, for whatever reason, you can't sustain for 10 straight days. Don't bother asking why, and don't make excuses. ("Why oh why" and "I couldn't because..." are rat chatter.) Just drop back one behavior per day, and make sure, all over again, that you can sustain it for 10 more days—just like you did a couple of weeks ago. If you can't, drop back one more. At the rate of one behavior per day, keep dropping back 'til you hit a sustained 10-day streak. That's your new bedrock baseline. After 10 days, try adding one behavior per day again. Train, don't strain.

How many prospects have you got? What's your N? Who knows, and much more important, who cares? (Hell, I'm not even sure which *week* it is.) It's still way too early to be asking those questions. You shouldn't even be recording the number of prospects you get, at this point, because the statistical sample is still too small. And you're never going to have a meaningful sample until you *slowly but surely* build your prospecting activity back up to the point where the numbers reliably tell you something. For the first 90 days of this experiment, your only job is to calibrate and incrementally raise the level of your prospecting activity *as an end in itself.*

Step five:

For the second 90 days, keep raising your acitivity level when you can, in one-behavior/10-day increments. But now, begin recording the number of prospects you get. Do not try to leap ahead to an analysis of your closing ratio (i.e. how many prospects it takes to get an account). That involves working on a very different set of skills, and it has to come later. Getting prospects is the horse; converting them to clients is the cart; in heaven's name, don't put the cart before the horse.

During the second 90 days, continue to "jog a little farther" every couple of weeks if you can. And always take the time to make sure you can sustain each incrementally higher level of activity, before going on to the next one.

But now, start recording a different type of hash-mark, each time you get a prospect. It's still too early for those numbers to prove anything, but they will begin to give you some sense of your prospecting effectiveness.

For instance, suppose I found, after my first week of baseline-data-collecting, that my initially sustainable number of behaviors was only five a day—one genuine attempt to start a conversation every two hours or so. After 90 days, let's say I had that number up to 10 a day, or just over one per hour.

Well, 10 behaviors a day is 50 a week, so I suppose I'm getting at least one prospect, and maybe two, out of that. But if after three months I only put down one or two prospect hash-marks per week on a big blank page, maybe I'll get depressed and go back to sending out mailers. I don't want that to happen. So I don't record prospects at all until the second 90 days.

During that period I'll be raising my baseline from 10 prospecting behaviors a day to (at most) 16...and I'll bet you I'm so psyched that there are days I can do 30. (*But never less than the baseline. Never.*) At that point, I'm officially back in the habit of prospecting—I can *feel* it—and I'm getting a prospect every couple or three days. Now, *those* are some hash-marks! But I still don't get seduced into focusing on results. I know that behavior—the slow weaving of the iron cable of habit—still has to be my main focus, *one day at a time.*

Step six:

During the last 90 days, keep raising the bar when you can. Count your prospects carefully. As this experiment draws to its inevitably successful conclusion, I'm committing a prospecting behavior no less than about three times an hour...and I've probably stretched myself to an average of one every quarter hour. (I have to bunch them, of course, because I'm going out on a lot of appointments.) Call it 30 a day, with time off for good behavior. I've had to cut back on a lot of my old avoidance behaviors, that's for sure. But somehow I don't mind. My prospecting activity is yielding a quality account (and sometimes two) just about every week. And I'm starting to get referrals again...

Oh, I almost forgot:

Step seven:

Divide all the prospects you got in the last 90 days into the number of behaviors you committed during those days. The resulting number is your N. Now, go have a successful life. Which is to say, try to "fail" as many multiples of N-minus-1 as you possible can. Then, try to "fail" a little more.

Those of you who've accepted this message may now skip ahead to the next chapter. I have to hang in here for another minute or two, and deal with the doubting Thomases...

OK, those of you still here shaking your heads: let me address your three concerns (one still lingering from a few pages back, and the two new ones):

(1) If I keep score the way I do, doesn't that inevitably inflate my N? In other words, if I count, "He's in Guam" or even "He's on the other wire" as hash-marks, don't I have to perform that many more behaviors/hash-marks to get one prospect? Yes, and that feels real good to me. I love to—and seem to need to—see that growing army of hash-marks marching across my call sheet all day, every day. That's what keeps me excited: I like high-scoring games.

Still, if you've got another scorekeeping system that works better for you, *and that you will stick to*, by all means be my guest. Your system is actually better than mine, because it works for you. There are no rules to this; there's only *what works for you*. If you wanted a life of externally imposed rules, you picked the wrong business. You should have joined the Army.

(2) Nine months is too long, you say? Apparently nature doesn't think so, when she creates a new human being. (And if you don't think this process creates an entirely new and different you, then I just don't know what to tell you.) But again, if you've got a quicker way that works for you and yields the same or better results, have at it. I won't take it personal.

(3) You're complaining because I haven't told you how to prospect (phone, letter-with-a-phone-call-follow-up, knocking on doors, seminars) nor what to say? That's because there's no right way to prospect; there's only the one you like best (or hate least), so that you'll stick to it. In my experience, that's as individual as fingerprints. And, as we've already seen, it doesn't matter what you say, because almost everybody's going to say "no," anyway. (Ah, there it is again: the golden "almost.") Say whatever's in your heart, and then ask for a 20-minute appointment. Are we just about done on this? Because I have to go catch up with the people who went on to the next chapter.

If you will give this seven-step program the requisite nine months—calmly, slowly, consistently, patiently and non-judgmentally, with your ego and emotions well out of it—you will inevitably discover your N. And then you will quite literally be set for life. Prospecting will become a career-long, joyful game which—since you already know you're going to win every $\frac{1}{N}$ times—you'll never stop playing.

In Summary

- The Excellent Investment Advisor is the author of his prospecting style; the journeyman is the victim of his. Your N is therefore driven not so much by who you call or what you say, but by who you are.

- Acting always accretes your energy; reacting always depletes it. Prospecting has to be done pursuant to your agenda. If you were a character in *A Chorus Line*, who would you be? If you named any one of the dancers—vying with all those other terrific dancers for too few jobs—you got it wrong. You're the director. You're auditioning 50 million dancers for 250 spots in the play that is your professional life. They're not interviewing you; you're interviewing them.

- The Excellent Investment Advisor knows that she has little or no ability to change prospects' behavior, and almost limitless ability to change her own behavior. Therefore, she invests all her energy in changing her behavior.

- All long-term production issues are behavior issues. Want to change your production? Change your behavior. You are responsible.

- There are no miracle cures. Activity frenzy is just another way of denying that one has a problem. The only answer is slow, cumulative behavioral change.

Even from a state of near-total paralysis, you can discover your own personal N in nine months. It's a seven-step process.

Step 1: Resolve to record all your prospecting activity, even if it's just a hash-mark on a blank piece of paper. This is just another way of saying: face your inactivity honestly.

Step 2: Spend a week collecting baseline data on your currently sustainable level of prospecting behavior. Assuming you already know that you're not going to like the number you come up with, resolve not to be self-judgmental. Self-recrimination at this point—or at any point, come to think of it—is tantamount to self-sabotage.

By my definition, a hash-mark-worthy prospecting behavior is any genuine attempt to start a conversation with another human being, whether the conversation actually happens or not. You can't control outcomes, you can only control your own behavior. Reward the appropriate behavior with a hash-mark.

Step 3: Test your first-week baseline for 10 additional days to make sure it's real. If it's not, drop back one behavior a day, and try again for 10 days. Find the real bedrock: not what it "should" be, but what it is.

Step 4: When you've been on bedrock for 10 days, add one additional behavior for 10 more days. Keep adding one additional behavior every 10 days until you falter. Then drop back. You should find that the bedrock level is rising beneath you.

Step 5: In the second 90 days, keep raising your activity in one-behavior/10-day increments, per Step Four. But now, start counting prospects.

Step 6: In the third 90 days, continue raising the bar and expanding your activity. Keep very good prospect records but do not concern yourself with your closing ratio. (Different set of skills.) Do not put the cart of results before the horse of discovering your N.

Step 7: Divide all the prospects you got in the third 90 days into the number of behaviors you committed during those days. That's your N.

Now, go out and "fail" as many multiples of N-minus-1 as you can possibly stand. You're set for life.

It doesn't matter how you prospect; it only matters *that* you prospect. The method you'll stick to is the right one for you. And it doesn't matter what you say; almost everybody will still say "no," anyway.

This chapter can be summed up in seven words: train slowly to withstand progressively more "rejection."

6

Training to win the "Rejection Olympics" . . . .

"You play basketball against yourself. Your opponent is your own potential."

—**Bobby Knight**

It should be clear to you, from a thoughtful reading of the last two chapters, that as an advisor seeking to arrive at the top of this profession—say, the 95th percentile of assets under management and earnings—you need ultimately do only one thing. And that is simply to get "rejected" more often than do 95% of your peers.

And the converse is also true: no matter how brilliant your work is, unless you are prepared to have N-minus-1 people say "no" to it every time you want another prospect...you will simply never get another prospect. (Or, if you do, it will be a statistical fluke which you won't be able to repeat at will.)

Once you know what your N is, then, your basic job is just steadily to increase the number of multiples of N-minus-1 you can endure in a given period of time. For example, suppose that, after nine months of gradual behavioral change, you've determined that your N is (just to pick a number off a bus) 15. That is to say, you have proven by dispassionate Edisonian experimentation that all you ever have to do in this world to get another prospect is to get "rejected" 14 (i.e. N-minus-1, where N equals 15) times.

If you can do that—get "rejected" 14 times every day, let's say—then you'll average a prospect a day. The challenge, then, is simply to see how quickly you can *sustainably* arrive at the point where you're being "rejected" 28 times per day—so that you can get two prospects. After that, although it may take a considerable uptick in your work disciplines and your efficiency, you'll want to strive to get "rejected" 42 times every day...thereby netting three prospects between sunrise and sunset. And if excellence is truly the only acceptable outcome to you, one glorious morning you'll have arranged your life so that 56 people "reject" you that day and every day. You'll thus average four prospects a day. At that point, my guess is you'll be opening at least one account every day. And you'll be on your way to achieving all your professional hopes and dreams, because you won the gold medal in the "Rejection Olympics."

Now, even I will admit that "rejection"—whether it's as benign as "She's still in a board meeting" or as malignant as "I hope you freeze to death in the dark, and your dog dies with you"—is just never going to be a lot of fun. You won't ever grow to actively *love* it, no matter how much you may accept it as the statistically necessary means to a highly desirable end. So the act of steadily increasing your daily dose of "rejection" is going to take more than just stoicism and discipline (though it'll certainly require those as well). As with all true excellence, winning the gold medal in the "Rejection Olympics" takes that special quality called *heart.* And heart, to me, is an indefinable combination of desire, determination, courage, and unshakable faith in oneself and in the quality of one's work.

This chapter is a collection of practices—each and every one of them entirely within your control—which you can employ to develop your heart. No one can stop you from doing these things—or can even limit your ability to do them—other than yourself. Some of them are things to do (and to think) every day, one exercise is to be performed once a week, and some are steps to take as infrequently as once a calendar quarter.

But I promise you that these 13 principles/practices, taken together, will surely give you, over time, the quality of heart that you need to be the ultimate victor in the "Rejection Olympics." They are the result of nearly 30 years of experimentation, aimed at distinguishing between "good to do" and "*got* to do." And they form, for me, an integrated whole, without which I could never have achieved what I have.

I'm better at some of these practices than at others (and you will be, too, although you and I will be better at different ones). And there are times when I get rusty or unfocused about one or another of them; at those times, I have to stop and put them back in good working order. But, when all is said and done, their combined effect is invaluable to me. The first time you read through them, they may seem like a menu, from which you can pick and choose. I sincerely believe you do so at some risk. After you've read them through once, please go back and do so again, this time with an eye toward how they interrelate. Try to see, in other words, the golden wire on which these 13 beads are strung.

1 Permit no one to have a higher ethical standard than you do—in your own best interest.

While admitting that all ethical advisors may not be successful, I believe that no Excellent Investment Advisor is unethical. Stated another way, I accept the possibility of an ethical journeyman, but not of a venal excellent advisor. In my experience, the excellent advisor has a finely developed ethical sense, *purely in her own selfish interest.*

Cutting corners is the first stage of the ultimate downward spiral, because it says, "I don't have enough faith in myself to believe that I can succeed cleanly and honestly." Since your courage and self-esteem are dependent on your faith in yourself, they begin to wither when you make an ethically shabby choice. The result is that you have less, not more, tolerance for "rejection." Your prospecting activity slows down, and you open fewer accounts. So you end up making an even shabbier choice in order to "make a living." And the downward spiral takes yet another awful turn.

The turn-of-the-century American author Elbert Hubbard always said, "Men are not so much punished *for* their sins as *by* them." The journeyman doesn't consciously see, at first, that his questionable ethical behavior is costing him his sense of self-worth. That's because the immediate payback may feel so good that it deadens his sense of shame. He prospects an old couple, whose debt portfolio is fighting a losing battle with rising living costs. So he shows them a junk bond fund, realizing that, while people always *say* they want safety and income, what they really want is all the income they can get *and the illusion of safety.*

The old fellow repeats that they need more income, and that the junk bond fund sure yields more than the intermediate-term, investment-grade bond fund they've got now. Then comes the moment of truth: the prospect says to the journeyman, "But these bonds are still *safe*...aren't they?" The journeyman launches into a 15-minute soliloquy on the high-yield bond market—the Milken theory in monosyllabic words. He uses jargon to mislead, without actually lying. And sure enough, the prospects hear "yes"—not because the journeyman said it, but because they so desperately wanted to. The journeyman goes home with a $175,000 ticket.

But the next morning, he wakes up feeling kind of blue, and he doesn't know why. And he just can't seem to get his baseline-level number of approaches done that day. Maybe tomorrow...

I'm sure you can see what's already beginning to happen here. The journeyman has started to lose his nerve, because, as Shakespeare promised, "conscience doth make cowards of us all." In the same situation, the excellent advisor might have shown a systematic withdrawal plan from an equity income fund...and if the old folks had said no, he'd have taken a walk. And since the excellent advisor draws the strength to play the numbers game from his own inner resources, each good ethical decision adds to those resources, and to that strength.

You need all the self-reliance, courage and confidence you can get. So always do the right thing (or, at least, avoid doing the wrong thing), out of rational self-interest. *Tell everybody the pure, unvarnished truth all the time.* "Labor to keep alive in your heart," said George Washington, "that little spark of celestial fire called conscience."

2 Go the extra mile.

Quick: write down the names of your top 25 accounts, in any order at all. Now: next to each name, write the person's birthday.

Gotcha! If you know people's birthdays, you can go the extra mile by sending out birthday cards. If you don't, you can't.

Have you ever heard anyone complain that he gets too many birthday cards? Let me ask the same question in another, perhaps more acute way: in this atomized, mobile society of ours, what percentage of people, after four decades on earth, get fewer than seven birthday cards? (I don't know either, but I'll bet it's an astronomical number.) And, just to put as sharp a point on this as possible, let me ask you: how many birthday cards did *you* get last time? OK, now: if you'd gotten one more, albeit from a business acquaintance, would you have been happy or angry?

Are we just about done on this? I mean, I don't want to drive it into the ground like a tomato stake...but do you think *anyone* would ever say, "Yeah, she sent me a birthday card—pretty nice one, too—but it doesn't count, because her fund only has three stars"? No, I don't either.

Everybody gets 900 holiday cards from businesspeople in December—the soulless, printed, secular kind, with no reference to Jesus, or Moses, or Santa, or anybody, so as to give no offense...and not a scintilla of genuine human warmth. And the huge preponderance of these cards instantly return to the garbage from whence they came. (They may be totally insincere, but at least they're recyclable.)

But a hand-signed birthday card—maybe one out of 10 (or fewer) that year? Excuse the heck out of me, but that's just naturally gonna ring the recipient's chimes so hard they'll be heard over in the next county.

Your ability to go the extra mile is constrained only by your willingness to do so, and by your ingenuity in thinking of new ways to do so. I knew a broker once who was the Birthday Bomber: forget the top 25 or even the top 100 accounts, this guy sent birthday cards to every one of his clients *and even to prospects.* He became a legend in his office for doing this, and all the other brokers started to do it, too.

This incensed the Bomber, who was so competitive—and leave us not forget that all champions are competitive—that he couldn't stand doing the same thing everybody else was doing, even if it *was* his idea to begin with. So he came up with a secret weapon: he *called* people on their *wedding anniversaries!* Each year, hundreds of people got one anniversary card from their spouse (maybe), one from their kids (maybe)...and a call from their broker! Extra mile? *This guy went the extra light-year!*

Going the extra mile is attitude aerobics: it oxygenates your soul. And, like physical aerobics, the more of it you do, the more of it you want to do...and the more you find you *can* do. I've gotten to the point where I simply will not put my head on the pillow every night until I've written a nice note to somebody about something—I no longer care what.

In general, these days, people either never write letters at all, or write them only when they're outraged about something. But I look for things I appreciate, and write to the people who do those things, or—and this is *really* a winner—to their bosses. For instance, when one travels as much as I do, one can't help but be worn down by the thousand small indignities which business travel heaps upon all of us. And the cumulative effect of that will really shrivel you up inside, to the point where you're actually looking for bad things to happen. This is attitudinal suicide, because you almost can't help exhaling all the negativity when you get to where you're going.

My defense is to force myself constantly to be on the lookout for somebody who's trying to do it right—whatever "it" may be. I'm searching, in other words, for the diamonds among stones who can be the recipient and/or the subject of that day's note from me. Some days this is harder than others. But if I look carefully enough, I can always find that diamond—and, because I focus on diamond-mining, I don't seem to notice or mind the stones as much. (And the converse is also true: when I allow myself to focus on the stones, I usually get buried in a landslide of boulders by day's end.)

It's just an attitude. (Which is a little like saying, about the stuff you breathe, "It's just oxygen." Yes, it is, and it's the most common element in the earth's atmosphere. But four minutes without it and you become seriously dead.) And, like any attitude, **(a)** ultimately you control it, and **(b)** it can be learned.

Suppose you're prospecting a fast-rising executive, and not really getting anywhere—but certainly not getting told to go away and never come back. You look around his office, and there's a framed picture of his son in a soccer uniform. One question and a 10-minute answer later, you've learned that the kid is a high school star, and is seriously working toward playing college soccer on scholarship.

"Two last questions, and I'll be on my way," you say. "What's his birthday, and who's his favorite player?" "September 7, and Roberto Baggio of Italy," says the already smiling prospect. "Have a nice day," says you.

You pick up a soccer magazine at a newsstand, send away for a couple of catalogues, and eventually find out that there's a cool Baggio poster you can get for $10. (Or, if the guy is a monster prospect, an autographed Baggio soccer ball for $50.) Or you find that, for $30, you could buy the kid a year's subscription to *Instep* magazine, for young people serious about playing college soccer.

You call the guy up, and ask, "Your son ever hear of *Instep* magazine?" Prospect says, "Sure, it's his bible. Why?" "I was just checking. I remember you said he wants to play college soccer, and I ran across the magazine," you say. "Well, listen," says the prospect, "it's awfully nice of you to think of him. Say, what can you tell me about investing in emerging markets?"

Or he says, "No. What's *Instep* magazine?" You say, "Near as I can make out, it's a magazine for high school boys and girls who are real serious about playing soccer in college. Think your guy would want to see it?"

The prospect goes nuts, obviously, and asks for the information. "No, it's my pleasure," you say, "I'll have it sent to him at home for a year. What's your address?"

Or you dimly remember that the great John Huston directed a movie about a dozen years ago called *Victory*, in which a bunch of Allied POWs (including Sylvester Stallone, Michael Caine and soccer legend Pélé) play the soccer team from the Wehrmacht in WWII. So for $20 you send it to the kid for his birthday.

Or your heart's in the right place but your budget is tapped out. OK, so you see in the soccer magazine an ad for a big mail order retailer of soccer gear called Eurosport. You call for the free catalog, and send it to the prospect with a note saying, "I saw this and thought of your boy." Costs you postage, and it's a total no-lose proposition. Kid already gets the catalog; you still get very good vibrations from the prospect. Kid doesn't already get the catalog; father and son go nuts.

You didn't have to know anything about soccer going into this exercise to make a friend for life—and maybe two generations of friends for life. You just had to be open to the idea of tuning into what the prospect really cares about. Nor did you have to be Sherlock Holmes to figure out how important the kid is to him (chances are he didn't put the picture in his office for target practice), and how important soccer is to the kid (chances are the father didn't choose this *particular* picture if the kid's major extracurricular interest is ballroom dancing).

Go the extra mile by getting to those places in the heart where people really live. This business isn't simply about making money. It's about making money *as a means to an end*—even if the end is just, "I want to *be* somebody." The journeyman, who doesn't actually want to find out where people really live, in part because he doesn't want them to find out where *he* lives, focuses on the money. The excellent advisor is always searching for the real human ends—the interests, loves, wants and needs for which the money is a funding medium. And, because she is genuinely interested in really knowing good people, the excellent advisor becomes someone that good people really want to know.

3 Get a year's living expenses in a money market fund.

You have to have the courage to walk away from ethically dicey situations, and from accounts who have turned abusive, even—and especially—when you have no idea how you're going to replace that business. It is extremely difficult to do this if you aren't quite sure where your next mortgage payment is coming from. And the self-loathing that arises from "needing" corrosive people is inimical to your self-esteem. The antidote: a war chest with a year's living expenses in it.

Start this plan at once. If it means some sacrifice on your family's part, go home and call a family meeting. They'll not only understand, they'll probably volunteer some economies of their own. In return, make monthly written reports to the family, with copies of the money market fund statement. In each report, remind them of the dollar amount of your goal, tell 'em what you saved this month and where you are so far, and don't forget to thank them.

If this means you yourself have to live on coffee and rice one day a week for a year, do it gladly: how good can anything taste if it's costing you your sense of self-worth? If you and the family need to have dinner at home once a week when you'd otherwise have gone out, calculate the savings and write out a check to the fund—even if it's only $20 or $30—that very evening. You have to give yourself visible, tangible rewards every time you make a sacrifice like that; you have to see that every such sacrifice gets you that much closer to freedom. The pain of the sacrifice is immediate and specific; so, therefore, must be the reward.

The knowledge that you and your family can live for a year without a dime of earnings, without borrowing, and without impinging on your essential lifestyle, is literally the most *encouraging* thing you can do for yourself. And when you reach your goal—when a whole year's living expenses are in the fund—I strongly suggest that you get that month's statement laminated, and carry it around with you in your briefcase.

Look at it as often as you need to; hey, look at it as often as you like. Because it doesn't just mean you can tell an individual account to go to hell and make it stick. It means you can tell the whole world to go to hell and make it stick.

4 Have your own financial plan; fund it with the investments you recommend to clients.

Saying "You ought to buy these funds/annuities" is one thing. Saying "I think you should own the funds/annuities (my family and) I own, and for essentially the same reasons" adds tremendous moral weight to your recommendations.

When you have your own financial plan, you're able to see, and to show the people you love, what you're working for. Accumulating wealth for yourself and them is, after all, the primary motivation of most really successful people in our business. As that wealth builds up month by month, in keeping with an organized plan, you're able to say, "This is what it's all about; a little more all the time." And it can make your family a consciously cohesive economic unit, rather than a group of people competing with "the office" for Mommy's or Daddy's time and attention. The plan allows the family to see themselves as shareholders in a growing business, rather than as its victims. And few things are more effective than your own financial plan in teaching your children the value of work, of discipline, and of systematic investing—life lessons which everyone must learn.

Moreover, there's an essential falsity to prospect/client interactions in which you're telling them to do something which you claim is indispensable, but that you yourself haven't had the discipline to do. And all falsity saps your confidence and courage, thereby limiting your effectiveness. Having your own financial plan allows you to say things like, "I can tell you from my own experience how a financial plan dispels my anxiety about the future, and allows me to work better. Also, it's really brought my family together, and formed us into a team." You're able to make emotional as well as financial common cause with your prospects and clients by saying, in effect, "Come join me in the marvelous adventure of building wealth for ourselves and for the people we love." (Alternatively, I suppose, you could still try to wow the guy with how all your recommended investments are in the northwest corner of the scattergram, whatever the hell that means.)

Owning the things you're recommending also enables you gently to turn aside all the left-brain, bottomless-pit objections prospects learn from financial journalism, which has made an art form out of isolating on the wrong variables:

prospect: The expense ratio of this Pacific Rim fund you're recommending is too high.

eia: Well, it's certainly higher than most; that's a fair observation. And as an investor in the fund, I was struggling with that same issue a few months ago. So the last time I had dinner with the fund's manager, Grey Trueheart—did I mention that I meet regularly with the managers of all the investments my clients and I own?—I was critical of the expense ratio. But Grey made a couple of interesting points. He reminded me that his firm does its own research, sending their analysts to visit those countries and companies. He said it'd certainly be cheaper just to buy local brokerage-house research, but the idea of all those analysts sitting around all the same clubs in Hong Kong, telling each other all the same stories, makes him real queasy.

prospect: Gee, that makes a lot of sense. You pay a little more, but you get the story first-hand, and you get to make your own business judgment. Hmmm...

eia: Exactly. The other thing Grey said to me, which I certainly can't argue with, is that the expense of primary research is always going to be high in a relatively small—$500 million—fund such as ours. But with a smaller fund like that, when one of our major holdings is an out-of-the-park home run, the whole fund can go into second base standing up. When—heaven forbid—the fund is $5 billion, the expense ratio'll probably drop like a stone, but the effect of any one great stock will become negligible.

prospect: Of course, of course. I wouldn't want it any other way. Who wants to own a glorified index fund?

eia: Well, I sure don't, and I was pretty convinced that you wouldn't, either.

prospect: So really, what you're saying is that none of these variables can be intrinsically good or bad. They're all business trade-offs. I understand that; I make business trade-offs all day long.

eia: Here in the real world, we all do. That's what journalists—who aren't business people, and who often aren't even investors, because they don't make enough money—tend to miss.

prospect: Of course. Don't just tell me what I'm paying; tell me what I'm *getting* for what I'm paying, and let me make an informed business decision as to whether I think that's a good trade.

eia: You just stated my entire portfolio philosophy.

I trust you observed the huge emotional flashes of warmth and light which the excellent advisor detonated during his answer. **(1)** He got on record the fact that he owned the fund. **(2)** He was clearly on top of the issue which the prospect raised. (As how could he not be; if you own the fund and you're even halfway diligent, you can't get surprised by an objection that's got any rationality to it, because you yourself have been over the same ground.) **(3)** He made the point that he meets regularly with all his managers, and challenges them on the issues. **(4)** In making the case for the higher expense ratio, he clearly demonstrated that it was, at least potentially, the source of superior returns. And **(5)** he blew the prospect's doors off, by showing that he (the advisor) and the manager were exactly the prospect's kind of smart businesspeople. Above all, please see that the excellent advisor was not merely scoring debating points. He was proving beyond a reasonable doubt that he is value-added to the prospect, by virtue of the relationships he has forged with excellent managers while creating his own plan. He's not, in any sense, selling mutual funds anymore. He's quite literally offering to share the wealth.

Telling someone with very young children to invest for their education by buying a small-cap aggressive growth fund is one very specific kind of emotional interaction. A completely different kind of experience occurs when you take out your own statements, and say:

> "We've been investing in this fund for our own children's education—our kids are a bit older than yours—for several years. And I'd just like to show you the powerful effects of dollar-cost averaging on our results. You see, the increased volatility inherent in small-cap works **for** you when you're dollar-cost averaging. Look how we were able to pick up a very large number of shares at bargain prices when the market got killed in the summer and fall of 1990."

The day-in, day-out accretion of courage that you draw from being the genuine article—having your own plan, funded with the investments you love to recommend—makes this a must for anyone striving to be an Excellent Investment Advisor.

5 Tell people what to do.

You're a superbly qualified financial advisor, not a clerk in a department store ("How do you like this dress? No? Well, how about this one? Or this one?") and not a waiter ("I'd like to acquaint you with our many dinner specials this evening, so you can pick the one that suits your fancy"). If the President (the client) is going to charge the Chairman of the Joint Chiefs of Staff (you) with winning the war for financial independence/multigenerational wealth, he's got to let you pick the forces, the battleground and, above all, the weapons. (When LBJ started personally choosing bombing targets in Vietnam, you had to know we were going to lose.)

Clients-For-Life who are smart enough to pick you to fight that war for them have to be smart enough to let you fight it your way. Moreover, if you go back to Steve Moeller's psychographics of the desirable client, CFLs either don't have the time, or don't have the interest, *or don't have both*, to want to go over a long list of bombing targets. They don't need to be educated, they need all their investing problems solved, and one thing with the other got nothing to do. *Tell people what you want them to do.* Then tell them as much of the whys and wherefores as they want to know—and only as much as they want to know. Most importantly, in all your prospect/client interactions, *strive never to answer a question that nobody asked you.*

Once again, it is a hallmark of virtually all CFLs that they do not seek to *understand how* everything is going to turn out all right, but rather seek to be secure in the *belief that* it is going to be all right. *Their* belief, in turn, is inspired not by the excellent advisor's intellectual mastery (square peg, round hole) but by *her* belief. Indeed, all the excellent advisor's experience leads her to conclude that when she believes, she is believed.

Do you believe? Then don't try to explain why you believe (unless you're asked). Simply have the courage to ask the people to believe you. Offer them, in other words, both the opportunity and the encouragement to make an act of faith in you. *Give the trust a chance to happen.*

If it doesn't, answer the direct questions you're asked (within reason; don't let this turn into a cross-examination). Then try again: "Well, Mr. President, I'm sure you've got a lot of pressing domestic legislation to attend to, so if you'll give the order, we'll launch Operation Overlord at 0600 on June 6th."

If you're still sitting there an hour later, with the President asking for the third time how you're going to handle the machine gun emplacements on the bluffs above Omaha Beach, you know it isn't going to happen. But a CFL will identify himself as such by giving you the order—you should pardon the play on words—when you ask for it with confidence and authority.

If the prospect hesitates—and even CFLs hesitate sometimes, particularly in the early going—I always find it useful to remind him that he has to distinguish between giving me the *management* of his account and giving up *control* of it. He's certainly doing the former, but not the latter—not in any way. He's still the Commander-In-Chief (after all, it *is* his money), and the Joint Chiefs serve at his pleasure. The ultimate authority remains the client's. At that point, don't be surprised to hear first a sigh of relief, and then the order to launch the invasion.

Finally, don't forget that you always have the right (and even the duty) to go back to the client at times when the war isn't going so well, and to tell him not to worry. Again, don't try to prove to him *why* he shouldn't worry—unless he asks. Try to remind the President, when the bear counterattacks, that we may take some casualties and lose some ground temporarily—but that our strategy is sound, and that the outcome of the war is not at all in doubt.

Tell people what to do. Deep down, that's what the good ones really want.

6 Never compromise your business plan or your belief system.

Codifying your belief system; making a three-, four- or even five-year business plan based on that belief system; and steadily increasing your tolerance for "rejection" in pursuit of that business plan: those are the actions of a potentially excellent advisor. And they'll take every ounce of courage, determination and persistence that you can muster. (Some days, they'll take even more than you can muster, and that's when your "heart" will be put to the test.)

Stand by your plan, no matter how severe the temptation to compromise it "just this once" may be. I can't take that $7 million bond account; I'd be selling my soul to get it. And when I got it, what would I have? Maybe half a point a year in fee income—i.e. 30 pieces of silver—and a bad conscience. If you've set a $250,000 account minimum, and a no-brain, low-maintenance $100,000 account washes in over the transom, you're going to be sorely tempted. (If you're not, you ain't human.)

Don't do it. If you're really serious about getting X number of $250,000 accounts in a fixed, finite time period, taking the smaller account will make you feel a traitor to your standards. And one day, while you're having to serve that account (because low-maintenance is never actually *no*-maintenance) you'll have to put a CFL on hold...or actually see one slip away. You need your focus; you need your self-esteem. Hold to your standards.

And if you've said you'll only handle the whole account or none of it—and, believe me, there's no other way; the buck can never stop here and/or there—a day will surely come when you'll win $2 million of a $5 million estate. And then your whole life is going to flash before your eyes. On that day, your sense of yourself will hang in the balance. Don't succumb. If the President says that it's only reasonable to have one general running the war in Europe while another runs the campaign in the Pacific, tell him: neither of those generals is going to be you. If your career plan calls for you to be responsible for the entire war or for none of it, stand by your plan.

If you don't have enough faith in yourself to see your plan through to completion, how can you credibly ask other people to believe in you? And if you do believe in yourself, prove it (if only *to* yourself): *stand by your plan.* Excellence, by definition, precludes compromise. Compromise, then, is the first step on the long "strategic retreat" to mediocrity. But all you have to do—in order to be sure of never completing the retreat to mediocrity—is to fail to take that first step. **Don't compromise.** You'll never forgive yourself.

7 Start every business day with three specific acts of courage.

Call somebody you do not want to call, see somebody you do not want to see, and do something you do not want to do, at the beginning of each business day *without fail.*

This profession, as the film star Bette Davis said about old age, ain't for sissies. It takes courage—great courage, if you ever expect to be an excellent advisor—and courage takes constant, conscious practice. But courage, for the aspiring excellent advisor, is like Vitamin C for all of us: to wit, the body doesn't store it.

Unlike most other vitamins and nutrients, the unused Vitamin C in your system gets flushed out, so that every day, when you need more, you have to ingest more. Every day, I believe, advisors who are pushing the limits of their prospecting capacity burn up every iota of courage they've got, just doing their job. So every morning, when you look at that blank piece of paper that's got to have a whole lot of hash-marks on it by nightfall, your courage gauge—whether you realize it or not—is on empty.

And just as you have to drink some fruit juice every morning to get more Vitamin C, you have to *practice courage* every day in order to generate more courage. Knowing this,

⟨eia⟩

The excellent investment advisor practices courage every day.

You can miss a day of jogging, or doing sit-ups, or even flossing. But, if you want to become (and remain) an excellent advisor, you can never miss a day of practicing courage.

And indeed, it should be a source of tremendous comfort to you to know that courage is something you *can* practice—that it isn't something you had to have been born with, like blue eyes. Everyone has the capacity to practice courage, just as everyone has the capacity to be excellent. (These are, in fact, two ways of saying the same thing.) And there's no better way to practice courage than by starting the day off with the Courage Trilogy: calling and seeing people, and doing something, we'd prefer to avoid just then.

Ducking people and things we don't particularly want to face is always the beginning of a downward spiral; you can't preserve courage (much less add to it) by avoidance. The converse is (wonderfully) also true: that in three acts of expending courage every morning, we actually build up a reserve of it that may carry us through much of the day. The reward of courage is courage. And, if you're like most people, you'll need to figure out the night before who you're going to see, who you're going to call and what you're going to do that you'd really rather not. This has the effect of ending even the most dismal day on a high note. ("It wasn't much of a day, but the heck with it: look how brave I'm gonna be first thing in the morning.") And, of course, the morning trilogy of courage tends to banish unpleasant memories of yesterday that might otherwise have washed over into today. ("Both my appointments cancelled yesterday. What if that happens again?")

Please note that, when I say you should see and call people you don't want to, I'm certainly not suggesting that you speak to people who chronically abuse you. [*That's not courage, it's masochism.*] Let's say your firm came out with an emerging markets fund in 1992 or '93—such things are not unheard of—and the fund took a licking in 1994 and early '95. Maybe you have one client who bought at the top and panicked out at the bottom. (This, too, is not unheard of.) But now, every time you speak to him, he passes a snide remark. Not only should you not make exposure to such abuse a part of your morning courage trilogy, but you should take immediate steps to shut the abuser down, hard.

My approach would be, "I sense that this incident is a source of continuing distress to you. But I'm not sure how your bringing it up every time we speak is helping either of us. I think I've made it clear that the fund has recovered considerably from its meltdown lows, and that the emerging market meltdown itself was by no means specific to our fund. I've also tried on a number of occasions to make the point that, had you not sold, you wouldn't have suffered the loss you did.

"This is all water over the dam, however, and for both our sakes I'd like to find a way to put some closure on it. How about this: let's sit down together and go over all the investment decisions involved in that incident, to make sure we've learned everything we can from it. After that, I'd really prefer that we not talk about it anymore, because doing so doesn't help me help you. So please: let's set a date for our meeting, or tell me this subject is closed."

Shutting down a chronic abuser is, itself, an act of courage, of course. And it can be a part of your Morning Courage Trilogy, if you like. But only once, obviously. And incidentally, if there's just nobody you can see on a given day in this context, make sure you replace that behavior with either another call to a second person you'd rather not speak to, or by doing a second thing you'd really rather let slide. Three's a charm.

You'll find the Morning Courage Trilogy oxygenates your sense of self-worth in much the same way that early morning aerobic activity—a jog, a power walk, 20 minutes on the stationary bike—energizes your body. In fact, a combination of the two kinds of activity is absolute dynamite.

8 Compartmentalize your day; put all your energy into just one activity at a time.

Establish a set prospecting time every day. Devote that prospecting time, as nearly as is humanly possible, to doing nothing but prospecting. Same for client contact time. And the same—with a vengeance—for all administrative/paperwork.

Answering a client's phone call, and stopping to figure out his cost basis in Gronsky Incomprehensible Technology Fund, during peak prospecting time is an obvious avoidance behavior. **(A)** It isn't that urgent. **(B)** An assistant should be doing it. But what if the call is about investments, or the effect of some scary headline on "the market"? My answer: "It won't have any effect on your long-term investment plan, and it may not even have had an effect on the market, three days from now. If you need to talk about this some more, may I call you back at 11:00 this morning?"

Train your clients to know that they can speak to you virtually any day, but only during certain hours. This builds your courage, because you know you're not going to let anything interfere with your business-building agenda. It also sends your clients a clear message that you are a busy, successful professional with significant demands on your time and attention. (Can their attorney come to the phone whenever they call? Can their doctor? And are you less of a professional than those people?)

Take some time to examine your work flow with a critical eye. If you find that you might be doing literally anything at literally any hour of the day, you can be sure that that chaos is significantly diluting your effectiveness. And the self-recrimination that follows from this will just naturally shoot a hole in your courage tank.

This isn't merely a time management issue; it's an inquiry into what you're doing for (or to) your self-esteem. Identify the behaviors that you substitute for the real work of our profession (especially the prospecting part). Box them inside certain blocks of time. And never let them out again.

9 Make a reward system out of your old avoidance behaviors.

This is another way of getting a rope around your unconscious, low-level avoidance behaviors, and of actually turning them into self-esteem builders instead of sappers.

Suppose you smoke cigarettes. Without you actually having to do anything at all, this has turned into a jim-dandy avoidance behavior in recent years. Because, in this new age of smoke-free environments, you have to step outside your building to smoke a cigarette. Don't you love it? Cigarette smoking doesn't just kill you, it lets you drain your courage by avoiding your work. Because, after all, *you can't pick up the phone and call a referred lead while you're standing outside the building!* (Unless, of course, you're standing out there with a cigarette in one hand and a cellular phone in the other. If you are, don't call the lead. Call a psychiatric referral service.)

Now, suppose you like to drink coffee. You do a prospecting behavior, then a second and a third, but you don't hear a "yes," and you're starting to feel a tad anxious. So instead of immediately doing another prospecting behavior, you just duck down the street to the local gourmet coffee shop...where your favorite brew, double decaffeinated Kenya AA latté grandissimo with mulled skim milk, takes 12 avoidance minutes to make.

I think you may be starting to see that all kinds of seemingly natural, "innocent" things we do all day are actually avoidance behaviors. Now suppose, for a moment, that you either can't or won't stop doing any of 'em. And suppose further that you're in a place in your head where it's just very, very tough for you to do the things you need to do. That happens. Committing large numbers of prospecting behaviors every day sometimes feels like the gauntlet, even to the excellent investment advisor.

But what if you took all those unconscious avoidance behaviors, and made a reward system out of them? What if each and every one could be turned into an immediate, pleasurable payback for every appropriate behavior you commit? Maybe it would go like this:

> Do a prospecting behavior; read the C section of the *Journal.* Another prospecting behavior; read the B section. A third prospecting behavior; get a cup of coffee. Fourth prospecting behavior; the A section of the *Journal.* Fifth behavior; have a smoke.

When you've done your 20th prospecting behavior, you may be fresh out of rewards/avoidance behaviors. If so, invent yourself a new one. How about: taking a five-minute walk. Anything that gives you a breather, *but only as a reward for a set number of appropriate behaviors* (as opposed to, "If one more person whacks me with a tomahawk, I'm gonna lose it; think I'll duck outside for a five-minute walk").

You can also, of course, select perfectly appropriate (non-avoidance) behaviors from your everyday life, and make a reward system out of them. Let's say you saw in the paper this morning that a movie you've been dying to see is on cable tonight. And let's say the number of baseline prospecting behaviors you're up to at this point is 30. Seems pretty obvious to me: do your 30, get to watch the flick. If you don't—in addition to having to drop back to 29 behaviors for the next 10 days—no flick. (I will, however, suggest an Aaron Hemsley "get-down-off-your-own-back" technique for use on such occasions. If you've hit your 29th behavior and are in danger of missing your commuter train, grab the phone. Call information. When the operator says, "What city?" you can say, "Listen, you don't want to buy a mutual fund, do you?" When the answer is "no," thank the person, hang up, have a good laugh at yourself, and go home to the flick.)

The critically important thing here is that you key all your rewards to a variable you can control: your behavior, *not someone else's reaction to your behavior.* You've already got one "reward" system that's keyed totally to other people's reactions. It's called your compensation plan. You make a magnificent presentation to a seemingly eager, affluent prospect, and he says, "You'll hear from my accountant if we have any questions. Goodbye." Nobody pays you. Next minute, a referral you've never even heard of walks in with a $700,000 estate. You've done nothing. And for this they pay you. It's random; it makes no coherent sense. What useful feedback does it give you about your behavior? Not much.

But your *own* system of rewards, which you get every time you commit the one indispensable behavior of trying to start a conversation with another human being—*that's* a formula for increased capacity and healthy change. Play the numbers game; get an immediate reward. Play it again; immediately get another reward. Outcomes, shmoutcomes: invest your energy in the behavior, *get your rewards from the behavior.*

And if the little rewards you receive each day are precisely those behaviors that used to make you feel bad about yourself...I ask you: how delicious is that?

10 Undersell. Undersell. Undersell.

Overselling always sets you up to fail. It's transaction-oriented, and therefore is good for your month but bad for your life. (And make no mistake about it: even a financial plan, if oversold hard enough, ceases to be the basis of a relationship, and becomes just another transaction.) Underselling is always relationship-oriented, and always sets you up to succeed, in that it's denominated in a sustainable investment reality, and always focuses on the client's long-term comfort level.

Overselling always sows the seeds of a relationship's destruction. ("Buy this new fund *now* because it's *hot* and it's going to go straight up *starting this afternoon!")* Listen to how different underselling sounds:

> I'm not sure any of the funds in the portfolio I've chosen for you will ever be at the top of *Money* magazine's pick-hits-of-the-week list. One of the funds' managers, Grey Trueheart, has said to me on several occasions that no one can be consistently hot. So if it's a choice—and it is—he'd rather be consistent than hot. That's been my guiding principle in selecting a portfolio that fits your risk-averse attitudes: slow and steady wins the race. Does that make sense to you?"

Where underselling really earns its stripes, of course, is in a lousy market. That's when the hollowness of overselling shows up in all its ugly, recriminatory aspects. And it's where the underseller shines. You get to say, "We always agreed that the temporary declines are the price you pay for the permanent advances. And, as the old song says: here's that rainy day. They're rallying both the yields and the values of just about everything we own—which is a nice way of saying that the prices are falling. Is there any chance you could put some more money in at these bargain levels, before the sale ends?"

Selling will always be an intrinsic part of what we do, because being a good investor doesn't come naturally to Americans. (If most folks had good instincts, most folks would be rich. Since most folks clearly ain't rich, getting people to invest well will always be a sales job...no matter how consultative the selling is.)

One thing I've always found useful, in this context, is to draw financial plans using index returns, and ask people if they could live with those results. If so, the added returns they get from having superior managers and from dollar-cost averaging will be very happy surprises. That's what underselling buys you, in the end: a career full of happy surprises.

All issues of overselling and underselling come back to the question of how many prospects you've got. The fewer prospects you have, the more you tend to oversell. This depletes your energy because it makes you feel dirty, so you talk to even fewer people...and "have to" oversell them even harder. Downward spiral.

The more people you talk to, the more the business is a numbers game, the less you have to press any one prospect to do something, the more you can undersell...and know that you'll get your share of the good people...who respond to you because you undersell. Upward spiral.

And even though you have to prospect more people, you'll find you have enough energy to do so. Why? Because when you see underselling for what it really is—a form of moral leadership—you're energized by the pride you take in your work. Being the kind of person you always wanted to be increases rather than depletes your energy!

Thus, in the final analysis, underselling is great for the clients... but even better for you.

11 Organize your week, as completely as possible, on Sunday night.

Yes, you take a lot of time away from your family, and you're very loath to use any weekend hours for business purposes. But if you don't organize the week on Sunday night—lay it all out, look at it, think about the major things you want to accomplish, check on the logistics of your outside appointments—when are you going to do it? Monday morning is too late; by then you should be in the thick of the fray—executing your plan, not trying to figure out what it is. (And if you're still organizing on Monday morning, I submit that organizing has itself become an avoidance behavior for you.)

Very accomplished people from all walks of life have the Sunday night discipline. (Lee Iacocca, in his self-titled best seller, is particularly good on the subject.) They get to make the emotional transition from weekend leisure to business focus before they go to sleep on Sunday—and often wake up with a new idea on Monday morning. That's because the computer that is your unconscious doesn't sleep; it will often chew on the last issue you gave it to work on at night, and present you with a solution in the morning.

Most of all, an hour or two of quiet thought on Sunday nights allows you psychologically to take command of your week, like a general surveying the field before a battle. It lets you deploy your "forces" of time and energy in the most advantageous way. Sunday night sets you up to act, rather than react, for an entire week. You may come, in a very short time, to regard this as the most productive clip of time in the whole week.

12 Every 90 days, replace 10% of your wardrobe.

Ultimately, your product is yourself, and it's very important that you continue to invest in the appearance (as well as the content) of that product. The practice of programmatic replacement/upgrading of your wardrobe is an instant self-esteem booster, and an important way of investing in your appearance, which is a form of investing in yourself.

Every 90 days, lay out your entire business wardrobe. Take the tiredest-looking 10%—suits, dresses, shirts, shoes, whatever's most clearly not up to par—and give it away. Then go out and replace it *with something slightly better than the best stuff you now have.* For instance, say you've got five winter suits. Four of them cost between $350 and $400, but there's this older one that probably didn't cost more than $225. Clearly, you're going to give away that last suit. The point, though, is that you have to replace it with a suit that costs more—even if it's only a little bit more—than $400.

Thus, every 90 days, you begin wearing something that is not only the best thing of its kind that you own, but that may be the best thing of its kind you've *ever* owned. And, since this is a slow, rolling upgrade of your wardrobe, you never really have to spend all that much money at one time.

Make a game out of this; share the experience of laying out the wardrobe with your family or a significant other, to bring a fresh eye to the culling process. It's terrific fun, and it's another way of involving the people you care about in your career. And best of all, just three months from now, you get to do it again.

13 Be here now.

It may sound corny, but try to live this business day as if it were going to be your last. That way, you probably won't drag a lot of yesterday's resentments and frustrations into today. And you won't either fantasize about, or worry about, tomorrow—because there is no tomorrow.

Not long ago, I visited Pearl Harbor, and stood on the Arizona Memorial, looking down at the sunken ship in which 1177 American servicemen are entombed. And I wondered, as everyone must sometimes wonder: how could this have happened? So I bought Gordon W. Prange's book *At Dawn We Slept*, surely the definitive account, and one of the most fascinating books on any subject I've ever read.

As the Japanese fleet races silently across the Pacific toward its target, Prange describes the mounting anxieties of the fleet admiral, Nagumo, and contrasts him with his chief of staff, Kusaka, a better warrior and a better man:

> Kusaka wrapped himself in his usual kimono of ascetic calm, believing that at times the individual becomes caught up in problems he cannot solve by his own efforts. He thought that by concentrating on the immediate task to the exclusion of fruitless worries and speculations, the human being could tap a pure stream of spiritual strength to carry him through.”

This whole passage jumped right out at me as being perfectly evocative of the mind-set that you and I need to have in our business. Will the Fed lower or raise interest rates? Will the economy slow further, or re-accelerate? Will your favorite mutual fund manager go cold for a season or two? Will your biggest account move away or die? Will your very supportive branch manager get promoted and transferred away? Will the groundhog see his shadow?

You can't know. And like Kusaka, you can't solve these problems by your own efforts. But there is tremendous strength to be gained by concentrating solely on the task at hand, and by denominating your goals only in terms of variables you can control. (I cannot say for sure that I'll increase my business 50% this year, so that's a dumb goal. I can say with absolute assurance that I will increase the number of times I get "rejected" every day by 50%. And the latter will inevitably lead to the former.)

Take out a three-by-five card. Write on one side the five things you love most about the business. Get the card laminated and read it aloud to yourself every morning, as soon as you get to your office. If you reconnect, each and every day, with the glories of our career (rather than its mundane problems), you may find that you get a surge of energy that will help you concentrate solely on the task at hand.

St. Francis of Assisi was hoeing his garden one day, when one of the other monks asked him what he would do if an angel came down and told him he was going to die that night. Francis thought for a moment, and then said, "Finish hoeing my garden." That perfect state of being in the moment—without either regretting or futurizing—has tremendous power to purify your work. **Be here now.**

Two important addenda (not exceptions) to this rule: vacations, and the occasional illness. It's imperative that you take real, getaway vacations. Don't stay home, and don't try to splice a vacation with a business trip in any way. Make your vacation a special and specific event, discrete from literally everything in your life.

And while you are on vacation, try to have no contact with the office whatsoever. If you have to, take vacations that make such contact prohibitively difficult. Sail the Caribbean, ski the Chilean Andes, go on safari in Kenya. Also, do not go on a vacation that you have not already saved up for. If you're watching those credit card bills mount up in your mind's eye, you can't relax. (My children's mother always had a unique but effective way to enforce this rule, when we used to go to Europe each summer. Unless I showed her the passbook with the total budgeted cost of the trip in it, she wouldn't get on the plane.) And, as long as you're going to be saving up for your vacations for a while, save a little extra and fly first class. After all, do you want to save for a whole year to go on a spectacular trip, and then sit in the back of the bus?

The other addendum concerns illness. We are only human, and sometimes we get sick. The flu, a virus, a real bad cold, whatever: your job doesn't exempt you from illness in the way that it may from jury duty. And being the congenital overachievers that we are, we will always try to rationalize a way to walk through it ("I'm young; I have meetings I can't cancel; it's probably just a heavy cold").

Don't even think about it. When you try to fight your way through an illness, you're going to make mistakes. You'll look bad, you'll sound bad, you won't be sharp, you'll get stressed out, negative, self-pitying...and then, one fine day, you'll say something you really shouldn't say, to someone you really shouldn't say it to. Or you'll forget something really important. Oh, and by the way: you might make yourself *really* sick, in the bargain.

Be sick now. Put your heart and soul into it: see a doctor, take the medicine, unplug the phone, and sleep around the clock. And then do it again, the next day. And the next, as long as it takes to get *all better.* Then go back to work with everything you've got. It takes courage to admit that you're (albeit temporarily) licked. But he who fights and runs away lives to fight another day. *Be sick now.*

* * *

At the beginning of this chapter, I asked you to read these 13 very disparate suggestions with an eye toward perceiving their common denominator: the golden wire on which these beads are strung. I hope you see now that these principles and practices are all geared toward preserving and enhancing your courage—the "heart" it takes to win the "Rejection Olympics." As Coach Knight put it, you play this game against yourself. No one but you can prevent you from winning the Olympic gold.

In Summary

☞ Once you know your N, all you need to do is steadily expand the multiple of N-minus-1 "rejections" you can withstand.

☞ In addition to a strong belief system, a sound business plan, and a knowledge of your N, excellence requires a set of standards and behaviors that will sustain you on a day-to-day basis. Their function is to replenish and increase that indefinable quality called "heart."

☞ Maintain the highest ethical standards at all times, if only from a purely selfish motive. "A good conscience," said Benjamin Franklin, "is a continual Christmas."

☞ Go the extra mile by relentlessly seeking the personal connection with prospects and clients. Perform gratuitous acts of kindness and concern, the main characteristic of which is that they are above and beyond the call of duty. Write a terrific note to and/or about someone every day; this will aerobicize your attitude, and vent the resentment that can build up when you're hearing "no" a lot—which you always should be.

☞ Get a year's living expenses in a money market fund. The best defense against ethical shabbiness and corrosive people is not to "need" them.

☞ Have your own financial plan; fund it, as nearly as practicable, with the investments you want people to buy from you. This increases your overall effectiveness no less than 300%.

☞ Tell people what to do. Don't read them a menu. (Have you ever known a multimillionaire waiter?) People don't go to a doctor to learn the practice of medicine. They just want somebody to make them get well. Let the trust happen.

☞ Never compromise either your belief system or your business plan. As you must never break your word to a client, you must first never break your word to yourself. *Stand by your plan*.

☞ Start every day with a megadose of Vitamin Courage: call someone you don't want to call, see someone you don't want to see, and do something you don't want to do. The reward of courage is courage.

☞ Compartmentalize your day so that you are always totally focused on doing one thing at a time, as well as you know how to do it.

☞ Make a reward system out of your old avoidance behaviors. If you used to read the *Journal* and drink coffee *instead* of prospecting, train yourself to enjoy those things *because* you prospected.

☞ Undersell. You may have to prospect more people, but your life (and theirs) will be a series of pleasant surprises.

☞ Organize your work as completely as possible on Sunday night. If you hit the ground running on Monday morning, that momentum may very well carry you through the whole week.

☞ Every 90 days, replace 10% of your business wardrobe with better stuff than you now own. You're selling yourself. So plan to invest continually in upgrading the appearance of your product.

☞ Be here now. Yesterday is history and tomorrow is a mystery. The only reality is today, and the only thing you can control—or ever *need* to control—is your behavior today.

☞ Courage is the golden wire on which the beads in this chapter are strung. All the standards/behaviors herein are aimed at strengthening your "heart," because that's what's going to win you the gold medal in the "Rejection Olympics." And the only one who can beat you is you.

7

Leveraging up

"Each man is a hero and an oracle to somebody."

—**Ralph Waldo Emerson**

Here you are, very nearly halfway through this book. And you've surely noticed that—other than an anecdotal example now and then—you've seen no specific discussion of how to talk to prospects and clients. So far, we've worked only on your own beliefs and behaviors.

This is no accident. (And, if you'll permit me to say so, it's no mistake, either.) Everything we've covered up to this point is everything that really matters—belief system, business plan, behavior modification as it relates to prospecting. And everything that really matters takes place between your ears, not across a prospect's desk or a client's coffee table.

What you say, how you say it and whom you say it to are merely *refinements* of the things that really matter. Your interactions with the rest of the world, in other words, have to be driven by your core beliefs and by your behavioral values (sometimes called your "work ethic"). If you let the refinements take over, you are unconsciously ceding the agenda to the outside world, which no excellent advisor ever does.

For example, given my belief system, I have a very specific way of reacting to the objection, "Stocks are too risky." The journeyman, handing over the agenda to the prospect *and* taking the objection at face value—in other words, making two mistakes simultaneously—will whip out the Ibbotson chart. He'll then attempt to *prove intellectually* (two *more* mistakes at once) that while stocks are fairly volatile over shorter periods of time, in the long run the megatrend is always up. The prospect replies, "I haven't got 60 years" and/or "This time it's different." And the journeyman suddenly finds himself with both fists, both feet, his left knee *and* his forehead stuck to the tar baby, and he can't figure out how he got that way.

When someone says, "Stocks are too risky" to me, there's a moment of stunned silence on my part—just enough to communicate non-verbally that this is, to me, an almost alien concept. Then I reach into my pocket, and take out my business card. If I'm talking to husband and wife, I take out two cards, one for each of them. I place the cards face down in front of them—and they see that laminated to the back of each card are two first-class US postage stamps, one from the current year and one from 20 years earlier. At this writing, I'm using stamps from 1996 and from the glorious year of America's bicentennial, 1976. The 1996 stamp says 32 cents. The 1976 stamp says 13 cents. (If I were a sandbagger, I'd still be using my 1975 stamp, which said 10 cents. But I'm not a sandbagger.)

I look at my prospects, right in the eye, still not saying anything. Then I glance down at the stamps—which pulls their eyes down to the stamps, as well. Next, I reach out and very gently move the cards a fraction of an inch closer to my prospects. When that's done, I look at them once again, and ask,

> **"Please help me understand your concern. When you say stocks are too risky, how are you defining risk?"**

Yes, this approach has the effect of gently re-setting the agenda—of drawing the focus off investments and putting it back on real life. But that's almost beside the point I'm making. You see, what I've done here isn't some mechanical objection-handling "technique." It's a non-argumentative re-statement of one of my most deeply held beliefs: that in the long run, "risk" isn't principal loss; *it's the extinction of your purchasing power while you're still alive.*

One's most effective methods of interacting with prospects, then, grow (like everything the excellent advisor does) directly out of one's deepest belief system. And that's why we've spent so much time and energy working on your own beliefs and behaviors, before talking about your relationship to the outside world. If you try to do it the other way around, you end up an other-directed "technique" junkie, totally out of touch with your real self, and questing endlessly for some magic formula that will make all sales resistance melt away.

I despise the whole notion of "technique," because I reject any notion that what you do can be separated, in any meaningful way, from what you are. "Technique" is probably OK for people new to the business, in that having a track to run on reduces anxiety. But as you get a body of experience—which can only come from dealing with the hopes and fears of real people, and never from a computer screen—"technique" should begin to wither away.

In its place comes a deepening confidence in your own prospecting/selling/counseling style. "Technique," then, is what you do while you're waiting for the differences between your selling style and your personal style to disappear. At that point, your financial plans and investment portfolios cease to be your product. Your product—the thing you are fundamentally inviting people to buy—is yourself. So you reach inside yourself for the strength and skills you need, rather than looking outside yourself to empty, mechanical "techniques."

(And still I hear endless drivel about dividing prospects up into four—or nine, or skatey-eight—"personality types," so you can completely change your approach with each type. This not only blinds you to the infinite richness of human variety, it robs you of your identity by suggesting that you would actually want to be different things to different people. Carried to its logical conclusion, when you look in the mirror there won't be anyone there. Then comes October 19, 1987, and every time the phone rings, you pick it up, hear someone's voice, and have to try to remember who you are to that person—while all around you the world's in flames, and if you haven't got an absolutely fireproof belief system, you're toast. Puh-*leeze! You gotta be who you are!)*

In this chapter, I want to have you look at a menu of ways in which you can begin to leverage your new, fully realized self. Unlike the last chapter, in which I said you should adopt the 13 behaviors as a coherent whole—not selecting from among them but employing them all—I invite you to pick and choose among this chapter's suggestions. The issues here are twofold: first, does a particular tactic in this chapter feel right to you, and second—since some of these ideas involve finding colleagues and other industry professionals with skills/proclivities complementary to yours—are the right kinds of people available? And are *they* willing?

The ideas in this chapter may seem wildly diverse. Some seek to utilize people inside our industry, some relate to interactions with prospects and clients. Some do both at the same time. And one is something you do all by yourself. But they have one common theme, and that is *leverage:* how to deepen, strengthen, refine and multiply the good that flows from your hard-won belief/behavior system.

So here are half a dozen major ways of leveraging up.

1 Create an informal "Advisory Board" of great wholesalers.

Wholesalers represent a huge pool of underutilized talent. They don't get enough opportunity to show what they can really do, because most of the time they're bogged down in unproductive interactions of the what's-your-beta-how-many-stars-do-you-have variety. But some wholesalers have terrific strengths, which they're just dying to use. You can leverage the growth of your business by recruiting and deploying those talents.

Of course, all successful professional relationships have to be two-way streets. As wholesalers help you build your business, they have every right to expect to be rewarded with the management of the incremental assets you're gathering. So you're not going to recruit a wholesaler to your "advisory board," no matter how extraordinary her personal skills, if you don't also believe that her product is a genuinely superior fit for the kinds of clients you want.

But the multitude of good funds, wrap programs, annuities and variable life policies out there—and the army of wholesalers who represent those products—are such that you'll easily be able to find plenty of candidates for your "board."

So look for good people who also represent good products. They won't be hard to find, because of the operation of Murray's Law of the Inexorable Justice of Wholesaling, which states that all money managers/ product sponsors eventually end up with the wholesalers they deserve.

Here are some examples of special skills that many good wholesalers have. Think about what you need in order to take your business to the next level. That way, you'll know which wholesalers to include in your new professional advisory group.

(A) Wholesalers Who Are Terrific Speakers. Few occupations give people the opportunity to develop their platform skills more than wholesaling. A wholesaler may, between office meetings and public seminars, give 500 group presentations in a year.

I wouldn't argue that some of them just make the same awful presentation 500 times. And I know that there are few things more depressing than Mumbling Morty Marblemouth, three-quarters turned away from his audience, reading verbatim from 37 incomprehensible slides. But the constant practice elevates many wholesalers into great speakers: warm, funny, thought-provoking and very human, so that clients come to you after a seminar and say, "I want to look further into that."

You can easily schedule half a dozen client seminars a year, using wholesalers who are terrific speakers. So next time you're sitting in an office meeting listening to a wholesaler's presentation, don't be looking to compare his Sharpe Ratio or standard deviation to every other fund's. Ask yourself, "How would my clients react to hearing this man or woman?"

Particularly if you aren't that hot a speaker yet, this is a way wholesalers can add tremendous value to your practice.

(B) Wholesalers Who Are Great One-On-One. Obviously, if part of your team should consist of a great speaker or two, you should also enlist one or more wholesalers whose forte is meeting with clients one-on-one.

Someone who's very accomplished at this can teach you a lot about establishing genuine emotional contact in interviews, about questions-and-objections handling, and about that mysterious skill called "closing." (You'll find that, with the great ones, closing isn't even as much a skill as it is an attitude.)

And here you begin to see the critical distinction between a wholesaler and his product. If you've got a client who's overweighted in debt and very underweighted in equities, it would certainly be wonderful if the best one-on-one wholesaler you know represented a five-star equity income fund. But that kind of luck is pretty rare.

So you may have to choose between a five-star fund represented by somebody who starts sweating through his shirt in the client's house, and a genuinely charming and empathetic wholesaler whose fund is temporarily at three stars.

That's when you see that even a three-star equity income fund is better for these folks than bonds, and infinitely better than a five-star fund that the folks don't buy. The wholesaler who can help you get people to do the right thing is the wise and valuable citizen, regardless of theological abstractions like relative performance.

(C) Older, More Experienced Wholesalers Who Wear Their Years Well. Many salespeople/planners in the industry today are relatively young and of recent vintage professionally. They find, quite predictably, that it's tough for them to make an impression on older investors. This is where a wholesaler with age and experience more like those of the client can be an invaluable asset—particularly if he or she represents a large company with a lot of history behind it. As people get older (and wealthier), they may value experience and continuity even more than they do "performance"—especially if an older, wiser hand is there to reassure them.

Wholesalers may tend to blur and run together for you. But I promise you that when you bring in a vice president of a $50 billion money management firm—someone with 25 years of investment experience and a reassuring style—clients intuitively know that this is a profoundly different experience from dialing 1-800-NO-HELP.

(D) Generators Of Good Sales Ideas. Wholesalers with good instincts are encyclopedias of smart sales ideas. Being good salespeople themselves, who go through four dozen offices a month and talk to hundreds of salespeople/planners, they hear (and remember) every interesting idea there is. If you'd stop arguing with them about their annuity's mortality charge vs. that of Gronsky Life, you might get to hear some of those ideas.

Ours is not, by and large, an industry that is managed by top-quality salespeople. (Top-quality salespeople don't generally find the management track very interesting, especially as the management function gets more and more mired down in "compliance.") Therefore, we usually have to look outward, rather than upward, for dynamic sales leadership.

Great wholesalers who love their craft—and who have nothing and nobody to manage but themselves—are constantly generating good ideas. And a great sales idea generator can be a critical element of your "advisory board."

(E) Wholesalers Who Are Willing To Mentor You. It's hard to get somebody with acute sales/interpersonal ability to spend time with you these days—to monitor your phone calls, to role-play with you, to counsel you on tough prospects. Your peers are too busy, and your manager is either recruiting or in an arbitration hearing.

Good wholesalers are just dying to do this with you, provided, of course, that you'll use their products when they're a good fit for the client or prospect. A fair exchange of value is critical to all successful business relationships, but the value you can get from some really good one-on-one mentoring may be, in the long run, immeasurable. And these days, there may not be anywhere else to get it.

(F) Wholesalers Who Can Do, and Teach You To Do, Really Useful Stuff. A fair number of wholesalers are actually pretty skilled at estate planning (or at least at holding their own with estate planning attorneys, which can sometimes be even more important). That's just one example of a technical skill that is going to be more and more important to your success as we head on into the 21st century.

Going to a meeting at your firm's headquarters and having this explained to you by a technical expert is one kind of experience. Seeing it done in the field by somebody with the gut-level, give-and-take experience of really doing it with real clients (and their skeptical advisors) is a completely different kind of experience...and a far more useful one.

Pick out two or three skills or specialties (charitable remainder trusts and systematic withdrawal plans would be high on my list, were I you). Find wholesalers with very highly developed skills in these areas. Put 'em on your team.

All the things I've said about outside wholesalers are equally true about your in-house coordinators and technical experts, as well. And perhaps even more so, because you're paying those people's salaries whether you're using them or not. Each of them is there, at least with respect to his own narrow specialty, to serve your clients better than you can—and to pay you for the privilege. Learn who the good ones are, and always be on the lookout for ways to use them.

Elbert Hubbard said, "There is something much more scarce, something finer far, something rarer than ability. *It is the ability to recognize ability.*" Cultivate the ability to recognize—and to utilize—ability that you don't have, and in some cases don't even want.

2 Learn to give good seminars.

We live in an atomizing world, in the sense that people spend ever more personal and professional time alone with only an electronic device—the computer, the TV, whatever. Seminars bring people together. They're restorative of more traditional human experiences, and they remind people that investing is much more about essential human needs than it is about numbers that come out of a machine. I don't believe that anything builds a prospect's confidence more quickly and efficiently than seeing you standing up in front of an audience of similar people—and feeling how much they like you and respect you.

Again, you don't have to be instantly eloquent to start doing seminars. In the early going, you can use your wholesaler team. That way, you get to learn from professionals, who have practiced hundreds of times, as they make superbly organized presentations. And you get to see what people react to—what I call the Nod Factor. Watch very closely to see when the audience nods, and what points they're nodding at. After the presentation, watch the audience lob questions at the wholesaler, and see how she handles them.

There are also a number of extremely professional, well-organized seminar systems you can invest in today. (You'll see their advertisements in *Dow Jones Investment Advisor* magazine and other industry publications.) These systems enable you to virtually build your entire business on seminars—provided you use them consistently. Moreover, they're just expensive enough that you can't afford *not* to use them consistently.

And indeed, consistency is what it's all about—in seminars as in everything else. For many journeymen, seminars are something they try once or twice, sending out 4000 invitations to people they don't know and putting an ad in the *Des Moines Register*. Then, when six totally unqualified people show up, the journeyman decides that "seminars don't work."

Any seminar program works if you work it. You have to make a long-term commitment to it—I'd say no fewer than four to six seminars a year over no less than two years. And in the end, I think the main attraction at your seminars must eventually become you. Anybody can deliver a canned, pre-programmed presentation on asset allocation, but only you can be you. And since the excellent advisor is always selling herself, I believe a program of doing seminars in which the main event is anything but you is misguided. So rather than going over a lot of mechanical rules for building seminar audiences (which you can get in half a dozen other places), I'd like to spend some time on the process whereby you can become an excellent speaker.

Just as I believe that any advisor can become an Excellent Investment Advisor, I believe anybody who wants to can become a terrific speaker. So let's analyze the process of becoming eloquent—of learning to speak, instead of just talking. In seminars as in every other aspect of this business, feelings are to facts as 19 is to one. For that reason,

The excellent investment advisor knows that the way he says what he says is even more important than what he says.

If a person with marbles in his mouth tells you The Great Secret of Life, chances are you won't get it. The pain of having to listen to the messenger blocks out the beauty of the message. Most seminars are like that: the content is fine but the delivery is flat, humorless and eye-glazing. So forget about content, and practice eloquence. Here's my system:

(A) Define eloquence in your terms. What is eloquence, anyway, and how do you feel about it? If you see it as some extremely rare quality that comes along a few times in a generation—in a Lincoln, a Kennedy or a King—you're (a) setting the bar too high, and (b) courting despair.

Eloquence, to me, is nothing more or less than the ability verbally to inspire in others some of the passionate conviction you yourself feel. There are only two alternatives to eloquence, and they are both unthinkable. One is to try to infuse an audience with an enthusiasm you yourself don't genuinely feel, which is quite impossible. (Yet this is precisely the journeyman's self-imposed burden, and the reason he always sounds strained.) The other is to feel the conviction, but not be able to inspire it in others. This is simply unprofessional, and you have to get over it.

Eloquence, then, is not some rare art form that you have to be gifted with at birth. It is a skill—or rather a set of skills—and the test of its effectiveness is whether the audience catches some of your conviction. "Those who would make us feel," said the 18th century English poet Charles Churchill, "must feel themselves." If, and to the extent that, your audience ends up sharing your passion—for an asset class, for a planning idea, for a manager—you are eloquent. If it doesn't, you're not. There's nothing abstract or ethereal about eloquence. It's as down-to-earth and practical as a hammer and a nail. Eloquence is a tool. And, as with every other tool, excellence in its use comes with time and practice.

My personal concept of eloquence, and the guiding principle of all the speaking that I do, actually rests on two definitions. Interestingly, they both come from clergymen of bygone eras before mass media, when most people heard eloquence only from the pulpit, and occasionally from the campaign stump. The first is by an American, Lyman Beecher (1775–1863); the other is by an Englishman, Richard Cecil (1748–77). Respectively, they are:

Eloquence is logic on fire. Eloquence is vehement simplicity.

For me, logic is empty without the fire; it may instruct, but it doesn't inspire. And simplicity without vehemence is merely obvious, if not actually patronizing. All great truths are surely simple. ("Over a quarter century of retirement, the principal risk of holding equities historically declines to zero, while the risk of consumer prices doubling—indeed, nearly tripling—approaches virtual certainty.") But it takes a healthy measure of vehemence to cause that truth to come alive, in a way that makes clients not only understand equity investments, but want to buy them. ("In 1976, a first-class postage stamp cost 13 cents.

Today it costs 32 cents! Consumer prices *much* more than doubled in the last 20 years…which posed *no problem* to patient, long-term shareholders of The Great Companies In America. For, while the price of stamps was going up two and a half times, the dividend of the S&P 500 stock index virtually *quadrupled!")*

Logic on fire. Vehement simplicity. The ability to inspire in others some of the passionate conviction you feel. Those constitute my idea of eloquence. If your definition is different, that's fine. But make sure you have clearly written down what your alternative definition is. Because your definition of eloquence is your target. That's what all the rest of these ideas are aimed at: making you eloquent, as you define eloquence.

(B) Believe in your capacity to become eloquent, in your own special way. Eloquence is as individual as any other aspect of your personality; no two people approach it in exactly the same way. You can learn a lot from other good speakers, but you can never *be* another good speaker. You have to be who you are.

And you have to believe that you're going to get there, slowly but surely. Belief in your capacity to become eloquent in your own way is essential to your success. "I just don't think I'll ever be really good at this, but I'll give it a try," is an absurdity on its face. Self-doubt is the ultimate self-fulfilling prophecy; it works 100% of the time. "I don't think I can, but…" is exactly the same as saying, "I can't."

Contrast this with, "I don't know exactly how I'll get there, but I believe I will get there, and I've made an irrevocable decision to get there, whatever it takes." In the quest for eloquence, as in all things, belief and decision are the essentials; everything else is a little methodology and a lot of perseverance.

(C) Always know exactly what you're going to say. Unless you are already very far along the road to eloquence, assume that you can *talk* extemporaneously, but not *speak* extemporaneously.

"How's business? How's that soccer star of yours?" That's *talking;* you can and should do it off the cuff. "There are five absolutely critical things for the risk-averse investor to understand about equity investing.

They are…" That, obviously, is *speaking*. So you better know those five things—and know precisely what you're going to say about 'em—before you open your mouth.

This goes way beyond having an outline. (An outline, to the striver after eloquence, is like taking a shower every day. It's a given. Now what?) The outline is to your presentation as the string is to a pearl necklace. It organizes the beauty, and holds it in place, but it is not itself the beauty, nor is it what anyone wants to look at. (On the other hand, without it there would be no beauty, only the chaos of a lot of pearls rolling randomly around on the floor.)

Or, if you will, the outline is to the presentation as the tracks are to the train. It's an indispensable means to an end, but it's not the end. *And it is still technically possible for the train to jump the tracks,* just as it's possible for the most exquisitely outlined presentation to go crashing off into the woods if the advisor forgets what he's supposed to say to the outline points.

Knowing exactly what you're going to say involves three things: **(a)** making an outline, **(b)** writing out, pretty much word for word, the text of your presentation, and then **(c)** tape recording yourself speaking (*not reading*) the presentation. This is an extremely disciplined and painstaking approach to the art of the presentation, and it yields huge benefits. General Chuck Yeager, in his autobiography, says that when he was named chief test pilot for a new aircraft, he and his team would go into the hangar, literally take the plane apart, and put it back together again. Thus, even before flying the plane, Yeager almost always knew more about it than did the engineers who designed and built it.

You can argue that this analogy is overstated, in that if Yeager didn't find a flaw in the plane until he was two miles up, he'd die, but if you foul up a seminar presentation, it's not fatal. Don't count on it; you may never get that audience back. And besides, where's your pride? Where's your commitment to excellence? Be here now; do every single presentation as if your life depended on it, because in a sense it does. Every time you get up to make a presentation, see Yeager climbing into that cockpit, knowing that his craft was mechanically perfect, because he himself had made damn sure it was.

(D) Build your presentation on a very few great boulders of truth. When the Spanish conquered the Incas of Peru, they tore down all of the great buildings of the Inca capital, Cuzco, and built their own structures on top of the Inca foundation walls. Today, 450 years later, the Spanish structures are gone, or have had to be rebuilt many times after each great earthquake. Silent and mocking, the Inca walls stand exactly as they always have, undaunted by nature or man. "Civilization" exterminated the engineers of those walls, but could not learn what they knew.

Remember this when you build your seminar presentation. The Inca walls are the foundation stones—the elements of your outline. You want to build your walls out of a very few immovable boulders of truth, and then frame up the details of the presentation on top of those unshakable truths. For instance, if I were going to do a seminar on small-cap investing, my great boulders of truth would be:

▶ Small-cap has historically provided a 20% premium long-term return over big-cap. The compounding effect of that big a spread is enormous over time.

▶ The premium return is there to compensate you for premium risk/volatility. (Markets are, above all, supremely efficient in the long run.) So you only do small-cap with the portion of your portfolio you'd virtually never need to sell.

▶ Professional management and diversification are even more critical in small-cap than in other aspects of investing. Small companies are individually too risky, too hard for the investor to research and too costly for him to trade.

▶ This is the manager/these are the managers I use, and why.

▶ Think about the longest-term portion of your portfolio, the part you can leave alone to grow for 20 years and more. Then rent the movie *Apollo 13*, and watch the top rocket scientists in the world using slide rules, because it was 1970 and the microprocessor—the whole computer on a chip, mankind's greatest invention so far—was still a year away. Eighty-five percent of the scientists who've ever lived are not only still alive, they're still working. What will they invent in the next 20 years? I don't know either, but small-cap is where a lot of it will happen.

▶Any questions?

That kind of presentation is just good for my soul. It doesn't try to prove anything. It's a virtually statistic-free environment. And all it says is: how big can you dream?

(E) Keep it very, very light. Enlighten people; don't overeducate them. There is a world of difference. When the journeyman puts up a slide of the Ibbotson chart, which nobody can read, that's *education*, or a vain attempt thereat. (The journeyman always tries—and fails—to connect with the audience's heads, because he lacks the courage and the genuine human warmth that it takes to connect with their hearts.)

In my public seminars, I make the Ibbotson-chart point, 10 times more powerfully—and without the chart:

I see that most of you have something to write on, so I'd like you to jot down these two critically important dates in modern investing history.

On the left side of your note paper, I'd invite you to write the date July 8, 1932. Over on the right side, please jot down October 14, 1996.

On Friday, July 8, 1932, for one day only in this century, the Dow Jones Industrial Average recorded an intra-day low of...(*here I see the heads go down and the pens get ready to pounce, so I say*)...no, please look up at me when I say this. I promise you'll have time to write it down in a moment, but you almost have to see it to believe it...are you ready? **40**! Yes, I'm rounding to the decimal point; the precise statistic is 40.56. But for purposes of the broad sweep of investing history: **40**!

On Monday, October 14, 1996, the DJIA closed over 6000." (I always see people shaking their heads in wonder, and whispering to each other about this miracle.)

Now, 6000 is 150 times 40. [*Author's note: I hope I will not insult your intelligence when I point out to you that, if the DJIA is 7000, or 8000, or whatever by the time you read this, you'll use the last big round number, and adjust the other details accordingly. It's just that, at the time of this writing, the symmetry of the 64-year 40/6000 run is so lovely.*]

This is particularly interesting in that the 64 years in question are, by many important measures, the worst such period in human history. If you doubt this, try to remember another six decades marked by a larger global economic depression, followed by a larger global hot war (in which about 55 million people lost their lives). And top it off with a global cold war that threatened the planet with extinction, enslaved about a third of the earth's population, and diverted heaven knows what percentages of the world's wealth and human ingenuity into the black hole of defense!

And during this protracted global ice age, the DJIA went from 40 to 6000! You may well wonder, as I do, what's going to happen now that things are good—now, in other words, that capitalism is the organizing principle of most of the human activity on the planet. But that's just speculation; let's stay with what we know.

We know that they went from 40 to 6000 during the worst 64 years in history, and we have reason to think that—economically, at least—things are tending to get better rather than worse. I conclude from this that the great risk of American common stocks remains tonight just what it has always been: **Not Owning Them!**"

What you just read takes three minutes and 30 seconds to say. But in it, I think I totally capture the moral high ground, and begin liberating people from their fear of equities. That, if I may say so, is eloquence.

And it is the pure, distilled essence of the difference between education and enlightenment.

(F) Use lots and lots of symbols. Symbols are always better than words. The journeyman points, with his little red laser pointer, at the (illegible) line on the (illegible) Ibbotson slide that describes inflation. *I hold up the stamps.* (Perhaps we can compromise on this one: how about...a slide of the stamps!?)

The journeyman puts up the (illegible) slide of the University of Michigan study of "The 40 Best Days." He uses this to "prove" that you have to sit through any and all blood-curdling decimations of your retirement nest egg, in order not to miss that golden handful of days that take your return from passbook to paradise. In other words, he invites the audience to subordinate its most visceral, primal terror to some professor's intellectual abstraction. (God, what a *jerk.*)

I hold up a can of tuna fish. (OK, OK, if you insist: you're allowed to put up a slide that's a picture of a can of tuna fish.) I say, "I bought this in the Piggly Wiggly supermarket down on Third and Main just this afternoon. Paid $1.39 [*or whatever*]. Think that's about what it usually costs?" [*Folks say, "Yup."*] I say, "OK, suppose you went in the Piggly Wiggly tomorrow, and there was a big sign: Today Only, Tuna $4.98 A Can." [*Folks laugh, groan, say ixnay.*] "Right; everybody'd say that, so the market would get stuck with a lot of tuna fish. And next time you went in, that old sign might say, Tuna $.79 A Can. What would you do then?" [*Folks: "Back up the truck."*] "Right! Anybody here shop January white sales?" [*Lots of nods.*] "Anybody ever buy a new car at the end-of-the-model-year clearance sale?" [*More nods.*] "Thank you. *Now will somebody please tell me why you won't invest that way?*

"When they mark the tuna down to 79 cents, are they having a *bear market?* No, they're having a *big sale!* OK, here's the message [*I hold up the can of tuna in one hand, and the NYSE listings in* The Wall Street Journal *in the other*]: *It's all tuna fish!*" [*Rueful laughter, nods, even sometimes a smattering of applause.*]

Make a long-term commitment to doing seminars. (Or commit never to do them at all.) Get professional help, if you need it, in learning how to build an audience. Then, teach yourself to speak eloquently—not in the jargon of investing, which people hate and fear, but in symbols that explain the mysteries of investing in terms of their everyday life. People will come to love your seminars, and when they do they'll come to love you.

3 Build a peer network.

Once you have a clear picture of the kind of business you want to create, ask the internal and external wholesalers who travel your firm to help you establish a network of like-minded advisors who are striving for excellence.

Suppose there turn out to be five other people a lot like you. Imagine how a half-hour weekly conference call might accelerate all six of you up the learning curve. You'll hear (and improve on) each others' portfolio strategies, sales ideas, prospecting skills, presentation styles, Q&A/ objections handling and war stories. To be reminded regularly that others are going through exactly what you are means a lot. A "support group" can take the sting (not to mention the loneliness) out of the frustration and disappointment you feel when you hit a dry spell.

Plan a weekly conference call with your network. To make this call a focused, effective exchange and not just a telephone bull session, follow these guidelines.

Limit the group's size. Seven is the limit to have everybody participating in the call. Also, more than seven makes the telephone arrangements unwieldy.

Limit the call to 30 minutes, no matter what. Any more probably isn't worth doing anyway and can wait until next week. Don't let this call turn into an avoidance behavior.

Have an agenda, or at least a regular format. Every couple of months, review the format to make sure everybody still feels it's working.

Agenda items can include: each member's best answer to a key objection; one member making his presentation each week so the group can learn and/or critique; a pot every week for the most assets brought in that week, etc. Be creative; make it *fun*.

A member who misses three calls in a row is excused from the group. (He clearly wanted out anyway, and just didn't know how to tell you—or maybe himself.)

Hostility, excessive competitiveness and/or a negative attitude are grounds for being excused from the group. The weekly call only works if the call is a real "up."

The late Napoleon Hill (whose book *Think and Grow Rich* is to the literature of motivation/self-help what the Book of Genesis is to the Bible) called such arrangements "Master Mind Groups." Aaron Hemsley calls them "Performance Groups." Regardless of what it's called, **networking is an organized, relentlessly positive way to make each member better and smarter.** The whole turns out to be much more than the sum of the parts. Your learning curve becomes shorter and less steep, which helps you produce more assets sooner. And networking may acquaint you with colleagues and friends who can leverage each other's careers for years to come.

4 Become a student of the business.

You set yourself apart from your competition—and add great value to your client relationships—by being a real student of our business, of markets, and of long-term economic reality. This may be more true now than ever before, because a whole generation of the financial services industry has never seen a meaningful bear market in financial assets—nor a bull market in hard assets like real estate and energy.

By 1996, two out of three Series 7 licensed people (and an even larger percentage of Series 6 licensees, many of whom work in bank programs of very recent vintage) had entered the business since the birth of the great financial bull market in the summer of 1982.

Thus, a seasoned veteran of a dozen years or more might have accepted, as "permanent" reality, any or all of the following highly anomalous circumstances:

(a) The sextupling of US equity prices in 14 years, punctuated by only two declines, in 1987 and 1990, both of historic brevity and no lasting consequence.

(b) Rates of total return in the bond market nearly triple their long-term (Ibbotson) pace.

(c) The greatest crash in real estate values since the Great Depression of the 1930s.

(d) A secularly falling real price of energy (indeed, by the end of 1995, the inflation-adjusted price of oil was back where it had been in 1974).

(e) Inflation barely perceptible, at or below the long-term (Ibbotson) 3.1% rate.

(f) Falling personal income tax rates, at least until the '93 Clinton uptick, which nobody seemed to notice.

(g) A great, soaring arc in American productivity, which carried us from being a global non-competitor in the '70s to our current status as the world's low-cost producer of just about everything.

(h) A secularly falling dollar, which, combined with (g), above, turned America into an almost hegemonic global exporter, far and away #1 in the world.

(i) Cutting-edge leadership in technology, particularly at the high end, eclipsing our erstwhile nemesis, The Land of The Rising Sun, whose stock market meanwhile executed a 60% swan dive off the high diving board.

These, and many other unbroken trends of similar stripe, form the entire professional acculturation of a significant segment of today's industry participants. In fact, many of the early recruits to this peacetime army are now part of the officer corps; today, there are whole offices full of advisors with between nine weeks' and nine years' experience, being managed by old veterans with a dozen years' service.

Now, I don't go so far as to say that anybody who wasn't in this man's army during The Big One (the Vietnam/Watergate/OPEC Bear of '73–'74) is a pantywaist. [*Much as I might like to.*] I merely suggest that, if all your professional education has been derived from a decade or more of driving down a one-way street, **(a)** you may have forgotten that there are streets on which traffic can go in both directions, and **(b)** you may not react appropriately if, one night, you find yourself driving into the headlights of an oncoming 18-wheeler.

Similarly, if you joined the US Army right out of high school 10 years ago, you are certainly a grizzled veteran...but all your combat experience is Desert Storm. I submit with respect that, based solely on your experience and that of your immediate superiors, you cannot even conceive of Iwo Jima, much less know what to do if you suddenly find yourself in a recurrence of it.

And if ours has become an industry of weekend warriors, a look at the combat experience of our investors has to make your blood run very cold, indeed. At mid-year '82, just before the bull was born, mutual fund assets (excluding money market funds) stood at $54.2 billion. After 14 years of virtually non-stop Nirvana, that number was $3 trillion, and rising. And why not? "Reality" has not only been a one-way street, but that street has been paved with solid gold.

Now, loath as I am to kill anyone's buzz, I'm constrained to point out that life wasn't always like these 14 years. And that, given the cyclical nature of things, it may not always be quite so benign in the future.

Indeed, if you go *back* 14 years (or so) from the summer of '82, "reality" was actually quite different. From the summer of '66 until that of '82, in fact, the Dow Jones Industrial Average went from 1000 to...you guessed it...1000. (One may deduce from this that a sextupling of equity prices every 14 years may not be a natural law quite on a par with, say, gravity, or tides.) In the 16½ years to mid-'82, in fact, the annual return of the S&P 500, excluding dividends, was something like 1.5%. (With dividends, it was a bit more than 5%.)

Oil went from $1.50 a barrel to $40, completely blindsiding the US auto industry and everything that feeds off it. Nixon took the dollar off the gold standard and instituted wage and price controls. Inflation pushed Americans into higher and higher tax brackets, with no improvement in their living standards (hence: stagflation). We lost 55,000 men and a piece of our national soul in Vietnam, and still went down to defeat. The unemployment rate got to 10%, inflation got to 15%, and the prime rate got to 20%. Bonds turned into wallpaper. Our diplomats were held hostage in Iran for a year. And we gave away the Panama Canal.

It was a mistake, during those dark days, to extrapolate pessimism in a straight line, forever into the future. (Most people didn't see that, which is why most people aren't rich.) Similarly, it is probably a mistake to extrapolate Nirvana. But that's what most people are doing...because that's all they've ever experienced.

You're only human. If oil went up every day of your professional life for the first eight years that you were in the business, you probably thought oil was going up, at some greater or lesser rate, forever. Likewise, if stock prices sextupled over your first 14 years, and if the only two "major" setbacks you've ever seen were laughers, you probably think...well, you know.

Here, then, is where the excellent advisor can add immense value, simply by being a student of the business, and of markets. In the country of the blind, the one-eyed man is king. And in the country of the Extrapolators, the advisor with the character and courage to keep talking about The Cycle is the wise and valuable citizen.

Nor is it a requirement that you yourself have been in the business for more than these dozen-or-so years. As the want-ads say, this experience is desirable, but not necessary. There are lots of 25-year veterans who never were and never will be students of the business. And there are certainly people with five and 10 years' experience who already realize that, to a very great extent, if you study what's happened, you'll know pretty much what's going to happen (though not necessarily how, or when). The excellent advisor's value is not measured in years.

Seeing that all straight-line extrapolation is the enemy of Truth also begins the process of liberating you from the malignant fiction of "performance." American investors (and, all too often, their investment advisors) are "performance" junkies, but "performance" is just a variation on the theme of extrapolation.

The basic myth of "performance" is itself an extrapolation: to wit, that which overperformed in the last block of time will continue to overperform, and the converse is also true. Thus, when small-cap (or value, or emerging markets) has done twice as well as large-cap (or growth, or domestic US) for the last five years, Americans—egged on by the Great Demon Extrapolator, journalism—will go crazy for the immediate past overperformer...just as that cycle comes to an end.

Investing like that is like enlisting in the Japanese navy the day after Pearl Harbor. Yes, you are joining the proudest fighting force in the world *on that day*. Yes, your outfit just pulled off one of the greatest strategic coups of all time, and the single greatest coup *ever* in the short history of naval aviation. And yes, it's all going to go straight downhill from here on in. And yes, you are gonna get killed.

"Performance" selling is a treadmill to oblivion, and extrapolation always involves driving forward while staring fixedly into the rear-view mirror. By the time the gangbuster performance is there for all to see—when funds go from $50 million to $3 billion, and then nobly close to new investors—it's usually around three minutes to midnight, and Cinderella's golden coach is just about to turn back into a pumpkin.

Being in a red-hot sector can be a terribly addictive drug, particularly if you've never been to the mountaintop before. And sometimes that asset runs for years and years. Oil never left a skid mark from its initial tripling after the Yom Kippur War in October of 1973 until it finally topped out in 1981. Real estate rose phoenix-like from the ashes of the construction-loan-REIT debacle of '74–'75, and ran until tax reform burst its balloon in 1986 (and still its momentum kept the corpse staggering forward, until the '87 Crash finally brought it down).

The bond market soared, virtually uninterrupted, from 1982 until late in 1993. And here you had the classic case of a track record that looked its very best, and sent you exactly the wrong signal, just moments before Armageddon. For, by the summer of 1993, bond fund marketing essentially said just two things: 14% average return for the last 10 years, and not one down year in over a decade. (Utility stock funds told the same story, and to the same yield-starved audience. And utilities' average annual return was closer to 20%.)

Of course, this analysis only captured one side of the cycle, neatly clipping off the holocaust years of 1973–81. But there's something magic about 10-year returns, and all those people disintermediating out of 3% CDs didn't seem to want to be burdened with the Truth. So, starting in the fall of '93, and running for the next six months, we had, quite simply, the biggest bear market in bonds of all time. When your eyes are glued to the rear-view mirror, you don't notice until way too late that you've just driven off a cliff.

The excellent advisor sees the whole picture, so she tries to keep her clients from indulging their appetite for greed. And she willingly, if painfully, foregoes some business—maybe a lot of business—in the process. But she literally saves people's lives.

And if the excellent advisor's character is most evident at cyclical tops, his courage comes to the fore at panic bottoms. Just by being a strong and positive presence, he can inspire his clients when they're paralyzed or even panicked by the apocalypse *du jour*.

The excellent advisor thrives on "bear markets"—which he, as a student of the business, knows should always be looked upon as "big sales." If his knowledge of market history teaches him one thing above every other thing, it's that all value is born out of fear, and that the greatest value is born out of sheer, unreasoning panic. (Sir John Templeton, surely one of the greatest investors of the age, has always said that the time to buy stocks is "when others are urgently and anxiously selling them.")

So the more that markets, or sectors, or asset classes get killed, the more the excellent advisor loves them, and the more forceful and enthusiastic his interactions with his clients become. Meanwhile, of course, his "competition" is washing out on the evening tide, so he gets the increasing market share he so richly deserves. Rather than become infected with the prevailing pessimism, he himself—through the medium of his courage—becomes the cure. "Bear markets" are always the making of the excellent advisor's career, just as wars are the making of war heroes.

Markets don't usually bestow great rewards on huge upsurges in public enthusiasm—at least not for long. Nor do markets permanently punish those with the patience and fortitude to dollar-cost average into quality assets and businesses that the masses are fleeing in droves. And no matter how elliptical, that's the long, inexorable orbit that virtually all asset classes are always on. Dirt cheap...fairly valued...expensive...bigger-fool-theory top...collapse...denial...panic...dirt cheap...here we go again. That's the thing about the cycle. It always...*cycles.*

It should go without saying that the longer you're in the business, the easier it becomes to see the cycle in all its forms. But that can be a long and very expensive education. So it's a good idea consciously to cut down on the amount of time you spend watching TV, and reading newspapers and magazines. Take the same time budget, and invest it in reading good books that serve instantly to give you years and decades of perspective about cycles. And every good book about economic history, business or markets is—whether it consciously means to be or not—an insight into cycles. (See **Appendix 2: Bibliography.**)

For instance, there are people who've been watching oil for nearly two dozen years—all the way from $3 a barrel to $40, and back (in real, inflation-adjusted dollars) to $6—and oil is just as mysterious to them now as it was when they started watching it. Maybe more so.

But I promise you that no one who's read Daniel Yergin's phenomenal Pulitzer Prize-winning book *The Prize* doesn't understand oil anymore.

(Bottom line: it's The Mother of All Commodity Cycles.) And the funny thing is, it's a *great* read, genuinely very hard to put down once you get into it. Robert Ludlum, Jack Higgins and Frederick Forsyth all writing together couldn't have made up some of the stuff that's happened in oil.

Moreover, as soon as you understand oil, you start to understand *all* commodity cycles. Just as, once you read about the first great mutual fund mania of the late 1960s in John Brooks's hilarious *The Go-Go Years,* you'll instantly see pretty much where we are today on *that* cycle.

And after you read the chapters on the South Sea Bubble and the Tulip Mania in Charles Mackay's 1841 classic, *Extraordinary Popular Delusions and the Madness of Crowds* (which I do once a year, whether I think I need to or not), it'll be very hard for the Serpent of Markets to get you to bite into the apple the next time 1929—or even 1987—rolls around. (Which it surely will, *the nature of the cycle being what it is.*)

5 Make generating referrals a part of your clients' job description.

Prospecting may be the single most anxiety-producing thing we're called upon to do, but asking for referrals runs it a very close second.

Seeking referrals just seems to be way outside most advisors' comfort zones. And it's awfully hard to be good at something you're very uncomfortable doing. Thus, the vague, defeatist way most advisors ask for referrals ends up being a self-fulfilling strikeout. The question, "Do you know anyone else who could benefit from the services I perform for you?" almost always produces the same response. The client gets a little uncomfortable, and says something like, "Well, no, not right offhand, but let me think about it." He never brings up the subject again...so neither does the advisor.

Part of the problem, I've always thought, is that we're not just asking the client to *give* us a referral; we're asking him to *think* of the referral.

We haven't given the client any clue as to who the referral might be, and I believe that's asking too much.

If I know my client is the Senior VP for Engineering at a manufacturing company, I don't have to be *that* much of a rocket scientist to engage him in this dialogue:

me: You're Senior VP/Engineering at Digital Datawhack. There must be a Senior VP/Sales & Marketing. What's his name?

client: "Marvelous" Marvin Micklethwaite.

me: Good guy?

client: Not a bad example of the species, I suppose, if your taste runs to sales types...meaning no offense.

me: None taken. Would you introduce me to him?

client: Sure.

[*or*]

client: Let me take a pass. The guy is just not my cup of tea, and I don't really want to get involved with him. In the long run, I think he'd wear *you* down, as well.

me: Thanks for the warning. Who on your level—Senior VP or above, let's say—*would* you recommend me to?

client: Probably Dr. Werner Von Sprocket, the guy who runs our testing laboratory. Solid citizen, been there for donkey's years. Extremely diligent about his work, and probably not real focused on financial/investment issues. Absent-minded professor type.

me: Would you introduce me to him?

client: Now that you mention it, I insist. You could probably do him a whole lot of good, and he's the sort of person who'd be grateful for it.

me: Thanks for thinking of him...and me.

The point here is simply to suggest that you not ask for referrals in the typical mealy-mouthed, open-ended journeyman fashion. Give your client very specific clues to the identify of the referral—and if the initial suspect doesn't pan out, then ask the client to nominate someone else.

As useful as this [*you should pardon the expression*] technique may be, though, it begs the essential question. The best way to dispel the surprise/confusion/embarrassment of the referral process is simply never to allow it to be a surprise in the first place.

We've already established that all successful long-term client/advisor relationships are based on a sharing of rights and responsibilities that is **(a)** fair and **(b)** agreed upon right from the get-go. The Excellent Investment Advisor makes quite extraordinary commitments to the client and his family—indeed, commitments the client not only has never been offered, but may never even have heard of. In return, the excellent advisor certainly has the right to ask her CFLs to serve as referral sources, particularly since she points out that *to do so is very much in the client's own selfish interest:*

My life's work may not be easy, but it is remarkably simple: broadly speaking, I really only have two professional functions.

The first is the nurturing of the wealth of my existing clients—the research, the monitoring, the extensive program of contact with our managers that I've talked to you about, the administration of my clients' accounts, and my scheduled client communications. Those are all the things I have to do in order to honor my commitment to you and your family.

My other professional function, of course, is seeking out new clients, in order to build my practice to levels that will ensure the realization of my goals for my own family. This is a process that's ongoing, and that will take me several more years to complete.

The problem is that I can only pursue one of these agendas at a time. My clients come first, of course; I hope I've made that clear.

> But it's also true that the less time I have to spend looking for potential new clients—which is at best a hit-or-miss process—the more time and energy I can expend on my existing clients. For that reason, I ask my clients—and am asking you now—to **help me help them** by referring me to potential new clients. This cuts down on the work I have to do in that area, and again frees me to serve you even better.
>
> From time to time, as you grow more and more comfortable with my work, I'll actively solicit your help in this regard. In particular, I do semi-annual Client Appreciation Nights, which always feature top investment professionals, and which are a lot of fun, too. And I ask each of my clients to bring along one new person or family to those get-togethers—entirely without obligation, of course—to see if there might be a fit.
>
> My question is simple: assuming (as I certainly do) that our relationship is financially successful, and pleasant for you as well, will you consider helping me in this way, if you can?"

Please note that (a) you merely asked them to *consider* referring people to you, (b) you told them you'd only ask them for this if they were happy with you, and (c), above all, you told them they'd be *helping you help them* by giving you referrals. And no matter how tentative and qualified a "yes" you get to this speech, *it's still a "yes."*

Ask for referrals the way the Boston Irish used to vote: early and often. The sooner in the relationship that you do it—and the more often you do it—the less anxiety-producing it will be to all parties concerned... and the better it'll work.

By the way, don't let that item about Client Appreciation Nights in the above script get past you. This is, for many people at the top of our profession, the single most productive referral source they have. That's because, in their own gentle way, these advisors are deadly serious about the client's price of admission being to bring along a friend the advisor doesn't know yet. The clients are never permitted to mistake this for a request. And again, it works not because there's any particular magic to it, but because *the excellent advisor made it part of his essential agreement with his CFLs right from the giddiup.*

The very best cure for "referral anxiety" is, of course, to do work of such high quality that you come to feel that referrals are almost your birthright. But the second-best is simply to state your right to referrals as a clause in your "contract" with your clients.

6 Capture assets, and increase their longevity with you, through multigenerational marketing.

It has always been an axiom of our profession that "your best prospects are already in your account book." This allusion to our transaction-driven past was intended to communicate that, no matter what you assumed, your clients always had more money.

The Excellent Advisor deserves, asks for and gets all the money, not least of all because he does not accept shared accounts. ("Mr. President, you have every right to have one commanding general in Europe and one in the Pacific. But with respect, sir, neither of those generals is going to be me. I'll accept responsibility for all of this war, or for none of it.") However, even the excellent advisor may tend to stop after gathering the assets of one generation, and/or may focus all his attention on just one family member. This is a fundamental mistake, with potentially serious consequences.

So I'd like to see you run your business in obedience to Murray's Law of Multigenerational Marketing, which simply states that

The excellent investment advisor knows that the percentage of a family's assets that he controls, and the length of time he controls those assets, are an absolute function of the number of family members he talks to on a regular basis.

In other words, I'm not sure your best prospects *are* already in your book. But I do know that your best prospects have the same last name (or at least the same maiden name) as the people in your book.

The classic example is an account where your contact is a successful 55- to 60-year-old businessman. You get along great; you chat nearly every day; you know each other so well that you can just about finish each other's sentences. The wife? In the background somewhere, and besides, as the client makes clear, he makes the financial decisions.

Everything goes along fine until one afternoon when the guy gets into an argument with an oncoming crosstown bus about who has the right of way. Your guy loses. And you no sooner see the obituary than you see the transfer papers.

The widow, it turns out, cordially despises you—and you've never spoken to her for five minutes at a stretch. Why the antipathy? Partially because the deceased liked you so much—and the widow holds you indirectly responsible for keeping her in the dark about money.

This scenario is played out every day. But you can easily avoid it if you make sure you've opened a channel of communication to all the prospective widows in your account book—even if it's just taking both husband and wife to dinner once in a while. And even if finances aren't directly discussed. Just by letting them both know that you're ready to be as helpful to her as they'll let you be, you may ensure that crosstown bus doesn't get you, too.

And clearly, stepping up your contact with potential widows—which, actuarially speaking, all married women are—isn't just defensive marketing. Particularly for women in our business, it can be a great, proactive prospecting device.

I've been recommending that advisors start doing "widow training seminars," although I'm still struggling to come up with something less blood-curdling to call them. (And maybe I should stop struggling; maybe the best thing to do is just call them what they are.)

You can get a whole host of pertinent agenda items for such a seminar from Alexandra Armstrong and Mary Donahue's wonderful book *On Your Own: A Widow's Passage to Emotional and Financial Well-Being* (published by Dearborn Financial Publishing). It would be hard for me to do justice to this terrific book in this space; suffice it to say that, whether you're planning seminars or not, everyone in our business should be reading—and giving clients many copies of—*On Your Own.*

Much has been made, in recent years, of the so-called age wave. In our business, we've taken the age-wave phenomenon simply to mean the huge shunt of the nation's 77 million "baby boomers" from their peak spending years to their peak saving years. We've been told (and re-told) to get ready for the crush of these pre-retirees out of their BMW phase and into their mutual fund frenzy phase.

This is all well and good—and it's right up in your face, so you can't miss it anyway. But the spending/saving shunt is only part of the story. The other, and potentially more important, point is that the baby boomers are also going to become the greatest legatees ever in history. And if you are not helping both generations plan that process, chances are you're going to get lost in the shuffle when the actual transfer takes place.

A recent Cornell University study states that baby boomers will inherit $10.4 trillion—nearly twice the current US GNP, and more than half the current sum of all household financial assets, including cash and checking account deposits. These bequests are estimated to have started out at around $85 billion in 1995 (in a million and a half separate transfers) and to peak out in the year 2015, with $335 billion in three and a half million transfers.

If you're proudly and busily helping some graying yuppie with his $1000-a-month dollar-cost averaging program, and haven't heard a peep about the half million bucks his father's got earmarked for your guy in a bank trust department, you just bought a one-way ticket to Palookaville. By the same token, if you're Dad's and Mom's advisor, but the kids have never heard of you and could care less, you may just end up being the pallbearer nobody recognized. You've just got to make the generational jump—in whichever direction is necessary—if you're going to be more than a one-generation way station for this family's wealth.

One of the easiest ways to open lines of communication to all parts of a family is via the fact that anybody can give anybody $10,000 a year without paying gift tax. So this is a great way to move significant amounts of money intergenerationally without waiting for the estate tax bite.

If you see a little child's photo in your client's home or office, you know you're looking not just at somebody's child, but also a number of people's grandchild or niece/nephew. So, even if this child is the offspring of your relatively less well-off 35-year-old client, she's also the grandchild of up to four people, and could, therefore, be accumulating up to $40,000 a year through you—if you'd just ask your client for the introductions.

This is multigenerational marketing at its simplest but most effective. And, of course, the grandchild is never going to be safe from getting a birthday card from you, is she? Because, after all, at $40,000 a year, she could be a millionaire long before she goes to college.

Another no-brain intergenerational approach traces the potential need the other way: up, to where your clients' parents may live. Try this two-step questioning process:

Question #1: *Are your parents still living?*

The dark star that's in a collision orbit with so many baby boomers' retirement plans is the financial status of their increasingly long-lived parents. Few people expected to see a day when the fastest-growing segment of the American population would be folks over 85. Now, that segment is growing five times faster than the population as a whole. The prevailing attitude of their children has, up until now, been one of denial, but I think you can sense that they're awakening to the true scope of this financial planning problem. Question Number One establishes whether your particular client is in this situation.

If the answer is no, that the client's parents are gone, I'll ask if they left legacies to the client or to his children, and if the client is happy with the way those monies are being managed. But if the answer is that one or more of the client's parents (or parents-in-law) is living, I ask…

Question #2: *Do you expect to become financially responsible for your parents at some point?*

This is, as I hope you'll intuitively see, the mother of all win-win questions. Guy says yes, you get to ask how he's planning to fund that responsibility, particularly in view of his own retirement needs. This can lead to a whole new round of the planning process, in which you get to capture more assets.

But if the client says no, I'll never have to support my parents, he's told you they have sufficient means to be financially independent come hell or high water. Immediately, you know they're substantial prospects. You can quite reasonably ask if the client is happy with the arrangements the parents have made for the transfer of that wealth to him and to his children.

In many cases, the client doesn't know what his folks have planned, and doesn't know how to approach them about it. It's dicey, but you can offer to have that conversation with the parents, either with or for your client. I'm betting that in most cases, the parents will appreciate the help. (Maybe they hadn't fully planned their estates themselves; most folks don't, even today.)

But even if you're rebuffed by the parents, chances are you'll have cemented the relationship with the client just by offering to go the extra mile. And if you discover, in the process, that there probably isn't going to be a whole heck of a lot left when the parents are gone, you can relay that vital intelligence to your client, so that he realizes, and can plan for, the fact that he and he alone will have to provide for himself and his children.

Note that this line of questioning can be applicable to anyone, and has nothing to do with the state of the markets or how many stars your favorite funds have. Places in the heart vs. places on some chart... remember? Get to the realities of your clients' emotional and financial relationships with their parents. You can't fail to build trust, open accounts, and gather assets, perhaps on a scale currently unimaginable to you.

Asking great questions about the hopes, dreams and fears of all the generations of a family is the subject of the next chapter. For now, simply see that, as the pendulum swings back from the transaction-oriented '80s and early '90s to the intensely relationship-oriented future, we all have to find a way to become what our profession used to be about: literally, the family financial advisor. To do that, you can't rest on your laurels when you get a new account. Instead, you have to keep asking yourself and your clients: how many people in this family don't I know yet?

In Summary

☞ Up until now, this book has focused entirely on your own belief system and behavioral values, which are the two things that really matter. What you say, how you say it, and whom you say it to are just refinements. Try it the other way around and you'll end up a "technique"-driven empty suit.

☞ "Technique" is what you do while you're waiting for the differences between your personal style and your selling style to disappear. *You gotta be who you are.*

☞ There are six immensely powerful sources of leverage available to you that will deepen, strengthen, refine and multiply the good that flows from your essential belief/behavior system.

☞ Wholesalers are, in some sense, limitless leverage, because there are so many wholesalers with so many different strengths. They offer you all manner of skills and knowledge you either don't have yet or don't want. Surround yourself with a wholesaler "advisory board" and reward them with management of the incremental assets they help you gather.

☞ Learn to give excellent seminars. It's good to make one person at a time like you, but it's very hard work. Making a whole roomful of people like you (not understand you;

like you) is much more efficient...and much more fun. Eloquence isn't a gift from on high, it's a skill to be practiced and mastered. Above all: the way you say what you say is much more important that what you say.

☞ Build a peer network. Somewhere in your firm there are six other good people, striving for excellence just as you are. In one half hour a week, together you could become The Magnificent Seven.

☞ Become a student of the business. Ours is the most instructive profession imaginable, because the same economic/business/market cycle keeps recurring. On any given day, a 50-cent newspaper or a "free" TV newscast can tell clients what just happened. But the excellent advisor who's a student of the business can tell people something far more valuable: *what happened the last time this happened.*

☞ An efficiently running referral machine is, of course, the ultimate leverage. The first, most important way to get referrals is to deserve them. The rest is just asking for them early—at the very start of your client relationships—and often.

☞ Leverage the good you can do throughout all the generations of a family. The percentage of a family's assets you control, and the length of time you control those assets, are an absolute function of the number of family members you talk to regularly.

8

Planning for the five great goals of life . . . .

"All problems become smaller if you don't dodge them but confront them. Touch a thistle timidly, and it pricks you; grasp it boldly, and its spines crumble."

—Admiral William F. Halsey

• • • • • • •

Management, it has been said, is doing things right. Leadership is doing the right thing.

Even when they themselves don't consciously realize it, potential Clients-For-Life are looking for an investment advisor who will not simply manage their accounts, but who will lead them and their families to a higher quality of life. The Excellent Investment Advisor intuitively grasps this unspoken need in good people; the journeyman isn't even aware of the distinction between management and leadership.

The journeyman advisor gets a prospect who's 52 years old, married with two children out of college, and who's just inherited $180,000 from his Aunt Sylvia, may she rest in peace. The prospect says, "I want to invest this money conservatively for my retirement. Make some recommendations." The journeyman goes happily to work, crafting a portfolio that's 48% stocks ("Hey, the guy's conservative, so I subtracted his age from 100 to get his equity exposure"), 43% bonds and 9% cash. And he thinks he's done a good job.

The Excellent Investment Advisor, presented with the same situation, says, "Before I go to work on this, would it be OK if I ask you one or two very important questions?" Prospect says, "Sure."

eia: *Ideally*, if everything else in your financial life works out the way you've planned it, *who and what is this money for?*

prospect: Gee, you know, that's actually a terrific question. I guess I just said "retirement" because that's the financial issue that's uppermost in my mind right now. But, you see, I never expected to inherit this much money from Sylvia, and I wasn't counting on it for retirement.

eia: So you have your own retirement plan that you've been funding all along?

prospect: Well, sure.

eia: Then I guess one option you have is to cut back on your future retirement savings, and let Aunt Sylvia's legacy take up the slack.

prospect: That just doesn't feel right to me. It'd be the same as if I kept investing what I'm investing now, and spent the inheritance.

eia: Yes, it would. Would that feel like a waste to you?

prospect: Totally.

eia: OK, so the challenge isn't primarily how to invest the money, but how to make believe the money isn't there.

prospect: What do you mean?

eia: Well, we've agreed that no way are you going to spend this money before retirement, and now you've said that you don't even want to rely on it *in* retirement. Is that right?

prospect: Well...yes.

eia: OK, here's what let's do. Let's say Aunt Sylvia didn't die. Let's say she lives another 10 years—by which time it's not hard to imagine the $180,000 having grown to $350,000–$400,000—and *then* she dies. I ask you again: *ideally,* if everything else in your financial life has worked out according to plan, *who and what is that money for?*

prospect: [*Beaming*] That's easy: it's for the education of my grandchildren.

eia: Forgive me, but you don't have grandchildren.

prospect: Yes, but I sure will by then. My son is already engaged, and my daughter seems pretty serious about this guy she's going around with.

eia: Can you imagine how you'd feel if you could walk into the hospital the day their children are born, and tell them their baby's education is paid for?

prospect: To a guy like me, that would simply be the greatest thing that could happen.

eia: Well, I'll tell you one thing: you and I can make it happen. But not until you get a whole new definition of "conservative" investing.

prospect: How do you mean?

eia: The College Board says the average total cost of attending a public college was $7414 for the '95–'96 school year; $18,232 for the average private college. You have any idea what those numbers will be when your grandchildren are ready to go to college?

prospect: I shudder to think.

eia: If you assume costs will inflate at 6% a year, even a kid born today—which your grandchildren sure aren't going to be—is looking at $92,000 for four years in a state school, and $227,000 in a private school.

prospect: My kids will never be able to pay that.

eia: No, but between you, me, Aunt Sylvia, and a portfolio of managed investments in the ownership of a thousand or so of the great growth companies in the Global Capitalist Revolution, we can do it.

prospect: Then that's what we're going to do. *Just tell me what I have to do.*

I suppose that, on a certain level, this colloquy is just another example of the excellent advisor's basic art form: distinguishing between an investor's *stated wants* and his *real needs*. But it's much more important than that. For here you see the excellent advisor take the focus off the money and put it where it belongs: on the real hopes and dreams of real people.

My point is that all intelligent financial/investment planning has to flow from The Great Goals of Life. Investments can be very complex; tax and estate planning considerations can be even more complex. But, at least on the really big issues, *people are basically pretty simple.* The journeyman gets completely mired down in the complexities; the excellent advisor focuses on her clients' overriding emotional/financial need for a fulfilling life, as they define such a life. The journeyman manages; the excellent advisor leads.

The chapter does not seek to be a guide to the infinite complexities of financial planning. Instead, it provides a step-by-step, thoroughly common-sense process for putting people's greatest fears behind them, and leading them to the realization of their hopes for financial independence/multigenerational wealth.

Insulating people as much as possible from their financial fears is the very first step in the creation of a successful plan. And it is a prerequisite to the rest of the plan; you can't skip over it, or even passively enable the client to skip over it because he's become so excited about investing in the Global Capitalist Revolution. I've made the point before in this book—and will surely do so again—that the great destroyer of lifetime investment plans isn't ignorance, but fear. If someone is constantly looking over his shoulder to see what financial peril (real or imagined) may be gaining on him, not only is he never going to be a good investor, but he's virtually sure, at some point, to make The Big Mistake at exactly the wrong time.

The three great risks to the success of a lifetime investing program are:

1. Death

2. Disability and/or catastrophic medical expenses

3. Loss of employment

The first two are relatively easy, though not inexpensive, to deal with. A will, adequate life insurance, and a basic estate plan are the first steps in any intelligent program. And I think that, whether you can provide those services yourself or have to refer your fledgling CFLs to other professionals, if you don't insist that people have these bases covered before you invest a dime, you don't really care about them. (Besides, those other professionals can and should become lifelong centers of influence/referral sources for you.)

Disability and/or catastrophic medical expenses are the next most insidious enemies of a long-term investment plan. Again, adequate insurance, though not cheap, is a must. Look at it this way: if you're a responsible advisor, your clients are going to pay those disability/health insurance "premiums" one way or another, anyway. Either they buy the insurance and pay premiums to the insurer, or (in good conscience) you'll have to keep a larger portion of their investments in short/intermediate-term debt, as a reserve against uninsured emergencies. And in time, the returns they'll have to forego in order to stay liquid may far exceed the insurance premiums. I vote for the insurance.

Loss of employment is the third great risk to investment plans, in more ways than one. The obvious risk is that, if a client loses her job and doesn't have sufficient cash reserves to carry her over until she finds a new one, she may have to invade her investments at a time when they're down. That's the *real* risk of unemployment. But the *imagined* risk can be just as deadly: suppose the client's company starts downsizing during a recession, when *USA Today* is full of the apocalypse *du jour*, **and** her portfolio's down 22%. In the absence of a comfortable level of cash reserves, she may pull the trigger on her investments *even if she herself doesn't lose her job*...because she's afraid the ax will fall on her tomorrow, when (an "expert" says in *USA Today*) her investments will be down even more.

For that reason, I think getting a year's living expenses in a money market fund is advisable for most investors. And if somebody really needs a lot of equity exposure but is still very nervous about it, I don't mind seeing him get upwards of two years' living expenses in a war chest. Because if I can keep showing him that, no matter what happened, he wouldn't have to sell anything for two years, chances are I can keep him from panicking. (Or else nobody can.) Rule of thumb: north of about 65% equity exposure in a portfolio, go to two years. The opportunity cost may be high, but not nearly as high as the cost of The Big Mistake.

I suppose I should also say a word, somewhere along in here, about debt. In general, I don't think that people should undertake major investment commitments while carrying a lot of debt. Better to punch out a big chunk—if not all—of the debt. Sooner or later, in every public seminar I do, this always comes down to the same question: to invest in equities or to pay down one's home mortgage. My answer is always the same: it probably makes more *economic* sense to buy equities, when the spread between the long-term return of equities and the tax-deductible mortgage interest is favorable enough (10½% vs. 7½%, for instance). But it probably makes more *emotional* sense for most folks to whittle down the debt. And the more nervous about equities people are ("Omigosh! My investments are down 28% *and I still owe $400,000 on the house!*"), the more I vote for whacking out the mortgage. ("Whew! My investments are down 28%, but at least I still have my job *and a free-and-clear roof over our heads!*")

Also, although this should almost go without saying: never let people invest in equities with borrowed money. Never, never, never. Again, the reasons aren't as economic as they are emotional: if one watches $200,000 worth of equity investments go to $140,000, that's one kind of emotional experience. It's very intense, but it *may* be bearable. But if one bought that $200,000 worth of equities in part with a $160,000 home equity loan...I think one's proclivity to panic (or, worse, to "get even and get out") goes up by a factor of no less than five.

Now: what's "adequate" life insurance coverage? Term or universal life? Disability insurance against loss of the ability to perform *your* occupation or *any* occupation? And what about nursing home insurance? My answer to all these questions is twofold. **(A)** Not my field. **(B)** Beyond the scope not only of this chapter, but of the whole book. There are at least two sides to these questions, and the answer often varies with the individual client. Again: I'm not trying to write a detailed financial planning manual, here. I'm just covering what has to be gotten out of the way before I get to talk about what I love: planning for the attainment of one or more of the five Great Goals of Life.

I say again: shining like a beacon through (and over) all the complexities of financial planning is that glorious five-pointed star called The Great Goals of Life.

I don't want to talk to people about Professor Sharpe's ratio, or the letter ratings of funds in *The Wall Street Journal*, or beta, or standard deviation, or any of that essentially meaningless trivia. In the end, that all comes down to, "I'll bet you five bucks—or 500,000 bucks—that Mutual Fund Raindrop A gets to the bottom of the window before Mutual Fund Raindrop B." First of all, nobody can prove that outcome in advance, so why put any energy into it? Second, at the end of the day, maybe 5% of your total lifetime return is going to come from fund selection within categories. The other 95% of your return will come from your answers to two questions: **(1)** How much of your portfolio was equity, and how much was debt? **(2)** What did you do when the equity portion went down 30%? If your answers to those two questions happen to be **(1)** 100% equity and **(2)** nothing, you'll end your investing career in the 99th percentile of real returns achieved by real investors regardless of what funds you owned. **I guarantee it.**

I want to talk about the five things that virtually everyone I speak with is trying to achieve with his money. Some people have only one of these goals (usually, though not always, the same one). Some have two or three. And, not infrequently, I meet people who, with a little prompting, turn out to have a bit of all five. These goals represent the most primal emotional/financial needs of real people; they speak to the deepest yearnings of Americans for their own financial well-being and that of the people (and institutions) they love. And since these five issues are the main financial concerns in my own and my family's life, I can effortlessly (and quite genuinely) spark a tremendous amount of empathy with potential CFLs. And so can you.

The five Great Goals of Life are:

1. The endowment of a long, comfortable, and totally worry-free retirement, with no compromise in lifestyle, and no real concern about ever running out of money.

2. The need/desire to intervene meaningfully in the financial lives of one's children, during one's lifetime and/or in the form of legacies.

3. The ability to fund, in whole or large part, the education of one's grandchildren.

4. The capability to provide quality care to one's parents in their later years.

5. The ability to make a meaningful legacy to a much-loved school, church, charity, or other institution.

Is it all coming back to you now? You know: places in the heart vs. places on some chart? These are virtually all the things that anybody worth knowing really cares about, financially speaking. And the central financial planning problem of our time is simply that *almost no one is investing enough capital to have a real shot at achieving all their goals.*

The Excellent Investment Advisor's primary task, therefore, is not to pick superior investments. Her first job is to guide people—gently, therapeutically, non-argumentatively—out of their massive denial. And then to bring them face to face with how much capital they really need to accumulate, and how (relatively) little time they have in which to do so. (This exercise will, I submit, make an equity zealot out of almost anybody, for the very same reason that Butch and Sundance come running out of that barn: because it's their only chance.)

As a leader, not just a manager, of his clients, the excellent advisor is supremely uninterested in theological abstractions like relative performance. He wants to help his clients face the potentially huge gap between what they're now doing, and what they need to be doing in order to get where *they say* they want to go. The critical issue isn't investment performance but *investor behavior*. And master psychologist that he is, the excellent advisor knows that all recovery begins only when the person with the problem *admits he has a problem.* So by asking a series of warm, deeply empathetic, people-focused (as opposed to investment-focused) questions, all of which touch the Great Goals, the excellent advisor gently causes the client to own his problem. As always, his questions are original, interesting and thought-provoking (just as, predictably, the journeyman's questions sound like they came out of a can).

1 **You're 52 now. Take a moment, if you will, to picture yourself 20 years from now. You're 72, and well into a comfortable retirement. Tell me: What are you doing? What does it cost to do everything you're doing? And where is the money coming from?** Almost as an afterthought, as the people are talking about all the things they picture themselves doing in an active retirement, the excellent advisor places the card with the current and 20-year-old postage stamps on the table, just as the talk turns to what it's all going to cost.

The stamps are, indeed, the centerpiece of all the excellent advisor's discussions with people about retirement. Two other questions that she may substitute for—or ask in addition to—the one above are:

▶**What are you going to be living on when you're 82 years old?**

and/or

▶**Do you have an investment strategy for tripling your income in retirement?**

Because, as you can see, your cost of living may very well triple after you retire.

The journeyman always asks questions like, "Have you figured out what income (or how much money) you'll need to retire on?" The prospects say no—and immediately dislike the journeyman for putting them on the spot like that. And the irony is, of course, that as usual the journeyman asked the wrong question. The amount of capital—or the number of dollars of income—people will need on the *first day* of retirement isn't the issue. It's how people are going to cope with upwards of a tripling of living costs in a normal retirement. That is, in Admiral Halsey's words, the thistle that one musn't touch timidly.

The excellent advisor then says, "Well, we'll come back to this issue later"—all the while leaving the folks to stare at the stamps—"but first I'd like to learn some more things about you and your family."

Please tell me: to what extent do you want to intervene in the financial lives of your children, either during your lifetimes, or as legacies to them?

This question appears to be pretty straightforward, but it has an important double meaning, which the excellent advisor will bring out depending on how the question is answered.

You see, if the parents aren't concerned with legacies to their children, they have the luxury of living on both principal *and* income in retirement—in effect, annuitizing their capital. But if the parents care enough about their heirs to want them to inherit the capital, then there's more pressure on the portfolio to produce an adequate income. (We'll look at this issue in greater detail in a later chapter, when we talk about systematic withdrawal plans.)

Of all the five goals the excellent advisor asks about, this one probably gives him the most insight into the emotional dynamic of the family—and may even tell him whether he wants to work with this family or not. (How? If people don't really like their own children, they live in a painful, angry place. And one fine day, I promise you, they'll take that pain out on you.) And, of course, if he senses any reluctance to discuss this issue—or any of these issues—he can always try to draw the people out with a reference to what he himself is doing. This, of course, closes some of the emotional distance between prospect and advisor—very important in the early going—and reinforces the impression that this is, after all, a conversation between people who have a lot in common.

Remember that, on this first pass through the five Great Goals, you don't want to get hung up in a protracted discussion—unless, of course, the prospects start unburdening themselves at length, because you've hit a sore spot. On the first run-through, you're not going to get involved in the mathematics of providing for the goals; you're just trying to establish which of the Great Goals these folks have, and to what extent.

3 Do you have grandchildren? Please tell me about them. Are you going to want to be—or need to be—financially involved in their education?

There has, over the last several years, been a considerable flattening of middle-class expectations; the baby boomers are the first generation of Americans who don't really expect their children to do as well financially as they themselves did. So as people become grandparents, there begins to be a very legitimate concern that their children won't be able to provide the grandkids with the same education they got—at least not without some help.

College costs, meanwhile, continue to rocket out of sight, particularly in the schools people really want to go to. (Moreover, in many professions an advanced degree is virtually a requirement now.) In the script at the beginning of this chapter, I made some specific projections of cost; they were based on the College Board's annually published average total cost of public/private higher education. I took the figures for the 1995–96 academic year, and inflated them at 6%—or about twice the inflation rate, which I think is a good, conservative way to do it. The College Board said the average total cost in 1995–96 was $7414 for a four-year public college and $18,232 for a four-year private college. So, if a prospect has grandchildren anywhere from newborns to 15-year-olds, the runout looks like this:

Child's age now	Years to college	TOTAL COST Public	Private
15	3	$38,629	$ 94,993
14	4	$40,946	$100,693
13	5	$43,403	$106,734
12	6	$46,007	$113,138
11	7	$48,768	$119,927
10	8	$51,694	$127,122
9	9	$54,796	$134,749
8	10	$58,083	$142,834
7	11	$61,568	$151,404
6	12	$65,262	$160,489
5	13	$69,178	$170,118
4	14	$73,329	$180,325
3	15	$77,729	$191,145
2	16	$82,392	$202,613
1	17	$87,336	$214,770
Under 1	18	$92,576	$227,656

As we noted in the last chapter, when we briefly touched in concept on the strategy of Multigenerational Marketing, each grandparent can give each grandchild up to $10,000 a year without incurring a gift tax. This also removes these monies from the grandparents' estate. Thus, particularly if they get started early enough, it's a virtual no-brainer for reasonably well-off grandparents to fund much or most of their grandchildren's education. It just takes an investment professional to ask them: do you want to? (Or to ask younger adults, "Would your parents like to help you with your children's education?")

Realize that this is an issue which, even if the grandparents are aware of it, they may be reluctant to raise with their children. That's because it may be difficult for them to bring up a subject which suggests that their kids aren't going to do as well as they did. The excellent advisor is often able to serve as the messenger on sticky issues like this, and to do an immense amount of good thereby.

4 **Are your parents living? Do you expect to become financially responsible for them at some point?** This is the fourth of the five possible Great Goals of Life. And, as we saw in the last chapter, it is a very rapidly growing financial planning issue for Americans, particularly those between ages 40 and 60. It's a thistle that's got to be grasped particularly boldly; when it's time for the parents to go to a nursing home, it's too late.

Especially now, when the baby boomers have gotten their kids through college and want to make a mad dash for retirement with every dime they earn, this question must be called by the excellent advisor. The boomers are looking for answers, but the excellent advisor first has to make sure they have the question framed right.

boomer: We're 50! Retirement's only 12 years away! We gotta get serious! We need growth! What about high tech?! What about the emerging markets of Latvia, Lithuania and Estonia?!

eia: [*Serenely*] Is retirement the only major goal you have to invest for?

boomer: What?! Well, sure it is! Uh...isn't it?

eia: Are your parents living?

boomer: Well, my mom is. And my wife still has both her parents. Why?

eia: Do you expect to become financially responsible for them at some point?

boomer: Uh, oh...

The journeyman would surely have accepted the boomer's agenda, and developed a terrific growth portfolio, only to watch it vaporize eight years from now when the guy's mom has to go in a nursing home. But by acting instead of reacting, the excellent advisor is able to save the boomer (and his mom) from his own denial. This is, to put it gently, not a skill you're likely to develop by studying modern portfolio theory.

And incidentally, on your list of Deeply Religious Experiences You Haven't Had Yet, But Are Going To, Any Day Now, consider this. With people getting married and having children later and later in life (not to mention having children in second marriages), you are about to start meeting prospects who are going to have a kid in college and a parent in a nursing home *at the same time.* And on that day, you can take all your charts, graphs and scattergrams, roll them up into a ball, and swallow them. Relative performance ain't gonna matter. The only thing that'll matter is: **are these people investing even remotely enough money to fund the huge responsibilities that are rolling down the hill of life, straight at them?** This is the question the excellent investment advisor was put on earth to ask (while the journeyman is vainly trying to answer the question, "Will Fund Raindrop A or Fund Raindrop B get to the bottom of the window first?").

5 **Is there a particular institution—a church, a school, a charity—that means a great deal to you, and to which you would like to leave a meaningful legacy?** I hope you see that this is as much a question about personal values as it is about financial planning. In other words, like the other four questions (only more so), this inquiry appears to be doing fact-finding, *but its real purpose is* **feeling-finding.**

Everyone's biography can be inferred from the list of people and things they care deeply about. And today, the same people who 30 years ago participated in sit-ins to close their college may be starting to think about endowing a chair at that college. As the population ages (and for other reasons), we are seeing a huge pendulum swing back toward traditional values and the institutions which represent tradition. (It helps that the institutions themselves have grown more tolerant, as well.) It is not at all coincidental to this point that for the last couple of years the hottest writer in the English language has been Jane Austen.

With this question, the excellent advisor reminds her prospects—or causes them finally to see for the first time—how sensitive she is to the things that matter most in the creation of a meaningful life...and even, in some sense, a life after death. For, like the education of a grandchild, a significant legacy to an institution may confer upon the giver a certain kind of immortality ("If what I did still benefits people, am I not in that sense still alive?").

And even if the prospects' answer to this question is "no," the advisor has clearly communicated to them that she's genuinely interested in the things that really matter, and not just in money as an end in itself. Thus, no matter what the answer, this fifth question is one which can't fail to enhance the advisor's stature in the prospects' eyes. (On the odd chance that the prospects *aren't* properly impressed with this question, they have, of course, disqualified themselves.)

When, as you increasingly will, you get a "yes" answer to this fifth question, explore the situation to see if a **charitable remainder trust** might be in order. If people have significantly appreciated assets on which a large capital gains tax would be due upon sale, they can contribute those assets to a trust, and get a tax deduction for the donation. The trust can then sell the assets and reinvest the proceeds so as to generate more income. The income is distributed to your clients, and upon their deaths the principal will pass to the institution.

Charitable remainder trusts are an elegant and increasingly popular way to help people help the institutions they love. And I submit that the advisor who brings that idea to a family has a client for life. But you have to ask the question.

Invest some time to learn about—or, better, to recruit a wholesaler or home-office staff expert who can help you do—charitable remainder trusts. They're not for everybody. But when they're appropriate, charitable remainder trusts never fail to hit a grand slam home run for the relationship.

* * *

On the second pass through the Great Goals, you just have to take all the questions to which the prospect said, "Yes; that's part of my program," and try to put a number on what pool of capital they need to make it happen.

For instance, let's say that, after Social Security and his corporate pension plan, a prospect says they'll need another $75,000 in pre-tax annual income from their investments in order not to compromise their lifestyle. But both husband and wife are vehement about wanting to live on their income so they can leave their principal to their kids. The conversation might go something like this:

eia: Do you think it would be reasonable to assume that you could recover 6% a year from your investments during the two dozen or so years after retirement?

prospect: But bonds are paying 7½% right now.

eia: [*Smiling*] Let me ask you two questions, in no particular order of importance. (1) Who said anything about bonds? (2) Who said anything about now?

prospect: But wouldn't we want safety and income in retirement? And doesn't that mean bonds?

eia: If I were a doctor, do you realize you'd be asking me what medicine I prescribe while I'm still only about a third of the way through the examination?

prospect: OK, OK. What did you ask me, again?

eia: I said, do you think that, over two and a half decades of retirement, you could withdraw 6% a year from your investments without drawing down your capital?

prospect: Without breaking a sweat.

eia: Good, so do I. In fact, I think you can get 6% and still be able to grow *both* your income *and* your capital. And growth of income is the only sane retirement investing goal, because you *know* your cost of living is going to grow. Now, all we have to do is figure out what amount of capital $75,000 is 6% of. Is that pretty clear?

prospect: Yup.

eia: OK, We divide $75,000 by .06, and we get...$1,250,000.

prospect: How in the world are we ever going to put another $1,250,000 together in just 10 years?

eia: $6000 a month.

prospect: What?

eia: Just to pick a round number, $6000 a month invested at 10% or so will get you there.

prospect: Where am I going to get $6000 a month?

mrs. prospect: Those two years when both the kids were at Boston U., we came up with $6000 a month. And we're making more money now than we were then. So what's the problem, if it means a retirement where we can do basically anything we want?

prospect: Er...uh...

eia: Good. That's settled, then.

This is basically all you have to do on your second pass through the Great Goals:

(1) Capitalize the income stream people will need at 6% (you'll see why when we get to systematic withdrawal plans).

(2) Subtract the capital and/or the income they can already count on, plus an assumed growth rate thereon.

(3) Figure out how much they have to invest each month at 10% to get to the required capital. (Yes, 10% is clearly an equity return, but don't go into that yet, until the prospects buy into the monthly number).

And just keep doing this with each of the goals that's a hot button with your prospects, until they yell "uncle!"

mrs. prospect: Forget about these moving college targets; they make my head hurt. Just tell me: how much do I have to invest every month, starting the day a grandchild is born, in order to be able to hand my kids $100,000 on the baby's 18th birthday?

eia: Assuming you pay the taxes from another source as you go along...about $175 a month.

mrs. prospect: It can't be that little.

eia: [*Smiling and handing her the calculator*] OK, you tell me.

mrs. prospect: I don't know how to figure it out.

eia: I do. Already did, in fact.

mrs. prospect: OK. Sign me up right now.

prospect: What?! On top of the $6000 a month we have to invest for retirement? Where is it going to come from?

mrs. prospect: Listen, hotshot. Do you remember how we sweated blood to put those kids through college, because we swore they wouldn't graduate with student loans?

prospect: Well...sure.

mrs. prospect: Do you want the kids to have to go through what we went through?

prospect: Well, no, but...

mrs. prospect: No buts about it, sport. And if you want, I'll even squeeze it out of the household accounts. You'll never miss it. [*To EIA:*] Now, where were we?

eia: You were saying something about signing you up, but you've gotten way ahead of me.

mrs. prospect: Fine, sonny. I'll just wait here for you to catch up.

And here you see the somewhat disconcerting spectacle of a prospect trying to buy something before the advisor tells her what it is. What's that you say? A lot of your prospect interviews don't actually sound like this? I ask you: could that be because you talk about abstractions like mutual funds, relative performance and asset allocation, instead of talking about the real hopes and dreams of real people (and the people they love), for which investments are merely funding media? And/or could it be that you waste a lot of time talking to the prospects you've got rather than the prospects you really want? (Can I offer you another soggy potato chip?)

There's an infinite variety of planning software around that'll do these and many other calculations for you like lightning; even a decent scientific calculator can rattle off most of this stuff. Or, if you're electronically challenged, as I am, you can just carry around a few printed tables. How you do the math can never be the issue, any more than which investments you recommend can ever be the issue. The issue is whether or not you have a carefully rehearsed, naturally flowing and genuinely empathetic way of inquiring into the prospects' positions on The Great Goals of Life, together with a facile, non-technical way of figuring out what it'll cost to do what they want to do.

This exercise can really only have three possible outcomes:

1. The prospects look at what it'll cost to do what they ideally want to do, and find that there's no way on earth they can do it. So you start back through the five goals, in order to distinguish between "good to be able to do" and "*got* to be able to do." Note that the issue isn't any longer whether they're going to work with you. They already are.

2. The prospects find that their goals and their capabilities are just about in Goldilocks Mode: not too big, not too small...but *just right.* Now you can play show-and-tell with your equity fund portfolio recommendations, stressing that the assumed 10% return should be conservative over time because of the combined effects of small-cap/international/dollar-cost averaging.

3. The prospects find that they can very comfortably do everything they could ever want *and then some*. Listen to what the Excellent Investment Advisor says:

eia: Before we get into specific portfolio recommendations—which may have some marginal impact on your ultimate results, but which can't possibly change the overriding fact of your ability to do everything you want—I invite you to consider the enormity of what you've already accomplished. You're one family in 100—if you're not one in 1000—in that your means are perfectly adequate to your most important ends. I congratulate you. You have tremendous options and choices, and as we go through them I'm eager to know what makes you comfortable, and what you feel is appropriate. I reserve the right to disagree with you, but only when I feel it'd be more helpful to you than agreeing. (In a sense, that's why you hire an investment advisor: to disagree with you when that would help you.) But above all, please realize that I'm just helping you negotiate the peace treaty with your financial life, because *you've already won the war.*

There are, of course, a couple of outcomes subordinate to these three. For instance, in Outcome 2: Goldilocks Mode, you may find that people don't want to go as heavily into equities as you want them to. The journeyman breaks out in a sweat, and starts trying to put the Ibbotson chart up the prospect's nose. The excellent advisor gently lets the people see that they're not objecting to equities (or to him) so much as they're objecting to reality.

eia: Sure, no problem. Would you feel more comfortable at 50% stocks and 50% bonds?

prospect: Much more comfortable.

eia: Then let's do that. Of course, bonds have only about half the long-term returns, so to end up in the same place, you'll have to invest quite a bit more money each month. Say, $7000 a month instead of $6000.

prospect: Impossible! No way, no day! We can never, *ever* come up with seven grand a month!

eia: I see. [Silence. And I mean silence. *If the prospect doesn't say anything for 20 minutes, don't you, either. This is the moment of truth.* The next person who speaks loses.]

prospect: Well, what do you recommend?

eia: [*Gently*] I already told you what I recommend. You didn't like it. So you've got a couple of options. I don't recommend them, but I'll be happy to spell them out for you.

prospect: Go ahead.

eia: Option One: Invest $6000 a month in some combination of stocks and bonds, and retire on less money. Maybe a lot less money, depending on the bonds/stock mix.

prospect: Retiring on less money is not an option.

eia: Option Two: Go 50% stocks/ 50% bonds, and figure out a way to come up with the extra $1000 a month to get you to the same pool of capital as $6000 a month in equities would have.

prospect: I already told you, with no little vehemence, that that's not an option, either. You can't get blood from a turnip.

eia: [*Gently*] That about does it for me, then. [*Silence*]

prospect: What you're saying is that it's $6000 a month in equities or punt, is that it?

eia: That's about it.

prospect: [*Sadly*] I think I might be gonna throw up.

eia: I'm familiar with that symptom. It's the uncomfortable short-term side effect of taking exactly the right long-term medicine.

prospect: [*Resignedly*] All right, we're in your hands, not because we like it, but because we seem to have no other option. Tell us what to do.

Never put yourself in the false position of having to advocate passionately for a reality that's obvious to begin with. It cheapens you. Just stand back and let the prospect bang his head against all the available unreality for a while. He either comes around or he doesn't. You've handled the input flawlessly; the outcome will be what it will be.

Remember that you got into the elegant position of having the prospect argue with himself rather than with you by letting him tell you what he wants to accomplish and what he can contribute to that process. Your role isn't so much to sell him anything as it is to reconcile his dreams with his capabilities.

Above all, you put yourself in this excellent field position simply by inferring a financial/investment plan from the prospect's own statement of the great goals of his life. Does this approach work all the time? Once again, nothing works all the time, and most things don't even work most of the time. What we do is like baseball (and like life, but I repeat myself): there are no lifetime .400 hitters.

But I think I can promise you that, in the 21st century, the Great Goals of Life conversation will work more often than everything else put together.

In Summary

- Management is doing things right; leadership is doing the right thing. The Excellent Investment Advisor doesn't so much manage her clients' accounts as **lead** them...because that's what the great client really wants.

- All intelligent financial/investment planning has to flow down from the clients' attitudes toward the five Great Goals of Life, not up from theological abstractions like relative performance.

- Before you can realize people's hopes and dreams, you have to insulate them, as much as possible, from their fears. Adequate life/health/disability insurance, as well as significant cash reserves for emergencies (real or imagined) are prerequisites to a successful investment plan.

- The less debt people carry, the better they'll invest.

- Maybe 5% of your total lifetime return will come from which investments you selected within the same categories. The other 95% will come from (1) what your debt/equity mix was, and (2) what you did when (not if) your equity investments went down 30%.

☞ The five Great Goals of Life are:

(1) retirement without compromise in lifestyle nor any real concern about outliving one's income;

(2) meaningful intervention in the financial lives of one's children;

(3) the education of one's grandchildren;

(4) the ability to care for one's parents if and when they need it;

(5) an important legacy to institutions/charities one believes in.

☞ Take (or make) every opportunity to show how the prospects' Great Goals are similar—if not identical—to yours. This banishes the feeling of "selling" and replaces it with empathy.

☞ The Great Goals prospect interview is conducted in two stages:

(a) interesting, thought-provoking questions intended to discover which goals are the prospect's, and

(b) calculation of what each of the prospect's goals will cost to fund, assuming index returns.

☞ The fundamental investment challenge isn't picking the "right" mutual funds. It's investing enough money to have any real shot at making one's goals a reality. The Excellent Investment Advisor concentrates on getting people to invest enough money.

☞ Journeymen do fact-finding. The Excellent Investment Advisor does feeling-finding, knowing that feelings are to facts as 19 is to one.

☞ Don't knock yourself out trying to sell the prospect the right asset classes; it's undignified. Let the prospect paint himself into the corner of *having* to make the right investments, because there's no other way to bridge his dreams and his wherewithal. Don't, in other words, try to force-feed people reality; let them bang their heads against all the available unreality, until they give up.

☞ Once you've gotten in front of a prospect, the Great Goals of Life conversation will work more reliably than just about everything else you've ever learned, put together.

9

The **new** *universal five-point managed money presentation . . . .*

"I would not give a fig for the simplicity this side of complexity, but I would give my life for the simplicity on the other side of complexity."

—**Justice Oliver Wendell Holmes**

• • • • • • •

One of the most thoroughly enjoyable books I've read in recent years is the actor Hume Cronyn's autobiography, *A Terrible Liar.* A passage that I find myself coming back to again and again concerns one of Cronyn's (and my) very favorite actors, Spencer Tracy:

> "I tried never to miss watching a scene when Tracy was playing. His method seemed to be as simple as it is difficult to achieve. He appeared to do nothing. He listened, he felt, he said the words without forcing anything. There were no extraneous moves. Whatever was provoked in him emotionally was seen in his eyes. He was praised for his naturalness, for being 'so real,' but it wasn't real. Acting never is. His was a finely honed craft."

I'd like you to keep this concept firmly in your mind as we begin, finally, to explore what the Excellent Investment Advisor actually says to people about investments. The organizing principle of the excellent advisor's presentation is, as Justice Holmes observed, that *there is a simplicity that lies beyond sophistication.* And it is that simplicity which we'll seek to systematize in this chapter.

The great cellist Pablo Casals gave a "master class" near his home in Puerto Rico during the last years of his life. A "master class" is offered to artists who have studied an instrument all their lives at the finest music schools with the best teachers, and who are ready to take their places in the very front rank of musicians in the world. Their training is completed with one of the greatest living masters.

On the first morning of class, Casals always said, "Now, we must please forget the notes." He was saying, of course, "You know the music; you have all the technical proficiency you need or you wouldn't be here. Now, if you're to become *artists*, you have to go beyond the obvious."

Another star in the musical firmament, Miles Davis, was probably the greatest jazz artist of the postwar era, and he changed the shape of jazz not once but two or three times in 40 years. In 1985 he gave an exceedingly rare interview to the poet Amiri Baraka that was published in *The New York Times Magazine*. Baraka asked him what went through his mind when he listened to his own music, and Miles Davis said, "I always listen to what I can leave out." That same year, in an interview in *Arts and Antiques* magazine, the painter Andrew Wyeth said very much the same thing: "The less subject matter in a picture, the better. If you can express it by just one thing, it's that much better."

Less is more. And you have to forget the notes: no one ever became an Excellent Investment Advisor until he learned to rise above the facts. Remember, the excellent advisor is a leader, not just a manager. And, as the educator John W. Gardner said, "If the modern leader doesn't know the facts, he is in grave trouble, *but rarely do the facts provide unqualified guidance.*" (Italics, I freely admit, mine.) Knowledge is good, as far as it goes, but in the end it doesn't prove anything. To reach people where they really live, and to induce them to respond to you from their deepest levels of trust, you have to let go of, and get beyond, what you know. And, like Miles Davis, you must always listen to what you can leave out. I say again: *there is a simplicity that lies beyond sophistication.*

What is the goal of a presentation? I'm sure you will answer that it's to cause the prospect or client to take the financial action you want him to take. The problem with that answer: it's so obvious that it doesn't tell you anything. The real question is, what state of mind are you trying to induce in a person that will allow him to commit himself? We've already seen (a) that people don't make their investment decisions in their intellects, and that (b) no future investment outcome can be "proven." So the goal of a presentation is not to create in the investor a state of intellectual certainty, nor even of virtual certainty:

(eia)

The excellent investment advisor knows that the goal of any presentation is to induce in his listener a state of informed belief.

Much as I might like to, I'm not asking you to seek an act of blind faith from your prospect/client. Blind faith is not the only alternative to intellectual certainty (though it *is* the ideal alternative). There's actually a spectrum of mental states in between proof and faith, and the excellent advisor aims for the place on that spectrum where her listeners arrive at a state of *informed belief.*

Please note that in the state of informed belief, when the prospect says "yes," he doesn't necessarily mean "I completely understand." (It's good if he "understands," but it isn't critical.) He means "I believe you." And that's why so much of this book has been devoted to codifying and strengthening your belief system. "When I believe, I am believed," says the excellent advisor. And he then presents his beliefs to other people, with just enough information to give them a strong sense of his reasons for believing as he does. But it is the advisor's belief that ultimately motivates his listener to act, not the factual underpinnings of that belief.

The journeyman doesn't make a presentation so much as he files the financial equivalent of a legal brief. "Let's make every single argument we can think of, backed by every single statute, every regulation and every precedent in case law that we can find. Then we'll see what, if anything, the judge picks up on." The flaw in this analogy is that the judge is also a lawyer, and can be expected to—indeed, is required to—understand, weigh and measure all those brilliant legal arguments.

But the investor may have neither the training, the temperament nor even the desire to process the journeyman's data deluge.

The excellent advisor asks herself, "How little can I burden these people with, in order for them to get a reasonable working knowledge of what they'll own, and in order for me to discharge my 'compliance' responsibilities?" In other words, what's the *minimum* amount of information necessary to bring your listeners to a state of informed belief, in which they will feel comfortable taking the appropriate action?

And by intuitively seeking the least amount of information necessary to achieve informed belief, the excellent advisor ultimately stumbles onto The Great Law of Presentations, which, as you may have already anticipated, states:

The quality of a money management presentation is an inverse function of its length.

Presentations are, in fact, no more than a necessary evil, to be gotten through as economically as you can, so that you can arrive at what really matters, which is Q&A. During the process that I call feeling-finding, you discover your prospects' hopes and dreams, and you quantify what those will cost. You then present the portfolio of investments that you believe will most efficiently get the prospects where they need to go.

When you are finished, the prospects usually begin asking questions and expressing reservations about your solution. The journeyman calls what the prospects are saying "objections." The excellent advisor sees that all the prospects are really doing is *trying to give voice to their deepest fears.* Remember: the greatest impediment to investment success isn't ignorance, it's fear. The journeyman tries to "educate" investors; the excellent advisor seeks to liberate them from their irrational fears. ("But what if the stock market goes down some day *and never comes back?*")

But you can't liberate people from fears and misconceptions you don't know they have. And the only way you can learn people's fears is by letting them articulate those fears. This, then, is the single greatest argument for short, economical presentations:

The excellent investment advisor knows that her chance of discovering her prospects' deepest fears while she is talking is zero.

In his unconscious dread of being asked a question he can't answer, the journeyman uses his presentation to anticipate every possible question and objection. Thus, he talks interminably, and actually causes the prospects to start worrying about things they weren't afraid of to begin with. He says things like, "Now, you may think that investing in emerging markets is too volatile and risky, but..." And the prospects, who actually thought that having some exposure to emerging markets would be wonderful, look over in newfound alarm at the bug-eyed, profusely sweating journeyman, who is just now babbling about a place they've never heard of called the efficient frontier. Game over.

The excellent advisor says, "When the Berlin Wall came down in 1989, we found—a hundred yards from West Germany, the world's most advanced economy after the US and Japan—a country, East Germany, that had exactly 40 (yes, *40*) international phone lines, and in which only 16% of the households had a telephone at all! I knew then that, even with all the turmoil that would probably be involved, the investment potential in converting former communist countries to capitalism would be very great. That's why my family and I have committed a portion of our equity portfolio to this investment theme, and why I've included it in my recommendations to you. That concept makes sense to you, doesn't it?" (Andrew Wyeth: "If you can express it by just one thing"—telephones, in this case—"it's that much better." Note, too, that the excellent advisor talks about investing in *economies;* the journeyman almost always talks about stock markets.)

The excellent advisor's presentation, then, is not meant to accomplish the "sale." The "sale" takes place only when the prospects say, "We're not afraid anymore" (or, "We're still afraid, but we trust you, and if you say this is what we have to do in order to realize our goals, then we'll do it"). The process of dispelling fear is always one of dialogue, never of monologue. So try to think of the presentation essentially as a mood-setter.

The excellent advisor's general theory of presentations is built upon three fundamental assumptions:

1 **Money management isn't a product, it's a service.** You use it to accomplish something that you want done, but either do not know how to do or simply do not want to do yourself. People who are not engaged full-time in the investment field (and even many who are) ought not to be managing their investments themselves. The stakes are just too high, and the investment management that's available today is just too good. (*Can* you, as Peter Lynch suggests in his two delightful books, *One Up on Wall Street* and *Beating The Street*, pick your own stocks and outperform institutional managers? Surely. Do you want to bet your family's financial fate on the thesis that you *will*? I think the answer is obvious.)

So, in creating a professionally managed investment portfolio, you aren't buying products, but engaging teams of very good people to perform a vital service for you. It is, above all else, the people you are hiring—their character, their beliefs, their traditions, their disciplines and their skills—who will determine what happens to you in the long run. For this reason, the excellent advisor's presentation, like his entire approach to the business, is people-focused as opposed to product-focused.

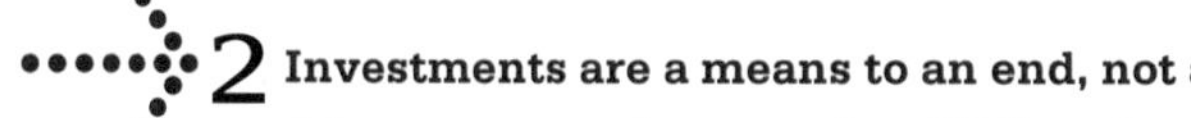

2 **Investments are a means to an end, not an end in themselves.** My answer to the question "What do you think of utility funds?"—or Pacific Rim funds, or junk bond funds, or Gronsky Incomprehensible Technology Fund, or whatever—is always the same:

Who are you?

Investments are, in and of themselves, neither "good" nor "bad." What they are is either appropriate or inappropriate for a particular person, and for his and his family's financial goals. If a 40-year-old woman (with at least 20 years to work, and perhaps 50 years to live) said to you, "I just got a bonus, and I want to invest it for my retirement; can you recommend a good bond fund?" I would expect you to say, "No." For while there are dozens of good—and even a few great—bond funds, there is no bond fund on earth that's "good" for this woman to invest her whole bonus in. (I would argue that there's no bond fund in which she should invest *any part* of her bonus, but then again, I'm a self-confessed Equity Zealot.)

In the bad old transaction-oriented days, of course, the investment *was* the end in itself. "Buy Hong Kong *now* because it's about to outperform *all other markets* starting in about *20 minutes!* Buy Hippocrates Pharmaceutical common stock *this morning* because the FDA is going to announce approval of their new anti-ugliness medicine *this afternoon* and the Street *doesn't know it yet* so the stock's *gonna fly!*"

But, in this new golden age of relationships, the excellent advisor's presentation of any investment stresses *where it fits into the plan* which the advisor and the clients have made for the realization of their Great Goals.

3 **The investment that the excellent advisor presents is good because he says it is good.** Not because some magazine agrees that it is good. Not because it went up 19.628% in the last three months and the average fund in its peer group only went up 18.962%. And not because the Children's Crusade Mutual Fund Rating Service And Storm Door Company gives it nine moons—their highest rating.

The more you use third-party endorsement in your presentation of investments, the more you devalue yourself, and the more you actually short-circuit the current of trust that is the *sine qua non* of all successful advisor-client relationships. Even when the investments you recommend are highly rated and/or endorsed in some third-party way, try to discipline yourself not to use that material as an inducement to invest. (I have no objection to your sending that stuff to people who already own the investments under discussion, if that's what floats your boat.)

Material whose primary focus is the comparison of an investment to others in its peer group totally confuses the basic issue, anyway. If people need a healthy dose of small-cap growth exposure in order to leaven their overall portfolio return, then the overriding issue is their acceptance of that need, and of the incremental volatility involved. Which small-cap growth fund they buy isn't that important, relative to the threshold decision to own small-cap growth as a high-return, high-volatility portfolio component. A piece of paper that says the particular fund I like did relatively better than its peers in the last block of time (a) muddies the issue and (b) doesn't prove anything. (My clients aren't going to own it in the last block of time, they're going to own it in the *next* block of time, which is probably going to be different from the last one.) Similarly, it doesn't matter that much to my physical well-being whether I breakfast on Total cereal, Special K or All-Bran. What matters is that I eat any one of them each morning rather than, say, cold pizza.

The excellent advisor is selling himself. If his relationship with clients is to succeed, they must implicitly trust him, and must believe that the investments that he says are good for them *are*, indeed, good for them, precisely (and purely) because he says so.

You may infer from these three points that the similarities in the excellent advisor's presentations far outnumber and outweigh the differences. Indeed, I think that the essential points that should be made in the presentation of any managed portfolio are fundamentally the same. I believe there are no more than five of these absolutely critical points, and that not infrequently you only need four of the five.

Why five points? For a couple of reasons. First, I don't think anyone alive can absorb and retain more than five important ideas *about anything* in one sitting. His circuits will overload, and you'll lose him. And imagine if you're trying to present a whole portfolio of funds, or of separate accounts inside a variable life policy or annuity. If you're planning on telling people more than five things about each of those accounts, you'll still be talking at daybreak. Second, and just as important, the sun has never shone on a managed investment which has more than five supremely important issues to it.

This chapter will prepare you to make that universal five-point managed money presentation. But nothing can prepare you for the surprise and delight with which people respond to simple clarity. After all, your prospects may be (and most are) daunted by, and a little defensive about, all the intricacies of investing about which they feel ignorant. So chances are they'll be intensely grateful to you for purifying the critical factors down to a precious, comprehensible few. "You make it all seem so *simple*," people will start saying to you. And you can reply, in your best Spencer Tracy deadpan, "It *is* simple. It's just not easy. That's why I'm here for you." Which is, of course, no more or less than the truth.

What five shining, universal points will make you an Excellent Investment Advisor? In the end, only you can answer that question. I'll tell you what *my* five points are, but you've got to let yours flow naturally from your personal style, and from your sense of the greatnesses of the investments you personally love. Ted Kurtz, the psychologist who writes so perceptively for *Registered Representative* magazine, told me a great story, in this context, about Louis Armstrong. Somebody asked him about his trumpeting technique, and how it could be learned by someone else. Satchmo shook his head and said, "You blows what you is."

Having said that, I do think there are five points inside which every managed investment fits, and which allow you to explain any investment easily and comfortably. They are:

1. **The concept/where this investment fits into your plan**

2. **Who's managing the money, and how I feel about them**

3. **What the investment does and why that's good for you**

4. **(Optional) How the investment works**

5. **Risks/limitations/what the investment isn't**

These five points, I'm happy to say, haven't changed all that much since *Serious Money*. The big difference is the context in which the universal presentation is offered. *Serious Money* attempted (and, I think, succeeded in the attempt) to be an encyclopedia of presentations. In other words, it put just about every kind of mutual fund there is into the Universal Five-Point Presentation format, (a) to show that it could be done and (b) to give you an easy way to present any fund you wanted to.

But, not long before I started writing this book, I had kind of an epiphany. I was speaking at a meeting somewhere, and after my talk a youngish wirehouse broker came up to me. He said that *Serious Money* had made him a lot of serious money, and went on to single out the Universal Five-Point Presentation as having been especially helpful. He described one occasion when he was presenting a new fund offering to someone over the phone, using the Five-Point Presentation. And afterwards his buddies came up to him and said, "Wow, that was great. *We'd* have bought that fund if you presented it to us like that."

Now, the broker clearly meant this story as a compliment. But it caused my heart to sink. "Oh, no," I thought, *"they're using my work to pitch the fund-of-the-month over the phone!"* And in that moment I resolved to let *Serious Money* go out of print, and to write this book.

(I mean, I *think* the guy was a broker. But maybe he was an angel, sent to me in human form by God to deliver this very important message. I can't be sure. So let me just say this. If you were the broker who shared this story with me, even though you didn't know what you were telling me, I'd like to thank you. Alternatively, if this incident *was* a message from God, I'd like to thank Her.)

So the big difference between the Presentation as it appeared in *Serious Money* and the way I'm using it here is *contextual*. My fundamental purpose now is to help you explain not so much the investment itself as how the investment becomes integral to a complete long-term investment/financial plan. Because in the fee-based, relationship-oriented, plan-focused 21st century, the context of an investment within the plan is the critical issue.

Logically, then, this is the point with which the Presentation begins:

Point # 1:

The concept/where this investment fits into the plan.

This point must contain two basic components:

(a) a statement of the investor's core financial need (or at least one of his most important needs), and

(b) a generic statement about how a particular kind of investing has historically met that need *when managed by superb professionals.*

The concept/The fit is the one critical, indispensable way to begin any money management presentation (and, in case I haven't already made this clear, variable universal life insurance certainly qualifies as money management). And since the very first things you say will often determine the outcome of any professional interaction, you'll want to be especially careful about the way you say what you're going to say—how you articulate **The concept/The fit.** Be sure to keep it very real-life, and packed with emotional resonance.

eia: The hallmarks of a successful retirement, to me, are dignity and independence. The financial key to continued independence over two decades or more of retirement is an income you can't outlive—an income that's rising even as your cost of living (gestures toward the stamps) continues to rise. That makes sense to you, doesn't it?

prospect: Good Lord, yes! That's what it's all about...or else why go on living?

Now, watch the journeyman take the very same concept and pulverize it into meaningless (if not genuinely disturbing) jargon:

journeyman: You'll continue to need growth in retirement, because of inflation.

prospect: But what about income? We need income in retirement...

We've already noted that the way you say what you say is even more important than what you say. Nowhere is that distinction more terribly critical than in **The concept/The fit.**

Why does the journeyman say the word "growth," for instance? If you've been in the business for more than about 72 hours, you know that older Americans always take the word "growth" to be the antithesis of "income" (if they don't take it to describe something that their sister-in-law had a while back, but thank God the doctors found it in time). And, while representing the opposite of "income," "growth" is also, for many people, synonymous with "risk-taking." So when the journeyman said what he said, the prospect actually heard, *"You need to take more risk and get less income."*

Then, just for good measure, the journeyman used the word "inflation," a hopeless abstraction that means a hundred different things to as many people. If you lived through the (for America, at least) hyperinflation of the 1970s, you tend to look at 3% inflation as virtually no inflation...even though it'll triple your living costs in 30 years of retirement, which is what a rapidly increasing number of folks are looking at.

The net result is that the journeyman is able to get the prospect actively, outspokenly confused and upset in less than 10 seconds, before he's even told the prospect about the investment. It takes a rare skill to be able to do this, but the journeyman rises (or, more properly, sinks) to the occasion. I'm sorry; I can't talk about this anymore. It's too painful. Now back to the excellent advisor's presentation, already in progress.

eia: [*Tapping the stamps*] Let's say you retired in 1976, and all you needed to buy every year was one first-class postage stamp. So you lent your capital to AT&T, General Electric, Pfizer, Coca-Cola...in fact, because you wanted to be safely diversified, you lent your capital to all the companies in the Standard & Poor's 500 Index. In other words, you bought these companies' bonds. And they paid you, let's say, 30 cents in interest. And since a stamp only cost 13 cents that year, you felt pretty good. Is this making sense to you so far?

prospect: Sure, sure. I was retiring, I wanted safety and income, so I bought a diversified portfolio of corporate bonds. That sounds like exactly what I might have done. So why am I suddenly getting a very bad feeling about this?

eia: [*Tapping the 32-cent 1996 stamp*] Because today those great companies are still paying you 30 cents, every year like clockwork, just like they promised. [*Silence*]

prospect: And it's not enough anymore.

eia: Bingo. [*Silence*]

prospect: OK, you have my complete and undivided attention. Is there anything you want to tell me?

eia: Why, yes, as a matter of fact. Let's go back to 1976. Suppose, instead of becoming a lender to those 500 companies, you'd become an owner of all of them.

prospect: You mean, I bought the stocks instead of the bonds?

eia: I mean, you became an owner of 500 of the greatest businesses the planet had ever seen up until that time. The difference is entirely semantic, but it always makes me feel better to say it that way.

prospect: I'm not sure it's my job to make you feel better, but put that aside for a moment. Could I induce you to cut to the chase, here?

eia: With pleasure. OK, we know that dividends on common shares yield a heck of a lot less than bond interest, for the simple reason that common shares can appreciate greatly in value, while bonds, at the end of the day, can't. So instead of getting 30 cents interest on your capital, let's say you got (just to pick a number off a bus) 13 cents in dividends.

prospect: I just don't think I would have done that.

eia: Neither would most people, which very neatly explains why most people aren't wealthy. So let me come straight to the point: if your dividend income from the S&P 500 was 13 cents in 1976, do you have any idea what it would be today?

prospect: Haven't the foggiest, old boy.

eia: Round numbers, half a buck.

prospect: Let me make sure I understand you. Are you telling me that the dividend of the S&P 500 has just about quadrupled in the last 20 years?

eia: That's exactly what I'm trying to tell you. Of course, your original investment is now worth five times what you paid for it, but never mind that. Just concentrate on your income. [*Takes out two quarters, and puts them on the table, next to the 32-cent stamp*] Remember, every year you only have to buy one stamp. This year, a stamp costs 32 cents and your income is about 50 cents. So what's happened to your standard of living?

prospect: I can't believe I'm about to say this, but...my standard of living has gone way up. Because this year I can not only buy my stamp, I've got 18 cents—more than half again as much as I need—to play with.

eia: Precisely. And the way you arrived at that enviable position is: you took a lot less current yield from dividends that could grow, rather than taking a much higher, but fixed, interest rate.

prospect: Then why have I heard, all my life, that as you approach retirement you're supposed to phase out of stocks and into bonds?

eia: Because it used to make sense. Even a generation ago, when the average guy retired at 65 and was gone by 73, bonds made sense. You're trying to retire at 62, and you may live into your early-to-mid 80s. Your wife will live into her late 80s.

prospect: I get it: the longer you expect to live, the more you'll need your income to grow, not just stay static.

eia: Exactly. To somebody with seven years to live, a guaranteed high fixed income was a blessing. To you it's a trap. A fixed-income investment strategy in a rising-cost world is suicide. It's suicide on the installment plan...but it's still a plan for suicide.

prospect: How does that translate into what I need to do?

eia: Simple. *Lend* to great companies, and they'll never pay you a penny less, *or more,* than they promised. *Own* those great companies, and your dividend income can rise as fast or faster than your cost of living. So a major cornerstone of a retirement portfolio has to be a professionally managed investment (or a number of investments) focused on dividend growth. Does that make sense to you?

prospect: It only makes all the sense in the world. [*And he thinks, if he doesn't say, "Where have you been all my life?"*]

I want you to know that the conversation you just read would have actually taken between four-and-a-half and five minutes. But in it—gently, non-technically, using lots of symbols—you turned around a whole lifetime of "conventional wisdom." And you set the investor on the road to an income he can't outlive, and to a growing capital base for his heirs. All in under five minutes.

The other thing I hope you noticed about this interchange is that *it isn't so much a presentation as it is a conversation.* It's a dialogue, not a monologue. You've got to get the prospect talking with you, agreeing with you, right from the get-go. If he isn't involved, then...he isn't involved, if you see what I mean. Perception is reality: no matter how intellectually *correct* your statements are, they aren't *right* until your listener says, "That's right." Or, "I can see that." Or just plain, "Yes."

(eia)

The excellent investment advisor knows that his chances of ultimate success are a pure and absolute function of the number of times he gets his listener to agree with him.

Nor are you looking for an unbroken litany of "yes," necessarily. In this conversation, the prospect asked about the age-old shibboleth about switching to bonds in retirement—and ended up embracing **The concept/The fit** even more warmly when he heard the answer. *Get the prospect talking.* It is, after all, his money. And you can't be really right about anything until he agrees with you.

The concept/The fit is the bulk of the new Universal Five-Point Presentation. It establishes a great need (one which the prospect may not have even known he had), and shows conceptually how a certain investment approach answers that need, and thus where it fits into an overall plan. Once the prospect strongly affirms the need, the presentation should already be rolling downhill, propelled by its own momentum.

The journeyman identifies himself as such by starting to talk about the product within the first minute of his presentation. But the excellent advisor knows that **The concept/The fit** *is the prospect's birthday present; the product is merely the box the birthday present comes in.*

Point # 2:

Who's managing the money, and how I feel about them.

The second presentation point is the strongest statement you can make about the people you've chosen to run the money, and about your and your firm's relationship with them. (If the most important bond between you and your clients is the relationship, why wouldn't/shouldn't the most important bond between you and your chosen few money managers be that relationship, as well? Otherwise you're going to be shuttling back and forth between left-brain and right-brain too quickly and arbitrarily for the client to follow.)

It is, as we've already noted, the character, beliefs, traditions and disciplines of the people you're hiring—as well as their skills—which will determine your clients' long-term success (in contrast to, say, which quadrant of the scattergram the fund is in year-to-date). Once again: portfolio management isn't a product but a service, and the critical issue is who's providing that service.

In particular, *stress the extent to which you've personally been exposed to the management.* If your firm has its own money management unit, and you believe in them, then stand up for them. If you're worried that your prospects will think "he's just peddling his own firm's funds because he has to," you haven't established any basis for a relationship to begin with. If they don't trust you, it isn't going to matter much which fund family/annuity/universal life policy you recommend, anyway. And if investors do trust you, imagine how warmly they'll respond to your pride in your in-house managers—in your statement, "This is a big part of why I work here."

The key issues in your recommendation of a manager have to be:

1. (My firm and) I know these people well.

2. We/I believe in them.

3. We/I can choose from hundreds if not thousands of funds.

4. I chose this investment for you primarily because I understand you and your needs, I understand the managers and their style, and the fit between you and them seems ideal to me.

Conspicuous by its absence from this list of essentials is, as I'm sure you noticed, relative "performance." "Performance" selling is a vain attempt to "prove" what no one who trusts you would ever need proof of to begin with: that you can (and objectively will) choose excellent managers whose styles are marvelously appropriate to the prospect's needs. Moreover, "performance" is the answer to a question no one has asked you yet, and I'm a passionate believer in not answering questions no one has asked.

Finally, relative "performance" has nothing to do with the success of the plan you and the prospect are making. Success is a function of whether the plan is sensible, whether the asset classes chosen are appropriate to the plan, and whether the investor sticks to the plan. (In the example above, the particular dividend growth fund you choose can never make or break the client's retirement.) It isn't your job to "outperform," whatever the hell that means. It's your job to endow the investor with a retirement income he can't outlive. And you never have to do the former in order to accomplish the latter.

This business is not about investments, it's about people. In this second presentation point, your goal is to cause your prospect to feel the depth of your belief in—as well as why you actively like—the people you've chosen to manage his money.

Point # 3:

What the investment does and why that's good for you.

This critical juncture never fails to distinguish the excellent advisor from the journeyman. The latter, unable to restrain himself any longer, starts explaining to the prospect what the investment *is*. He's so enthralled by his "product knowledge" that he totally loses sight of the critical issue: no one on earth has ever bought anything—a mutual fund, a vacuum cleaner, a set of pots and pans—because of what it *is*. People only buy a thing because of *what it will do for them*. Next, the journeyman launches into an elaborate description of all the ways the investment differs from other, similar investments (beta, standard deviation, etc.), apparently not seeing that he still hasn't yet made the prospect feel he really needs the investment.

The excellent advisor sketches, in her naturally artistic but economical way, the barest outline of the investment. But she spends real time and energy explaining what the investment will *do* for the client—how it will be the engine of **The concept/The fit.**

Forget the dozen sales points you learned in an office meeting. The purpose of that meeting was to convince you to sell Fund X instead of Fund Y. These points really aren't germane here. Again, you're not selling one investment vs. other, similar investments. You're describing a seamless conceptual fit between a particular need and a particular solution. In the example we've been using, even if the dividend growth fund you choose achieves only average results, that's still going to be better by orders of magnitude than if the guy owned the world's best bond fund for 25 years.

The greatest advantage of an economical, why-I-love-this-for-you style of presentation (as opposed to the kitchen-sink/legal-brief approach) is that *it presumes acceptance.* In a simple, understated way, you're saying, "We agree on your need; we agree on the conceptual fit between that need and a certain style of management. The vehicle I've chosen is the obvious choice. I won't bore you with the details. If you want to know more, just ask, and I'll be happy to fill you in on everything I know."

Point # 4:

(Optional) How the investment works.

The purpose of your presentation is to establish clearly how a particular investment meets a prospect's real needs. If necessary, *and only if necessary*, you can use Point #4 to explain something about how the investment does what it does. In other words, to paraphrase Miles Davis, always listen to see if you can leave Point # 4 out. Your prospect is asking you what time it is; it is rarely necessary to tell him how to build a watch.

Use Point # 4 only when to do so will meaningfully reduce the abstraction or complexity of the investment. *The acid test of Point # 4 is whether it is more likely to clarify or mystify*. If you are presenting an international equity fund, for instance, your manager may have a very sophisticated approach to the issue of whether and when to hedge the currency risk, and when to accept that risk. And you may even understand his strategic thinking. So there'll be a great temptation on your part to share this highly technical subject with your prospect. You'll be able to prevent yourself from tap-dancing into this quagmire if you ask yourself: is this discussion more likely to clarify or mystify? Clearly, the answer is that any significant discussion of currencies is much more likely to confuse the hell out of just about anybody. So stifle it.

On the other hand, suppose one of your favorite approaches to balancing the competing needs for growth and income is a convertible bond fund. I think it's fair to say that even most experienced investors don't know much (if anything) about convertibles. So to explain *that* convertibles soar like an eagle in rising markets but nest like a chicken in major market declines, you almost have to give people some idea of *how* they do so. This, then, is a case where some controlled use of Point # 4 is probably a necessity. Just be careful of giving the prospect more information than he either needs or wants.

Another caveat to the use of Point # 4 is that you must take care not to state an investment's attributes in terms of what the investment is not. If you're talking about a dividend growth strategy, for instance, you wouldn't say "...mature, solid companies with a long history of dividend increases, *not speculative high-fliers.*" And most particularly, you'd never say anything like "mature, high-quality companies, which means this fund is *less volatile* than funds that don't stress dividends." Telling most people that an equity fund is "less volatile" is like telling them they're going to get shot with a smaller caliber bullet. Inarguably, a .22 will put a much smaller hole in you than a .45. But most people really have their hearts set on not getting shot at all.

You can simply never sell managed money by negative comparison. Say to someone that he doesn't have to worry about volatility, and I can guarantee you that he will instantly start worrying about volatility. Please: no negative vibes. Your prospects are plenty worried enough. Let them feel the warmth of your enthusiasm for the investments you love by highlighting just a few of their wonderful qualities. Don't try to make your recommendations look good in relation to something inferior and/or scary.

The hallmarks of the excellent advisor's presentation are economy of dialogue, simplicity in concept, and an unstated but very palpable presumption of the ability to generate understanding and agreement.

Err on the side of underexplaining the complexities. If you leave something out that the prospect really wants to know about, he'll ask. And if your prospect simply elects to go ahead and believe you, you'll have saved both of you a lot of grief.

Point # 5:

Risks/limitations/what the investment isn't.

This is the journeyman's nightmare point—he's always afraid that if he's candid and forthright about an investment's risks/limitations, his prospect will take a walk. (Hype doesn't always have to involve the exaggeration of an investment's advantages; it can also be the understating of what you give up in order to obtain those advantages.)

Point # 5 is also, of course, the excellent advisor's very favorite point, because it's where her ethic, her courage, her deep knowledge of the business and of markets, and her passionate commitment to underselling *all* get to shine. Indeed, I know many advisors (including, if you'll permit me to say so, myself) who believe that this point is where the sale is made. For, just as the journeyman's all-roses-no-thorns presentation instantly arouses a good prospect's suspicions, the excellent advisor's straight-arrow, no-holds-barred presentation ("For everything you gain, you give up something; here's what you give up in this wonderful investment") convinces the prospect to trust her. ("She's not sugar-coating anything; she's telling it just like it is. *She's the advisor for us.*")

In the bad old transaction-oriented days, the object was to get a prospect to *buy* an investment. And, in the real world, it was merely human to accentuate the positive while (virtually) eliminating the negative.

But in a fee-based, relationship-oriented practice, where investments are the funding media for financial plans whose success will be measured over decades, *the critical skill is getting the client to* **hold** *the investment long-term.* And the ability to hold investments is directly related to one's capacity not to get surprised/scared out of them.

Thus, the more you can use Point # 5 to take away people's capacity for surprise and/or fear, the more likely you are to accomplish the goal of enabling them to hold their investments throughout the market cycle. This is perhaps most obvious in equities:

Since the end of World War II, the Dow Jones Industrial Average has declined 20% or more 10 times. The average of those declines was 28%. I'd love to believe that, in a new age of global capitalism, the market cycle would run somewhat more gently than that, but I sure wouldn't count on it. So I plan to watch about a third of my family's wealth melt away temporarily, about every five years or so on average, before the cycle turns and goes on to new heights.

It'd be nice to know when those declines were coming, so you could get out of the way, but no one's ever been able to do that consistently. So the only strategy that's ever worked for me is to accept the temporary downs as the price of the permanent ups, and to just hang in there.

If you're going to be an equity investor over the long haul, you have to accept that this is what you're signing up for. And I don't want to minimize the emotional challenges you'll face if and when you're just a couple of years from retirement, your investments go down by a third, and every talking head on every six o'clock news broadcast in the US of A is giving you 27 good and compelling reasons to believe the sky is falling.

When all that is happening, I can predict with a high degree of confidence that you're going to ask me—more than once—when and how this bloodbath is going to end. And you're going to get mighty sick of my two answers: (a) I don't know, and (b) it doesn't matter.

All I can tell you is: that's the price of all the potential benefits of equity investing: an income that rises with your living costs, a meaningful legacy for your children, and your granddaughter's education. And, as we've seen, there's no other way for you to reach those goals, other than with equities.

Please tell me you understand this, and that you accept it.”

And, frankly, this kind of reality check is even more important in bonds. For, as we saw in late 1993 and early 1994—when the interest rate on the 30-year Treasury bond went up 50% in less than six months—bonds are capable of far more volatility than most folks give them credit for. And, here again, investors probably did about as well or as badly as their advisors had prepared them for that volatility:

journeyman: All the bonds in this government bond fund are guaranteed by the US government, as to timely payment of interest and principal.

eia: All the bonds in this government bond fund are guaranteed by the US government, as to timely payment of interest and principal.

But, of course, the market prices of the bonds will fluctuate all over the place—up and down—with movements in interest rates. The benefit of owning a fund like this as opposed to rolling over CDs year after year is that the yield is substantially higher than CDs. And every benefit has a cost: in this case, the ability of your bond portfolio to fluctuate, which CDs (ignoring the withdrawal penalty for a moment) can't.

Since you've said you never intend to spend this capital, the yield advantage seems a greater benefit to you than fluctuation is a cost. Do you agree? Are you quite clear on the trade-off involved, here?

Tell the absolute, unvarnished truth all the time. It's better for your soul, your life, your career, your energy levels, your self-respect and the clients' wealth—even (and especially) when it may not be better for your month.

And don't just try to convince people of how smart you are. Let them—through the force of Point # 5—feel how *good* you are.

* * *

Any managed investment you choose can be presented with this simple, effective, generic, universally adaptable approach. Simply work up a clear, logical, compelling arrangement of the points…and then *start practicing*. Tape your presentation again and again. Role-play with the wholesalers; role-play with your networking group (incidentally, what are *their* five points?). Grind it, polish it, and just make the presentation as tight and seamless as you can. Because…

⟨eia⟩

The excellent investment advisor knows that the act of perfecting a presentation is more beneficial than all the product-knowledge sessions in the world.

Well, sure it is. You know that the fifth or tenth time you hear a story, you are able to chip away at it, to find holes and formulate questions the presentation just doesn't answer. Practicing so that you can spot the flaws prompts you to tighten the presentation even further. (As you begin to approach excellence, you may even consciously decide to leave some rough spots in the presentation because you'll know exactly what questions they provoke. And, you'll know just how terrific your answers are!)

Your objective is to get so good you can be shaken out of a sound sleep and be making the presentation, with the utmost warmth and conviction, before your feet hit the floor.

When you get that good, you can actually begin to detach yourself from the presentation, let the force of painstakingly acquired habit take over, and *devote your real attention to watching the prospect's reactions.* Remember the Nod Factor? I said that, during a seminar, you can observe which points in the wholesaler's presentation the audience is reacting to. Well, the next step in your presentation progress is to be able to observe the client's reactions to what you're saying. (A pro can read and adjust to those reactions, even while speaking.)

The seamless beauty of your presentation can, after all, only take you so far. In the end, what you say doesn't matter, only how the client reacts to what you say. But having a perfectly rehearsed presentation enables you to tune yourself out, and start watching the prospect's reactions.

Simplicity, economy, clarity, candor. These are the hallmarks of The Universal Five-Point Presentation. In succeeding chapters, we'll look at how different investment objectives/management styles can be fitted to the Presentation. But for the moment, you might consider going back and reading this chapter again, to let its philosophy and practice begin to knit together in your understanding.

Just before you do that, though, let me leave you with something from the memoirs of Thomas Jefferson. Speaking with awe and wonder of two of his most famous colleagues, Jefferson says, in this passage, literally the first and last word for me on the theory that less is more. And this observation has shaped my career:

> “I served with General Washington in the legislature of Virginia before the Revolution, and during it with Dr. Franklin in Congress. I never heard either of them speak 10 minutes at a time, nor to any but the main point that was to decide the question. They laid their shoulders to the great points, knowing that the little ones would follow of themselves.”

In Summary

- In presenting investments, less is more. There is a simplicity that lies beyond sophistication, and you can attain that simplicity through discipline and practice.

- The Excellent Investment Advisor knows that the goal of a presentation isn't to "prove" anything. It is to induce in the listener a state of informed belief.

- The quality of a presentation is inversely proportionate to its length. Ask yourself: what's the minimum amount of information I can give someone, such that I discharge my "compliance" responsibilities and bring my listener to the state of informed belief?

- The presentation is only a necessary evil, anyway. The sooner you get through it, the sooner you can get to Q&A, which is where the prospects' real fears are lurking. The journeyman answers objections; the excellent advisor dispels fear. And your chances of discovering your prospects' deepest fears while you are talking is zero.

- The New Universal Five-Point Presentation rests on three assumptions. First, money management isn't a product; it's a service. So the central issue is, who are you hiring to perform the service? Second, investments aren't the end, they're the means. So the central issue is, where does the investment fit into the plan? Third, the investments you recommend are good because you recommend them. If you hide behind a lot of third-party endorsement/"proof," you actually prevent people from trusting you. That isn't what you want.

☞ If your deepest, most passionate beliefs spawn a different presentation from mine, yours is, *ipso facto*, better…for you. "You blows what you is."

☞ The New Universal Five-Point Presentation is:

Point # 1: The concept/where this investment fits into your plan

Point # 2: Who's managing the money, and how I feel about them

Point # 3: What the investment does and why that's good for you

Point # 4: (Optional) How the investment works

Point # 5: Risks/limitations/what the investment isn't

☞ **The concept/The fit** must contain two basic components:

(a) a statement of a/the core financial need

(b) a generic statement about how one investment approach answers that need.

☞ **Who's managing the money** must stress:

(a) the character, beliefs, traditions, disciplines and skills of the manager— *not* his "track record," and

(b) the nature of your and your firm's relationship with, and confidence in, the manager.

☞ **What it does/why that's good** describes the investment itself: not what it **is,** but what it *does for the investor.* The conceptual fit is the important thing; abstractions like relative "performance" aren't.

☞ **How the investment works** is optional: offer it only when you're sure it will clarify rather than mystify.

☞ **Risks/limitations/what it isn't** is the excellent advisor's finest hour, and where the best sales are made. All investments are a trade-off; the excellent advisor makes sure investors are equally clear about what they're giving up and about what they're getting. The less people get surprised, the more likely they are to hold on to their investments, and holding on is 90% of the battle.

☞ Simplicity, economy, clarity, candor. These were good enough for Franklin and Washington. (Can you picture either of *them* talking about standard deviation?) Let them be good enough for you.

10

A passion for equities . . . .

"So first of all let me assert my firm belief that the only thing we have to fear is fear itself—nameless, unreasoning, unjustified terror which paralyzes needed efforts to convert retreat into advance."

—**Franklin D. Roosevelt**
First Inaugural Address
March 4, 1933

• • • • • • • •

The British philosopher Isaiah Berlin wrote of Franklin Roosevelt, "He was one of the few statesmen in the twentieth century, or any century, who seemed to have no fear of the future."

Indeed, on the day of his first inaugural address, FDR must have seemed as much the nation's chief optimist as its chief executive. And yet, looking back on those days, we can see that he was simply America's chief realist. It turned out to be the pessimists who were unrealistic. It always does.

That's pretty much the way life works, and the sooner you see that, the sooner you can become an excellent investment advisor. *Optimism is, finally, the only realism.* It is the only view of the future which squares with the experience of the past.

Pessimism, on the other hand, is quite literally counterintuitive. A pessimistic view of the future rests on the notion of an insoluble crisis—for which there is, quite simply, no historical precedent. So to be a pessimist, one has to believe not just in the possibility but in the probability of something that has never occurred.

Thomas Malthus declared in 1798 that population growth was exponential, but "the power of the earth to provide subsistence" finite; he foresaw "a gigantic, inevitable famine" (and, in so doing, earned economics its nickname, "the dismal science").

Of course, food production has outstripped population growth from that day to this. Malthus, as George Gilder has written, "failed to grasp that it is not the earth but man that produces food." Human ingenuity, from John Deere's first plow to today's giant combines, has driven the real cost of food down relentlessly. In the US today, the cost of food as a percentage of the average household budget is at its lowest point ever.

All pessimists are Malthusians, in that they extrapolate the problem—whatever the problem is—in a straight line, but they hold the potential for solution of the problem—i.e. human ingenuity and/or will—constant. "At current rates, the Social Security system will be bankrupt in 2019," cry the pessimists. This observation is **(a)** inarguably true and **(b)** utterly ridiculous, in that its premise ("at current rates") is that we lack the capacity or will to hit the brake before we hit the wall. This is [*I say it again because I can think of no better word*] **counterintuitive.** Humankind in general, and Americans in particular, are *always* at their best in a crisis. This isn't *a* lesson of history, it's *the* lesson of history.

Pessimism, then, is constructed of an exponential problem and a linear (if not non-existent) capacity for problem-solving. All the evidence is precisely to the contrary. Human ingenuity—the sheer volume of new ideas waiting to be thought of—constantly surprises us, because we always underestimate it. And it is that ingenuity (not the apocalypse *du jour*) which is exponential. From the dawn of human consciousness, man dreamed of flying. The Wright brothers finally did it—and within the span of one human lifetime, a man stood on the moon.

Johann Gutenberg had all the bugs out of his movable metal type by the spring of 1454. Over the next 18 months, he produced 200 Bibles, all exactly the same. Everybody thought that's what the new invention was for: to produce the same few books for the same few people, but much more quickly and accurately.

By the year 1500, just 45 years later, 1000 presses in Europe had turned out 10 million copies of 35,000 different titles. Exponential growth of knowledge was already leading to exponential progress, and the potential for universal education was just around the corner.

Moreover, progress is, in a very real sense, just getting started. As Michael Rothschild points out in his indispensable book, *Bionomics: The Inevitability of Capitalism*, our species—called *homo sapiens sapiens* (doubly wise man)—has been walking around for about 100,000 years. Compress that into a 24-hour day and the story of our species goes like this: from midnight until 10 p.m., we're hunter/gatherers. From 10 p.m. until 11:57 p.m., we're subsistence farmers and craftspeople. The modern industrial age, which Rothschild dates from Watt's steam engine in 1775, is three minutes old.

And the microprocessor—the entire computer on a microchip, the single greatest human technological breakthrough—was invented about 20 seconds ago, in 1971.

The microprocessor has already made possible revolutions in the workplace (personal computers, word processors, handheld calculators that cost $30 and have more computing power than ENIAC—the first "mainframe" computer—had in 1947), entertainment (VCRs, camcorders, video games), medicine (magnetic resonance imaging), communications (cellular phones) and a host of other areas, from supermarket scanners and bank ATMs to electronic fuel injection and anti-lock brakes.

Indeed, microchip technology is now merging with fiber optics to create a new information economy. George Gilder predicts that "the technologies of computers and communications will each advance roughly a millionfold in cost effectiveness in the next 10 years." Small wonder that Sir John Templeton recently said, "It has often taken 1000 years for the standard of living to double in the most advanced countries, yet it may double for the world as a whole in the next 20 years."

Finally, today's technological advances not only don't eliminate jobs, net-net they create jobs...and they're environmentally benign, in the bargain.

Gilder points out that during the past 30 years, the US has led the world both in technology and in jobs. "Deploying three times as much computer power per capita as Japan or Europe, the US has created some 35 million new jobs. Automation is its own remedy—by creating wealth, technology endows new work."

And, as our progress becomes more information intensive, it becomes more energy efficient. Microchips are, after all, made of the three most common elements in the earth's crust—silicon, aluminum and oxygen.

Crowning (and, in a very real sense, organizing) this accelerating progress is the triumph of capitalism. Indeed, the primary economic/historical trend of the last 10 years has been the collapse of centralized economies (communism, socialism) and their gradual replacement, however painful and spasmodic, with free-market principles.

In the developed countries of the West, led by the United States, large, interventionist central government is also on the wane. It was only natural that economic power should have flowed toward government in the three-quarters of a century from America's entry into World War I until the breakup of the Soviet Union. An almost constant war footing was a powerful centralizing force, and the apparent collapse of capitalism in the 1930s greatly enhanced government's role as employer/health care and retirement provider/goods and services purchaser of last resort.

But government doesn't really do any of those things efficiently or well, not least of all because it has no economic incentive to do so. Moreover, as Putnam's Dr. Bob Goodman demonstrates in his book *Independently Wealthy*, a social/democratic sense of "fairness" is different from, and antipathetic to, a concept of fairness based on enterprise and productivity. The former stresses human equality, and is therefore a leveler. The latter recognizes the essential inequality of talent and energy, and is therefore an incentivizer.

And, as the insupportability of vast social welfare schemes becomes ever clearer, we continue to move toward a new era of self-reliance. This, among its many other benefits, creates a great environment for the Excellent Investment Advisor, as his prospects come to realize that they can't look to government, unions or big corporations for either income or health care in retirement.

Looking around the globe, then, we see that capitalism (not democracy) is the dominant impulse of our time. Michael Rothschild, in *Bionomics*, argues that it's the dominant impulse of *all* time—that capitalism is a force existing in nature, and is the way human societies will spontaneously organize their economic life, unless they're somehow prevented from doing so.

I know that nothing in life calls forth human ingenuity and energy as efficiently as the opportunity to achieve wealth for oneself and one's family. So when I see the hurtling momentum of human ingenuity being organized (and incentivized) through a global capitalist revolution, I'm logically forced into an outlook of the most rampant bullishness. Capitalism, it seems to me, has become the gatekeeper of progress; common equity (and certainly not debt) is the gate. *And I own the gate.*

Again, this may strike some readers as very "optimistic." But to me it is the coldest-eyed realism imaginable. It is, in the end, the only worldview consistent with the facts. Dow 50,000 seems perfectly inevitable to me. (If you struggle with Dow 50,000, may I remind you that the Nikkei, which was almost exactly equal to the Dow at about 200 when the Tokyo Stock Exchange re-opened in 1949, has long since been to 40,000?)

To the extent, then, that you feel you're in the business of endowing families with wealth over long time horizons—particularly over more than one generation—your view of the world should start to take over your portfolio decision-making process. Yes, it's narrowly true that there's never been a 15-year period since 1926 in which equities have produced a negative return. And I suppose that gives you a certain dry, statistical comfort (or rather, an absence of acute discomfort) about the propensity of time to leach the "risk" out of stocks. But it so completely misses the glorious point.

The reason I want to own—and want everyone who'll listen to me to own—equities over the next 15 years (and more) isn't the statistical improbability of loss. It's my passionate conviction about the wondrous ways in which the global capitalist revolution and the accelerating pace of technological/scientific discovery may manifest themselves in the values of common stocks.

Moreover, when you take the long view of progress, and marry it to a multigenerational investment horizon, you suddenly find yourself—as I long since have—relieved of the necessity for a short- or even an intermediate-term market outlook. With the Dow at 6000, I am keenly focused on the move to 50,000, which I regard as inevitable. I have no idea whether, on its way to 50,000, the Dow will see 4500 or 7000 first. Nor do I care. (Well, that's not exactly true. In a way, I *do* care, because, like most people, I'm not finished buying yet, and I won't be for years. So I'd really welcome one of those 25%–30% declines that have come along every five years or so on average since the end of WWII. For it has been wisely—if cynically—observed that a bear market may be defined as "a period during which common stocks are returned to their rightful owners.")

Long-term, which is where most investors and/or their heirs are going to be living, the equity market's trend is inevitable; short- to intermediate-term, it's unknowable. It only stands to reason, then, that we invest our clients' capital and our own professional energies in the former rather than the latter. And the more we focus on the long term, the more optimistic (i.e. realistic) we're forced to become. Indeed, I think one of the most important functions we can perform is to remind people that, in the long run, it isn't just going to be all right. It's going to be absolutely terrific.

* * *

But it isn't necessary for you to become even remotely as bullish as I am, in order to develop a genuine passion for equities. Instead (or in addition), you can see equities as being an essentially *defensive* investment, in that stocks have historically provided the greatest margin of long-term protection against the ravages of that most pernicious enemy of wealth, inflation (and its evil twin, taxation). And, particularly for investors facing 25 and even 30 years of retirement, this is the critical issue.

In the last chapter, I telegraphed this punch in the example of the essential point of the presentation, **The concept/The fit**. (If you have any impulse to duck back and take another look at it, be encouraged to do so; you'll find it on pages 235 through 240. Take your time. I'll wait here for you.)

Got it? Good. OK, we know that the huge preponderance of investable assets are in the hands of people who were taught, from earliest childhood, to regard "risk" as the chance that they'd lose their money, and "safety" as a credible guarantee that they'd get their money back. And, until well within the last generation, this viewpoint was perfectly understandable...if not inevitable.

Let's go back one full generation—30 years, to 1966—and meet the person who gave our clients a lot of their attitudes toward money, risk and safety: their father. We'll call him Joe Average. We join him on the day of his retirement—which, being the average American male who retired in 1966, was his 65th birthday. *And on that day, he had less than eight years to live.*

Now, maybe he had a pension, and maybe he didn't—the private pension system in the US was only just then beginning to mature, and ERISA was still nearly a decade away. So there's a pretty good chance he only had Social Security, plus whatever he'd been able to save over his working lifetime. And he just had to get those savings to last for the few remaining years of his life. So he was absolutely sure of just two things: the big financial risk was losing his savings, and safety was the FDIC's guarantee that he wouldn't.

And if, in 1966, Joe Average's life *expectancy* dictated these twin certainties, his life *experience* had all but carved them into his soul.

After all, he'd been born in 1901—and not necessarily in this country. By the time he was in his teens, there was a pretty fair chance his own father was dead, and that he was a breadwinner, if not *the* breadwinner, in his family. Or he may have lost his parents in the influenza epidemic of 1918, which killed 22 million people worldwide, 500,000 of them in the US (including my father's older sister). In any event, on his retirement day, Joe could look back on nearly 50 years of *very* hard work.

Remember, too, that when he was just about 30 years old—the peak of his family responsibilities, with a lot of little mouths to feed—Joe went through the nightmare of the Depression. Add that searing experience to his *curriculum vitae*, and you can well understand why Joe (and Mrs. Joe) told their children (our clients) every day of their lives: *risk is losing your money; safety is being guaranteed to get your money back.*

And so a generation passed. And—perhaps on the very day you're reading this chapter—it's now time for Joe Average Jr. to retire. The average retirement age for an American male now, however, is 62. But the big change is that Joe Jr. and his wife are probably going to live into their eighties. And let's remember that our clients tend to have had better health care, better educations and higher-level jobs than the national averages, such that they're going to be retiring even earlier and living even longer than average. Suddenly, it seems, our clients have to get ready for 25 and perhaps even 30 years of retirement. That doesn't just mean they have to learn new definitions of "risk" and "safety." *It means they have to learn a whole new definition of "money."*

Back in 1966, when Joe Average said, "Safety is being guaranteed to get my money back," he meant that some institution promised to return to him *the same number of units of the currency* that he'd lent out. Observe this closely, please: Americans have historically never distinguished between currency and money. Once again, the issues are twofold: life *experience* and life *expectancy*.

From the standpoint of life experience, Joe Average's generation was from the "sound as a dollar" school of economics. In fact, Joe's whole adult lifetime up to his retirement in 1966 tracked the ascendancy of the dollar (replacing the British pound) as the world's reserve currency. Gold and the US dollar were literally interchangeable—at $35 an ounce, the one fixed star in a random and highly dangerous monetary universe.

Moreover, we have to remember that the defining economic event in Joe's lifetime, the Great Depression, was above all an episode of *deflation*: between the 1929 stock market crash and the end of 1932, the Consumer Price Index declined 24% (and has never gone down as much as 1% in any year since). In a deflation, the currency—the physical paper dollar—not only holds its value, but *increases* in value...while things like stocks and real estate are cratering.

And, from the standpoint of life *expectancy*, the prospect of eight years or so of inflation in the 2% range sure wasn't enough to get Joe thinking about anything but safeguarding his greenbacks, period. He could not, did not, and had no need to distinguish between "currency" and "money."

Joe couldn't know, of course, that even as he was retiring in 1966, Lyndon Johnson was starting to try to pay for the Vietnam war and the Great Society social agenda with the same money, and had decided not to inform Congress. Surging government deficits and accelerating inflation were just around the corner. Nor could Joe even imagine that, five years later in 1971, the dollar would have depreciated in world markets to the point where Richard Nixon would have to take it off the gold standard—whereupon gold would soar (or the dollar crash; same difference) from $35 to $350 an ounce.

But the tribulations of the currency during Joe's retired life aren't the point. It's the *definitions* that Joe's generation gave our clients—and the complete inappropriateness of those definitions to a quarter-century retirement—that must concern us.

Joe equated money with the physical paper dollar; when he said "safety is a guarantee of the return of my money," he meant, "if I deposited 50 pictures of Benjamin Franklin in the Gronsky Bank, the FDIC says

I'll get my 50 Franklins back, even when the Gronsky Bank goes belly-up like they all did back when I had hair." We don't have that luxury.

Because we know that, while it's a peerlessly efficient medium of exchange, currency was never really designed to function—and has never functioned—as a long-term store of value. Indeed, in every society and every historical epoch, the currency has always lost its value over time. (Nor is modern government any less prone to debase the currency than was some ancient king: "A democracy," observed Alexis de Tocqueville in 1836, "will always vote itself more benefits than it is prepared to produce.")

So even at the long-term (1926–95) inflation rate—let's call it 3%—we have to be expecting consumer prices to go up at least two and perhaps three times in a typical client couple's retirement. (Meanwhile, after 15 years, old Joe's conception of equity market risk—principal loss—has historically vanished.) So what is needed here is nothing less than a whole new long-term definition of money, and the excellent advisor has one:

The excellent investment advisor knows that, over long periods of time, the only sane definition of "money" is "purchasing power."

From that essential perception, the excellent advisor proceeds to new definitions of "risk" and "safety." He sees "risk" not as principal loss but as *the extinction of an investor's purchasing power within his or her lifetime.* Risk, in other words, is not so much losing one's capital as *outliving* it.

Once he's accepted that fundamental long-term risk is implicit in a decline in purchasing power, the excellent advisor re-defines "safety" as *increasing purchasing power.* He can no longer regard "safety" as a guaranteed return of the same number of units of the currency the investor lent out. That's because he no longer confuses currency with money. The excellent advisor correctly regards the currency as a fiction—and a fiction that becomes more malignant with the passage of time.

Instead, the excellent advisor develops a new way of testing investments for long-term safety:

"Does this asset class build purchasing power over time? And if so, to what extent?"

The question then becomes: how do you determine if an investment is building your purchasing power? My answer is stark, simple, and—if I do say so myself—elegant. I define accretion of purchasing power (and, therefore, safety) as *a positive long-term return net of inflation and taxes*. By that test, a lot of investments people have always thought of as "safe"—CDs, Treasury obligations, things like that—suddenly don't seem so safe anymore. And one asset class in particular that people have always thought of as "risky" looks very good indeed: common stocks. All kinds of common stocks.

Have a look at this chart:

Summary of Annual Returns	**1926–1995**
Small-company stocks	12.5%
Large-company stocks	10.5%
Long-term corporate bonds	5.7%
Long-term government bonds	5.2%
US Treasury bills	3.7%
Inflation	3.1%

Source: ©*Stocks, Bonds, Bills and Inflation 1996 Yearbook*™, Ibbotson Associates, Chicago (annually updates work by Roger G. Ibbotson and Rex A. Sinquefield). Used with permission. All rights reserved.

I daresay you've seen these numbers a time or two before, but now I'd like you to look at 'em in a somewhat different way. First, deflate the nominal returns into real returns by subtracting inflation. But then, reduce the real return for taxation. In other words, impute some tax rate to the nominal return—does 25% to 30% seem fair?—and *then* see what you've got in terms of a real bottom-line rate of return.

This isn't some abstract academic exercise. It is literally a matter of long-term financial life and death. Nor is it just a way of re-hashing the point that equity has a higher return than debt. ("Yes," answers the investor, "but at what cost?" Which is a much better question than even he knows. Because the answer is simply: patience.)

What you're seeing here is that equity is the only way to get ahead—and stay ahead—of inflation and taxes. In other words, by my admittedly very rigorous definition of "safety"—a long-term return greater than *both* inflation and taxes—equity isn't just safer than debt, *it's the only real safety*! (And small-cap is even "safer" than big-cap, because its net return after inflation and taxes is even greater.)

Yes, but...well, hold on a minute, here. This just about stands everything most folks have ever learned about investing right on its head, now doesn't it? **(A)** It sure does. **(B)** That's kind of how you know it's right: most people will almost intuitively disagree with it...and if most people were right, most people would be rich. Since most people are manifestly not rich (even after a 64-year run from Dow 40 to 6000), you can generally rely on any idea the consensus disagrees with. (Which is yet another reason why, if you would be an excellent investment advisor, you have to be a leader, not just a manager.)

Why do people, even today, struggle with the concept of equities as the only way to achieve real retirement "safety" and multigenerational wealth? I think it's clear: *because they can't tell the difference between fluctuation and loss.*

At all times, you have to keep in mind two ideas. First, the Depression (or rather, our family myths of the Depression, because the dragon tended to get bigger each time the tale was told) is the defining trauma in America's financial unconscious. The overriding concern is therefore disaster on a life-shattering scale, in which people "lose everything." Second, in our obsession with principal as an end in itself (i.e. the toxic illusion that currency is money), we tend to see any decline in our invested capital as "loss." If an American buys a mutual fund at $20 and it goes to $15, he won't call you up and ask you about "the 25% fluctuation in the fund's price." Rather, he'll start the conversation with, "I've lost 25% of my money," and then go on to demand an "explanation."

This is, purely and simply, an inability to distinguish between fluctuation and loss. And it leads to the psychology that says, "I've lost X% of my money; maybe I'd better sell out now before I lose a lot more" (or, "before I lose *it all*").

But is downward fluctuation really loss? Well, in an individual stock or bond, it could very well be. But in broadly diversified, professionally managed portfolios, fluctuation never has been loss, and I, for one, don't believe it can be. In fact, I'd like you to be keenly aware of a fairly staggering number:

$342,000,000

This is the actual amount by which Warren Buffett's personal shareholdings in Berkshire Hathaway went down in value on one day: October 19, 1987. My question to you (and, I believe, your question to doubting investors) is: *how much money did Warren Buffett lose on October 19, 1987?* I know that you'll immediately answer: none. And why? For one glorious, transcendent reason:

He didn't sell.

From 40 to 6000 in 64 of the worst years in the history of the species? How on earth do you manage to lose money in an asset class which behaves like that? There's only one way, really:

(1) You observe one of the significant but temporary declines with which the permanent uptrend is occasionally punctuated.

(2) For a variety of unconscious reasons arising from a Depression-based, principal-obsessed set of fears, you mistake the temporary decline for a permanent decline.

(3) You panic.

(4) You sell.

And therein lies the supreme secret of all investing, but especially of equity investing: losses—real, permanent capital losses—aren't created by markets. *They're created by people,* making an irrational and profoundly counterintuitive judgment. ("This time the sky really *is* falling!") This is well and truly The Big Mistake.

If you do not panic—if you do not fall victim to the toxic illusion of permanent decline—you will not sell. And if you do not sell—if you give the genius of capitalism, manifesting itself through the long-term uptrend in the value of great companies, time to do its glorious work—you will not suffer capital loss. This is not an issue of knowledge. At that hour before dawn when everything is always darkest, this is an issue of faith. *And faith is the Excellent Investment Advisor's stock in trade.*

Faith...and one more thing: a deep sense of the fundamental long-term efficiency—the *fairness,* if you will—of markets.

In an efficient market (which is to say: in the real world), the ability of an asset class to go up more than other asset classes over time must be a function of one primary thing: its ability to go down more than other asset classes. This is, or at least ought to be, **(a)** pretty obvious and **(b)** of little or no concern to the long-term investor. Higher return, higher "volatility"—in the *true* sense of the word "volatility," which, like leverage, cuts both ways. (A lot of the investing public uses the word "volatility" the way journalism does: as a synonym for "down a lot in a hurry." They seem not to see that whatever can go down a lot in a hurry can also—and more often does—go up a lot in a hurry.)

"Volatility," in an efficient market, is the friend and aider of real "safety," because the more variability there is in the value of an asset class, the higher an overall return the market demands from that asset class. And the higher the return, the "safer" the asset class, net of inflation and taxes.

But "volatility" isn't risk, other than in some academic model. "Volatility" is merely a measure of the efficient interplay between the temporary downs and the permanent ups. Risk, to me, is implicit in the danger that the investor will either want to sell or need to sell during the temporary downs. The ultimate value that the Excellent Investment Advisor adds is the ability to minimize both the desire to sell (through the strength of his belief/faith) and the need to sell (by creating a portfolio that's appropriate to an investor's need to spend capital).

Saving for a boat, a round-the-world trip, a daughter's wedding, or anything else where the capital will be spent within, say, five years? Then by all means *do* save for it; don't invest in equities. Buy yourself a nice CD or short-term bond. The safety of equities rises with the time horizon of the capital. If you don't *have* to sell, the temporary downs aren't "risk," but simply the price you gladly pay for the permanent ups.

The reason a lot of people who went into the 1929–32 holocaust rich and came out of it rich is simple: they weren't on margin, and they didn't have to sell. Because, after all, look what happened:

▶stock *prices* went down 86%, but

▶*dividends* went down only about 50%, while

▶the Consumer Price Index went down 24%.

So if you were living on the dividends from a broadly diversified portfolio of quality common stocks, you pretty much sailed right through that dark period. Granted, your income went down *somewhat* more than your cost of living, but not *that* much more. OK, so you garaged one of your two Rolls-Royces, and paid the chauffeur an hourly rate when you went out, rather than having him continue to live in. Cutting some discretionary spending like that was all you really had to do...*if you didn't "have to" sell.* Equities aren't just the way to *get* rich. Under an almost incredible variety of economic circumstances, they're also the way to *stay* rich.

Thus, "volatility" not only isn't risk, it's the one indispensable key to real safety. Try to think of it this way:

Imagine your car breaks down in the middle of Death Valley. If somebody doesn't come along soon, you'll die. Then, as the sun beats down and your tongue begins to swell...just when you're at wits' end...there on the horizon is an oncoming car. It's getting closer...closer...and...oh, no! It's *green. You hate green cars!* So...you wave the guy on.

Put this book down right now. Find somebody in the office who's good at calligraphy and have that person make you a sign. Get the sign framed, and hang it prominently in your office—where it should remain until I personally tell you to take it down. The sign says:

"Volatility" is the green car.

* * *

These, then, are the three keys to my passion for equities:

1. A belief in the ability of the twin engines of global capitalist revolution and technological/scientific change to drive superior equity returns.

2. A belief that only the *real* returns of equities, net of inflation and taxes, can accrete *real* wealth and provide *real* safety over time.

3. An acceptance of "volatility" as the efficient relationship between larger temporary declines and larger permanent advances.

Therefore, no matter what equity vehicle I'm plugging into The New Universal Five-Point Presentation, you'll find that it will be driven by at least one, usually two, and sometimes all of these three core beliefs. In the last chapter, for instance, you saw a dividend growth fund used to make the point that growth of income is the only solution to growth of living costs. (A secondary goal of that particular presentation was to begin to free the investor from a toxic obsession with "yield.") So in that presentation, I used a part of the second and all of the third point above, though not the first.

These three core beliefs are, for me, the natural laws that govern the financial universe I live in, and that the type of client who responds to me ultimately wants to live in. (You have to be who you are, and you have to sell what you love.)

And in a little while, when we talk about systematic withdrawal plans, you'll see that, even for investors who need more income than current dividends provide, equities still make much more long-term sense than debt does. But even if you never become quite the Equity Zealot that I am, please see that these three core beliefs have the power (just as the Universal Five-Point Presentation does) to purify and simplify your explanation of *all* equity investments.

The differences among equity management styles are far less interesting and important than are the common conceptual underpinnings of equity investing. The journeyman obsesses about the differences; the Excellent Investment Advisor stands serenely on the great conceptual commonalities. *Equity vs. debt is the essential issue.* All other issues (growth vs. value, big-cap vs. small-cap, Latin America vs. Pacific Rim) are merely refinements.

So let's begin to take the *mechanical* framework of the Universal Five-Point Presentation, blend it with the *conceptual* framework of a passion for equities, and see how to share our beliefs with the prospect in a way that (a) neutralizes his potentially instinctive discomfort with stocks and (b) maximizes the probability that he'll reach a favorable decision...*for the right reasons.*

Remember that the presentation is a mood-setter, not a legal brief. We're not litigators, we're therapists, managing prospects' anxiety first, and "educating" them only after that. (The antidote to fear isn't knowledge, it's trust.)

Remember, too, that most of what people register in any conversation (not just a presentation) is non-verbal. And very nearly everything else is verbal nuance: the way we say what we say, rather than what we say. (Students of language call this "paralinguistics.") Words themselves turn out to be a tiny fraction of total communication. In seminal studies by Dr. Albert Mehrabian, the exact relationships among the three elements of what "gets through" in a conversation were determined to be:

55% non-verbal communication

38% the way we say what we say/paralinguistics

7% words

In your presentation, I picture these elements as an inverted pyramid, with whole structure resting on the very small point of the words you use. The balance of this inverted pyramid is very delicate; it can easily be destabilized by very small miscommunications involving certain key words and phrases, which may mean one thing to you and another thing entirely to the prospect. In fact, we've already spoken, in this chapter and the one before it, about several of these emotionally charged words:

- growth
- inflation
- money
- risk
- safety
- volatility

You can see that you already associate very different ideas with these words than do most investors. (Indeed, I don't think it's too much to say that these words may even mean different things to you now than they did when you began to read this book.)

Bearing all these things in mind, let's start with a presentation of the most basic equity managed investment, a big-cap/blue chip "bottom-up" stock fund that's managed for total return.

eia: It seems pretty clear to me, from our discussion of your goals and where you are now, that a dignified and independent retirement is Priority One. You're 52, trying to retire at 62, last child just out of school—congratulations again!—and you're ready to do some very serious investing for retirement. Is that a fair summary of what you've told me?

prospects: It certainly is. We want to do something for the kids if we can, as we told you when you asked about that. But when you come right down to it, the phrase you used—dignified *and independent* retirement—really rang my chimes. And I thought: the first, best thing we can do for those kids is not to show up on their doorstep when we're 80, looking for their support.

eia: Is that what jumped out at you as being most important?

prospects: Absolutely. The instant you said it.

eia: Thank you; that's good for me to know. [*Writes down and underlines "Independence in retirement"*] OK, I think we've agreed that there's still a pretty significant shortfall between the income you can count on having in retirement based on your current investments and retirement plans, and the income you'll actually need. The figure we agreed on was about $1800 a month, wasn't it?

prospects: That's the number. It would make all the difference in the world to us to have that kind of a cushion.

eia: It's about freedom, isn't it? The freedom to do the things that, within reason, you want to do, without sweating your budget?

prospects: That's *exactly* what it's about. Sweating budgets is what we've done all our lives.

eia: Right. And a successful retirement means *to you* the absence of that kind of pressure.

prospects: We've worked *so* hard...

eia: And look at all you've accomplished! Believe me, you don't have that much farther to go. Let me show you how. I always start with the same number: 6%. I can't predict the future, and the last thing *anybody* can predict is interest rates, but 6% always seems to me like a percentage that you'll most probably be able to recover from your investments, almost regardless of the economic or market environment. Are you comfortable with that?

prospects: Sure. 6%...should be a no-brainer.

eia: Should be a no-brainer. So $1800 a month, which is $21,600 a year, is 6% of [*fiddles with his calculator*] $360,000. Looks like we have to endow you with an additional $360,000 over the next 10 years—or, a better way to look at it: the next 120 months, give or take a couple.

prospects: That looks like an awful lot of money.

eia: [*Smiling*] Then don't think about it.

prospects: What?

eia: I'm here to help you, so I give you permission never to think about that big number again, if it bothers you to do so. Instead, think about how much you have to invest every month, assuming a 10% annual return, to get where you want to go. And I calculate that number to be...$1800 per month, for 120 months.

prospects: That seems do-able. Not a walk in the park, but do-able. Where does the 10% figure come from?

eia: It's a plug number; it's what you'd have earned if you'd owned the Standard & Poor's 500 stock index, locked away in a drawer, for the last 70 years. Think of it as kind of the no-brain, long-term average return from a very large, unmanaged basket of quality companies.

prospects: Couldn't we do better than that?

eia: Sure, and there are a couple of reasons to think you will. But those are refinements, and I'd like to come back to them later, if I may. The important thing, I think, is that we *plan* conservatively. Hoping for better returns is a good thing; doing everything you can to achieve better returns is another good thing. But *planning* on better returns—i.e. betting your independence in retirement on getting a base hit every time you come up to bat for the next 10 years—that, to me, is a really bad thing.

And since I have to be responsible to you for getting you where you need to go, I want to do everything I can to make you successful. The first step in that process, for me, is making reasonable assumptions. I hope that's OK with you, because that's really the only way I can work for you.

prospects: Well, OK then…

eia: If the worst thing that happens is that we overshoot your goals, and you end up with an extra $2000 or $2200 a month instead of $1800, I assume that's not a problem?

prospects: [*Coming back down to earth*] No problem whatsoever.

eia: I'm going to recommend three to five managed portfolios in all, but the bedrock investment is the one I'd like to talk about now. [*The concept/The fit*] The critical investment issue for you, in my judgment, is *quality*. Your situation doesn't leave you a lot of margin for error, in that you have a finite amount of time to achieve a critically important goal. You can't speculate, because you haven't time to make up for mistakes. That's pretty clear to you, isn't it?

prospects: Couldn't possibly be clearer.

eia: Aside from quality, the other theme that I think is very important for you folks is *consistency*. You don't want a management style—or a manager—that's spectacularly right when it's right but very, very wrong when it's wrong. You want somebody who tries to hit 'em straight down the middle of the fairway. Does that make sense to you?

prospects: Quality and consistency make all the sense in the world.

eia: [*Who's managing the money, and how I feel about them*] My firm has a very close relationship with a money management firm headquartered in Philadelphia called The Gronsky Group. The firm was founded shortly after the end of World War II, originally as a portfolio manager for institutions and wealthy individual investors. In the late 1950s, they began to make their skills available to individual investors like us through mutual funds. Today they manage about $70 billion.

My firm can refer its serious, retirement-oriented investors to just about any money manager we please, but we've always been especially comfortable with the Gronsky people. That's because they've managed people's most important capital through all the fads and fears of the last half-century, and never lost their focus, which is the discipline of investing in a company's shares *as if they were acquiring the whole company.* I've always felt that, for the serious investor, the distinction between trading stocks and investing in companies is the critical one, and that's what the Gronskys are all about.

[*What the investment does and why that's good for you*] The Gronsky portfolio that I feel should be the foundation of your plan for capital appreciation is their flagship fund, Gronsky Capital Fund. It's managed by someone I've come to know fairly well—a man about your age, incidentally, named Grey Trueheart, Ph.D. His style is basically to ignore economic and market trends, and to focus on very large, mature companies that are experiencing fundamental change. His holdings will tend to be companies you know, and whose products and services your family may use.

One of Dr. Trueheart's main investment themes is globalizing capitalism, and he's particularly interested in companies that have rapidly growing earnings from overseas. That's why his largest holdings include PepsiCo, Viacom, Disney, Merck, Caterpillar and American Airlines. It's the blending of stability and opportunism that attracts me to Dr. Trueheart, and it's why I have my own/my parents'/a lot of my clients' [*whatever's true*] retirement money with him.

[*How the investment works*] I don't want to bore you with a lot of methodology, here, but Dr. Trueheart primarily analyzes large companies' free cash flows—rather than earnings, or book value, or any of the more textbook standards of measurement. He looks at those things too, of course, but he feels that real cash flow is the best measure of how a company is doing. The benefit to you of rising cash flow is that it lets companies do good things for their investors: expand, make strategic acquisitions, raise dividends and buy back stock. Does that strike you as an intelligent strategy?

prospects: Yes. And the best thing about it is: we understand it.

eia: [*Risks/Limitations/What the investment isn't*] Good. Now, make no mistake about it: the price of even the highest quality stocks will go down in a generalized stock market decline... *even when the values of the companies don't.* The ability of stocks to go down temporarily every so often is the key to their ability to go up permanently as much as they have since the Gronskys set up shop in the late 1940s, when the Dow Jones Industrials were about 200.

But beyond that, I want you to see stock price fluctuation the way Dr. Trueheart does, as the opportunity to buy larger pieces of great companies when they're on sale.

I recommend that you take the $25,000 CD you've got rolling over, plus $1000 a month of the money you're going to be setting aside each month, and invest it with Dr. Trueheart. Does that feel right to you?

Nine minutes. That's how long that whole conversation/presentation took, and I hope you can see a huge number of this book's major themes coming together in those nine minutes.

▶*A restatement of the prospects' most fundamental life situation.* "...a dignified and independent retirement is Priority One."

▶ *Moving from the conceptual need to an actual financial goal.* "The figure we agreed on was about $1800 a month, wasn't it?"

▶ *A trial balloon of the 10% long-term return of equities* to test for the presence of toxic levels of loss-aversion. (Fear of equities isn't really risk-aversion. We've already established that people don't know what "risk" is. Fear of equities is *loss-aversion,* which isn't the same thing at all.) Since quite the opposite is found ("Couldn't we do better than that?"), we have to tone down the expectations. ("Hoping for better returns" is OK; working toward them is OK; betting the ranch that you'll get 'em is not OK. Also note the restatement, "I have to be responsible to you...")

▶ *The concept/The fit are stated in purely right-brain terms.* Quality and consistency don't show up on a scattergram, but in the informed judgment of the excellent advisor. This is yet another reminder that the central issue in these folks' retirement planning is nothing more or less than *you.*

▶ *The traditions and beliefs of the management company are stressed.* "They've managed...through all the fads and fears of the last half-century." They follow "the discipline of investing in a company's shares *as if they were acquiring the whole company.*" (Speculators trade stocks; great investors acquire companies. A critical distinction.)

▶ *The emphasis is on your personal relationship with the manager, and on his beliefs.* "Very large, mature companies...you know, and whose products and services your family may use." Again: *companies, not stocks.* "Globalizing capitalism." Specific names of companies people have a bias to believe in. "The blending of stability and opportunism." (Let's see the journeyman graph *those* qualities.) The fund is good *because you/your parents/your clients own it.*

▶ *No mention of "performance."* The unspoken implication: we're just covering truths of the highest importance here. Since "performance" hasn't come up yet—and won't, unless the prospects ask—*it must not be of critical importance.* And, indeed, it isn't.

▶ *The* **how it works** *point is used only because it adds* **both** *clarification of* *the manager's style and how the methodology benefits the investor.* It passes the clarify/mystify test. But even then, you must never state a *feature* without stating the resultant *benefit* to your listeners.

▶*The inevitability—and the ultimate evanescence—of major NAV declines is stressed.* But stock prices are yet again distinguished from the value of companies. And "bear markets" are re-cast as big sales/opportunities. (Look: you know this is going to be an issue sooner or later. Use Point # 5 to shoot it even before it goes for its gun. Letting the bad guy draw first went out with the Lone Ranger.)

▶*You can't keep re-checking for the prospects' agreement too often.* In this presentation, the EIA checked for agreement nine times in as many minutes, not counting the closing question. If you weren't keenly aware of his doing this, please go back and read through the conversation again *right now.*

The combination of a passionate belief system and a "places in the heart vs. places on some chart" presentation discipline is the formula for winning—and keeping—quality clients and their families' assets.

But let it never be forgotten that what you say is ultimately meaningless. The only thing that matters is how many people you say it to.

In Summary

☞ No matter how finely crafted your presentation is, it's empty without a passionate belief behind it. Believe in equities. Optimism is the only realism. Optimism is the only world-view that squares with the facts.

☞ Pessimism, on the other hand, is counterintuitive. It presupposes an insoluble problem, for which there is no precedent in the vast, and often quite terrible, history of the human species.

☞ When you take the long view of progress, and marry it to a multigenerational time horizon, you end up being an equity investor largely because nothing else makes much sense. Moreover, you're relieved of the necessity for a market outlook. Don't worry about being in equities during the next 20% market decline; worry—a lot—about being out of the next 200% market advance.

☞ Currency isn't money. It may be a terrific medium of exchange, but it's no long-term store of value. The only sane long-term definition of "money" is "purchasing power."

☞ Equities are the only real long-term "safety," once you know what risk and safety really are—as opposed to what they used to be. Over a quarter century of retirement—and on into the lives of clients' heirs—risk isn't loss of principal. It's the extinction of purchasing power.

☞ And if risk is the extinction of purchasing power, safety can only be its accretion... *after accounting for inflation and taxes.* By that test—a positive return net of inflation and taxes—equities are the ultimate safe investment.

☞ Moreover, the more "volatile" equities are—i.e. the greater their potential for large temporary downward movement—the "safer" they will be—i.e. the higher the return net of inflation and taxes—in the long run. Markets are nothing if not efficient in the long run. And the temporary declines are purely and simply the price of the permanent advances. "Volatility" is the green car.

☞ No panic, no sell. No sell, no lose. The great enemy of long-term investment success, especially in equities, isn't ignorance. It's fear. The only known antidote to that fear is the Excellent Investment Advisor's faith.

☞ Organizing the *conceptual* truth of your passion for equities through the *mechanical* beauty of the Universal Five-Point Presentation will inevitably lead to success and happiness...but only if you do it often enough.

☞ Be ever vigilant regarding the inverted pyramid of communication. For, while non-verbal and paralinguistic (the way you say what you say) communication is the most important issue, *everything rests on the words.* Choose them wisely.

☞ Excessive optimism is as bad as (or worse than) pessimism. ("Couldn't we do better than that?") Don't let anyone make you responsible for more than the index return of the investment type you're presenting. This minimizes arbitration and maximizes pleasant surprises.

☞ You can't check for prospects' agreement too often. The more often they agree during the presentation's journey, the more likely they are to agree when it gets to its destination: the call to action.

☞ Consider using the **Risks/Limitations/What it isn't** part of your presentation to shoot an objection (or two) that's almost certainly going to come up sooner or later anyway.

☞ All of the above not a whit to the contrary, the passion of your belief and the precision of your presentation are ultimately meaningless. The only thing that matters is how many people you tell your story to. For many are called, but few are chosen.

11

Diversification: the unifying logic of an equity portfolio

"To every thing there is a season, and a time to every purpose under the heaven."

—Ecclesiastes 3:1

One crisp winter morning in beautiful Aspen, Colorado, I was standing on my skis together with a group of other eager students at the Aspen ski school. The instructor was going over some basic safety rules, and he especially cautioned us about getting overtired in the high mountain air. "Remember," he said darkly, "nine out of 10 major skiing injuries happen on the last run of the day."

I had to put my entire ski-gloved fist into my mouth to keep from laughing, because I knew if I started, I'd never stop. That was the single silliest statistic I'd ever heard in my life! Hell, I thought, *all* major skiing injuries happen on the last run of the day. Even at 8:00 in the morning, if they're taking you down off the mountain on a stretcher...brother, that was your *last run of the day!*

That's still the dumbest statistic I've ever heard, but in recent years I've been hearing another that's right up there.

It's the astounding conclusion—always delivered with an absolutely straight face by some professorial type—that 87% (or 91%, or 93%, or whatever) of your total investment return comes from the asset allocation of your portfolio, rather than from your selection of individual securities within an asset class.

Now, *there's* a Blinding Glimpse of the Obvious for you. Take another look at the index returns of the three major asset classes: stocks, bonds and cash, per Ibbotson Associates.

Stocks	10.5%
Long-term corporate bonds	5.7%
Cash (T-Bills)	3.7%

I infer from this [*as would, I believe, anyone who made it through sixth grade*] that the more of my assets I had in the thing that returned 10.5%, as opposed to the things that returned 5.7%, and 3.7%, the higher my portfolio return was. I just don't think you need a Ph.D. to figure this out all on your own.

Of course, if what the professors *really* mean by asset allocation is "moving into, out of, and among stocks, bonds and cash at just the right times," then what we have here is an academic theory that is of no practical utility whatever. Because that's the same as saying, "The key to superior returns is to be able consistently to time the markets." That's terrific in a computer model, and completely impossible in real life—as I presume even the professors know.

So I'm back to assuming that they're offering us overwhelmingly convincing evidence of what we all knew to begin with: the more stocks you own vs. bonds, and the more bonds you own vs. cash, the better you do. And, if you simplify that argument even further, you realize that, reduced to its essence, the asset allocation theory just says:

The higher your equity exposure as a percentage of your total assets, the better your overall return.

Why, then, has our industry made virtually a secular religion out of "asset allocation"? And—perhaps an even more important question—what does "asset allocation" mean to you, and what are you trying to get it to do for you?

If you believe in the myth of "higher returns with lower risk"—i.e. that by some alchemy one can mix the three asset classes in a way that returns more than 10.5%—you're beyond my help. "Higher returns with lower risk" isn't modern portfolio theory, nor even ancient portfolio theory. It's voodoo portfolio theory. It defies both logic and arithmetic.

What you *can* do—as the good folks at Bailard, Biehl & Kaiser in San Francisco have demonstrated over a long period of time—is produce *nearly* the return of equities with *not nearly* the volatility, if that's what floats your boat. As you can see from the chart on the following page, BB&K's "Moderate Norm" portfolio—35% US stocks, 15% international stocks, 15% real estate, 25% US bonds and 10% international bonds, *re-balanced [for all intents and purposes] annually*—has done just that.

This is the kind of chart that makes an institutional investor's heart go pitty-pat, but you and I have to remember a couple of things about it. (A) The key to its success isn't so much the asset allocation *as it is the annual rebalancing.* (B) In the real world, the individual investor would incur potentially significant transaction costs and/or taxation every year at rebalancing time, the net effect of which would reduce the returns to some potentially significant extent.

Major Market Indices

Year	U.S. Stocks	International Stocks	Cash Equivalents	Real Estate	U.S. Bonds	International Bonds	Moderate Norm
1970	03.9%	−10.5%	6.6%	10.8%	14.0%	6.5%	5.6%
1971	14.3%	31.2%	4.4%	9.2%	13.2%	15.5%	15.9%
1972	19.0%	37.6%	4.0%	7.5%	5.7%	9.2%	15.7%
1973	−14.7%	−14.2%	6.8%	7.5%	0.9%	−0.9%	−6.0%
1974	−26.5%	−22.2%	7.9%	7.2%	3.4%	3.5%	−10.3%
1975	37.2%	37.1%	5.9%	5.7%	9.1%	14.3%	23.1%
1976	23.9%	3.7%	5.0%	9.3%	17.4%	11.7%	15.8%
1977	−7.2%	19.4%	5.2%	10.5%	1.3%	33.5%	5.6%
1978	6.6%	34.3%	7.1%	16.0%	−0.5%	14.4%	11.2%
1979	18.6%	6.2%	9.8%	20.7%	3.4%	−8.3%	10.6%
1980	32.5%	24.4%	11.3%	18.1%	−0.4%	9.1%	18.6%
1981	−4.9%	−1.0%	14.1%	16.6%	7.7%	0.9%	2.6%
1982	21.5%	−0.9%	10.9%	9.4%	33.5%	14.3%	18.6%
1983	22.6%	24.6%	8.6%	13.3%	4.8%	7.9%	15.6%
1984	6.3%	7.9%	9.6%	13.0%	14.2%	8.4%	9.7%
1985	31.7%	56.7%	7.5%	10.1%	27.1%	22.7%	30.2%
1986	18.7%	69.9%	6.1%	6.6%	18.6%	21.1%	24.8%
1987	5.3%	24.9%	5.8%	5.5%	−0.8%	20.8%	8.3%
1988	16.6%	28.6%	6.8%	7.0%	7.2%	4.8%	13.4%
1989	31.7%	10.8%	8.2%	6.2%	16.2%	−0.4%	17.7%
1990	−3.1%	−23.3%	7.5%	1.5%	8.3%	9.9%	−1.3%
1991	30.5%	12.5%	5.4%	−6.1%	17.5%	15.4%	17.6%
1992	7.6%	−11.8%	3.5%	−4.6%	7.7%	8.9%	3.0%
1993	10.1%	32.9%	3.0%	0.9%	12.8%	16.4%	13.4%
1994	1.3%	8.1%	4.3%	6.7%	−5.6%	1.3%	1.4%
1995	37.6%	11.6%	5.4%	(e) 8.8%	23.0%	18.8%	23.8%
Cum. Return	1761.5%	2345.3%	472.9%	774.5%	991.5%	1211.4%	1516.1%
Ann. Return	11.9%	13.1%	6.9%	8.2%	9.6%	10.4%	11.3%
Std. Dev.	16.4%	22.9%	2.6%	6.2%	9.4%	8.9%	9.7%

Source: U.S. Stocks: Standard & Poor's 500 Stock Composite Index; U.S. Bonds: Lehman Long-Term Government Bond (1970–1977); Merrill Lynch 7–10 Year Treasury (1978–1994); Equity: MSCI Europe, Asia, Far East Stock Market Index (International)—Gross Dividends (U.S. $); Cash Equivalents: 91-day Treasury Bill Offering; Real Estate: Frank Russell Company Property Index (1978–1994), Ibbotson & Fall, Journal of Portfolio Management, Fall 1979, JMB Institutional Realty Corp., Real Estate, June 1986 (FRC Commingled-Fund 1971–1977); International Bonds: 1985–1994 Salomon Brothers (Non-U.S., 50% H); 1970–1984 composite consisting of Japan, U.K., Germany and France. Moderate Norm Portfolio is: 35% U.S. Stock, 15% International Stock, 15% Real Estate, 25% U.S. Bonds and 10% International Bonds.

Best Performing Asset of Given Year

At best, then, all you can reasonably ask asset allocation to do is to forego some of the return of equities in order (if you're very disciplined and/or very lucky) to protect you from a somewhat larger portion of equities' volatility. In other words, *asset allocation lets you give away some of the permanent ups so you can miss some of the temporary downs.* My question is: why would anybody want to do that? And my answer is: nobody would, *if he really believed that the downs were, in fact, temporary.*

So you'll have to forgive me if I conclude that most of this "asset allocation" hocus-pocus is just a way of pandering to investors' deep-seated equity loss-aversion. We give investors permission to have far less equity exposure than they and their heirs need—and we excuse ourselves for letting them do what they want to instead of what they need to—by cloaking the whole shabby affair in the empty suit of "asset allocation."

We actually dignify volatility—and in so doing allow the investor erroneously to equate volatility with risk—by going to such convoluted lengths to reduce it. This ends up being counterproductive, because, in pandering to people's susceptibility to panic, we reinforce instead of reducing that propensity.

The real-life problem with "asset allocation," of course, is that stocks and bonds correlate quite positively with each other. That is, when one is taking on water in a hurry, the other usually is, too—and for the same reasons.

The long-term value of companies is governed by corporate earnings, cash flows, dividends and book values. But the short- to intermediate-term prices of stocks (never to be confused with the value of companies) are more driven by liquidity than by anything else. When liquidity is flowing into the financial markets, interest rates fall and both bond and stock prices tend to rise. When liquidity is draining out of the markets, interest rates rise and both bond and stock prices fall—usually at the same time and for the same reasons.

Since asset allocation palliates the symptoms of loss-aversion without in any way curing the disease, I anticipate a deeply religious experience for the journeyman who proudly shows his fear-prone customers a mere 26.8% hit vs. 31.2% for the S&P 500. They'll not only panic out, they'll sue him. At the end of the day, it isn't going to matter how exquisitely nuanced your asset allocation models are. If you haven't taught your clients to distinguish between fluctuation and loss—or, at the very least, taught them to trust *you* to make that distinction—you've bought a one-way ticket to Palookaville.

And if you *have* taught them that fluctuation isn't loss—if you *have* taught 'em that volatility isn't risk—then why would you need to fool around with "asset allocation" in the first place? *Why would you ever part with any of your permanent ups in order to reduce the ultimately meaningless temporary downs?*

Like I said: you wouldn't. But there *is* something that you *might* do. **You might diversify.**

You can capture a good deal of the supposed benefit of asset allocation (i.e. some reduction of overall portfolio volatility), **without paying its awful price in permanently lost return,** *by diversifying an equity portfolio (a) by management style and (b) geographically.* A sturdy, basic, five-part portfolio, whose logic any serious investor can easily understand, might look like this:

Big-cap growth		Big-cap value
Small-cap growth		Small-cap value
	International	

Start 'em off evenly at 20% each, and rebalance them annually, if you're a purist. (Or just vector new money toward the laggards, if you're not.)

We know that growth and value tend to move countercyclically, and end up in about the same place in terms of overall return. We know, too, that big-cap and small-cap usually dance a contrapuntal minuet; the latter ultimately produces about a 20% premium return (with concomitant gyration) over the former.

Finally, we know that foreign markets do their own things at their own times, often (though not always) irrespective of US markets. So international investing—in addition to putting you on the front lines of the global capitalist revolution—can raise your overall portfolio return while reducing your overall portfolio volatility. (Foreign markets *themselves* are, of course, way more volatile than ours—anybody remember the Mexican Bolsa halving in a matter of weeks not that long ago?—so remember: it's only lower *portfolio* volatility we're talking about, here.)

Could you take this elegant, simple five-part portfolio and diversify it even further? Well, sure you could—although I'm not sure the incremental gain would be worth the trouble. You could, for instance, divide your international exposure into a number of more specific subcategories: Europe, Asia and Latin America, for instance, or mature markets and emerging ones, or big-cap and small-cap. But up around seven to nine different funds/accounts, I think you're at the point of diminishing returns. There's a finite limit to how thin you can slice a salami.

You're looking for the golden mean: diversified enough to be palpably effective against overall portfolio volatility, but still simple enough that the investor can understand and embrace the portfolio's unifying logic. (And, in the end, the latter is the more important criterion. No matter how gorgeous a portfolio's logic, if that logic is impenetrable to the investor it's worse than useless. Because if he doesn't "own" the logic emotionally, the investor will chuck the whole portfolio overboard when—not if—*everything* in it is down more or less.)

So the challenge to the Excellent Investment Advisor is to present equity investments not in the old transaction-oriented way ("Buy this because it's a superior investment") but in a new, truly *contextual* way ("Buy this because of the way it fits into the unifying logic of the equity portfolio that's going to endow your family with real wealth over time"). In the context of a diversified equity portfolio, the reason to own any particular equity investment isn't that it's going to shoot the lights out in the next 12 months (an outcome of which we can't be sure, and over which we have no control). It's that the investment will usually overperform just when another key component of the portfolio is underperforming. The critical effects of making this investment will thus be, in ascending order of importance, **(a)** to smooth out the bumps and the humps, and **(b)** to contribute to—and perhaps even enhance—the portfolio's overall return. **The Fit,** *rather than any factor intrinsic to the investment itself, becomes the Megaconcept.*

This is, to put it mildly, not the way we old-timers (i.e. those of us who've been in the business more than about 18 months) were trained. We were taught to extol the wonderfulness of the investment *itself*—which is no more or less than what you do when you're trying to get a transaction to take place. So presenting equity investments as components of a meaningfully diversified portfolio requires not just a different attitudinal emphasis but a different set of skills.

About the last thing you want a diversified portfolio approach to do is get people excited. Excitement junkies generally don't find such an approach very appealing, anyway. If they want a "portfolio" at all, what they usually mean by that is "a whole bunch of stuff all of which is currently delivering peak performance." By definition, a whole raft of investments that are simultaneously delivering peak performance (i.e. upside volatility) can also be relied upon to do a simultaneous NAV power dive (i.e. downside volatility) one fine day. This, then, is the pure essence of *non*-diversification. At the end of the day, true diversification is a whole lot of wonderful things, but "exciting" probably isn't one of them.

And do not fall prey to the illusion that you're necessarily getting oodles of meaningful diversification from a portfolio of funds that run from "aggressive" to "conservative." You can have five funds that look like this:

Growth
Growth and income
Dividend growth
Equity income
Balanced

And you'll think you have diversification by the carload, with some asset allocation thrown in for good measure. Then you'll look at the top 10 stock holdings in the five funds, and find out they've all got Pepsi or Coke, Merck or Pfizer, Disney or Viacom, Bank of New York or J.P. Morgan, and McDonald's or McDonald's (!). From the standpoint of real diversification, this is like eating a balanced diet of white bread, rye bread, whole wheat bread, pumpernickel bread and a sesame seed bagel. A "portfolio" like that will probably soar *and* dive in tighter formation than the Blue Angels!

Now, selling somebody a very mixed portfolio—or even one new component of such a portfolio—is inherently much more difficult than selling a single investment. ("Ms. Advisor, you want me to buy this thing that...let me be sure I follow you...this thing that'll almost certainly be going sideways or down...when this other thing you want me to buy is going up? Uh...meaning no offense...would it be OK if I just bought the thing that was going to go up? And...uh...which one *was* that, again?")

And of course, the fact that selling a truly diversified portfolio involves the maximum degree of difficulty is exactly how the excellent advisor knows it's the right thing to do. For, in this our life,

The excellent investment advisor knows that it is very easy to get investors to do things that will end up being bad for them, and very difficult to get them to do things that will ultimately make them wealthy.

This is just another reason why the excellent advisor is resigned to always having a high **N**: fewer prospects per unit of prospecting effort...but a higher closing ratio, and real clients (people who buy your advice) as opposed to customers (people who buy and sell investments through you, and blame you when any one investment is down, regardless of how well the rest are doing).

All of life is, on some level, the journey from victimization to empowerment. Thus, the career of the excellent advisor is a constant process of nurturing client relationships...and firing customers. *And only clients buy—and keep—truly diversified portfolios.* Customers may buy a portfolio, but they'll very soon call you about selling whatever components are down and reinvesting the proceeds in whatever's up. (And they'll keep doing so until, with all the exquisite civility at your command, you metaphorically shoot them in the back of the head at very close range with a large-caliber, soft-nosed bullet, so that your "relationship" becomes instantly—but quite painlessly—dead.)

So whereas *Serious Money* devoted upwards of 100 pages to the process of presenting virtually every conceivable managed investment on a stand-alone basis, I'd like now to examine the art of presenting equity investments *in relation to each other.* Once again: **The fit,** rather than the idea of any one investment, is the Megaconcept.

So let's take the whole concept of equity diversification itself, and put it into the Universal Five-Point Presentation. The purpose of this exercise is to make sure that you have, and can readily communicate, a core concept of what equity diversification (as opposed to "asset allocation," among other things) is, and of what it can and cannot do.

If these things seem so painfully obvious to you that you can't see any need for a discussion of them, feel free to skip over this section of the chapter. But just before you do, I'd like to caution you that it is, to me, a singular feature of the journeyman's pathology that he thinks a lot of things are totally obvious to investors which aren't really obvious to them at all. Diversification and "asset allocation" are two such concepts (and the very real differences between the two are a third). The critical input of a dispassionate professional investment advisor is yet another not-at-all-obvious idea—which is why the journeyman always plunges right into a discussion of investments before establishing what he brings to the table, and ends up stuck to the tar baby of the so-called "no-load argument." Finally, the transcendent beauty and truth of dollar-cost averaging—heaven's own engine of wealth-creation for the blissfully clueless—are, as we shall have occasion to see, intensely mysterious to most people…which is why most people aren't rich.

Now that I've got your undivided attention…

1 **The concept/The fit.** "We've established what your two overriding financial goals are: a retirement with no compromise in lifestyle in which your income grows right along with your living costs, and the preservation and enhancement of your principal as a legacy for your children. We've agreed that there's a natural tension between those two goals, and we've concluded that only by opening yourself up to the superior total return of equities can you hope to achieve both.

"The financial well-being of two—and possibly more—generations of your family rests on this decision, and on the way we put the decision into action. I want to remind you that I take this decision-making process every bit as seriously as you do—not least of all because I'm in the process of investing for the same goals for my family.

"In creating a managed equity portfolio that you can live with in good times and bad, quite literally for the rest of your life, my conceptual goals are twofold. First, I want to give you broad representation among great companies of all kinds: large and small, mature and rapidly growing, domestic and international. You deserve to, and can afford to, own a broadly ***diverse*** portfolio of the best businesses on the planet, managed by some of the highest quality investment managers in the world. A portfolio that's a major work of art, painted on a big canvas.

"The other goal of this diversified portfolio is not only to spread the risk of equity investing, but to smooth out, to the extent possible, the temporary ups and downs of different markets.

"The greatness of diversification lies in the fact that when major cyclical companies like Chrysler, International Paper and Alcoa Aluminum go into an economic downturn, money often flows into great growth investments like Coca-Cola, Disney and McDonald's that largely control their own destinies. Or, for another example, when Japan's economy is booming, ours may go into recession, and vice versa. Finally, emerging growth companies and large mature businesses tend to do well at different points on the cycle.

"No one can consistently predict the turn of these cycles, so trading in and out of them isn't an option. Besides, it misses the point.

"The point is how an equity portfolio that captures many or most of the major themes of modern global capitalism can build real wealth—in terms of both increasing your income and growing your capital—over time. And how the components of the portfolio—running on different cycles as they do—will tend to smooth out the peaks and valleys of equity investing somewhat.

"Can you see, in concept, how this kind of portfolio approach could be an elegant solution to your family's needs?"

This statement takes about three minutes. But look at all we accomplished in that brief time:

▶A total re-statement of the client's two major goals, and a reminder that those goals (income for one generation, capital for the next) have traditionally worked at cross-purposes.

▶The invitation to "open yourself up to" the superior total return of equities. Never mind which part of that return is dividends and which part is capital appreciation yet. The essence of the basic appeal of equities is the *total return,* which simply dwarfs that of debt.

▶Yet another statement of the ultimate similarity between the client's goals and the advisor's. *Keep moving to his side of the table.* You probably can't do this too often. You aren't "salesperson" and "customer." You're two caring people searching for the solution to a common set of goals.

▶A reminder that this will be, when it's done right, a portfolio "quite literally for the rest of your life." Not for the next 90 days, six months or year. Shoot the tendency to think short-term about "the current outlook" for the economy and the markets, even before that instinctive tendency has a chance to go for its gun.

▶A short list of the different categories of "great companies of all kinds" that you'll own in this portfolio. The journeyman always talks about "stocks" and "stock markets." Please note that these words appear nowhere here. The excellent advisor's client won't own "stocks." He'll own "great companies;" he'll own "a broadly diverse portfolio of the best businesses on the planet." The emotional impact of these essentially semantic differences is huge. Remember the inverted pyramid of communication, balanced on the point of the words.

▶"You deserve to, and you can afford to, own a world-class portfolio of great businesses," managed by "some of the highest quality investment managers in the world." When was the last time you put down your charts and scattergrams, and reminded your clients that they *deserved* greatness? And when was the last time you took a moment to focus on the fact that any American family of reasonable means can afford to invest in a thousand and more of the greatest companies around the globe? Neither Andrew Carnegie, John D. Rockefeller nor J.P. Morgan in their prime could ever have done that. There'll be time for the arithmetic later: touch the miracle.

▶"A portfolio that's a major work of art, painted on a big canvas." One of the world's great sociobiologists, Edward O. Wilson of Harvard—whose narrowly focused field of science might have made a lesser person very literal-minded—said, "The key instrument of the creative imagination is analogy." Jesus is not known ever to have discussed theology or epistemology, as such. He said things like, "The kingdom of heaven is like a grain of mustard seed." Think about that the next time you're tempted to start talking about standard deviation, much less about post-modern portfolio theory.

▶Specific examples of "major cyclical companies" and "great growth investments...that largely control their own destinies." Different types of wonderful businesses, waxing and waning at different times; this is "the greatness of diversification." Forget about the client for a moment: don't *you* find this soothing?

▶ "No one can...predict..." You don't try to flit from market to market, or from style to style. That's for journeymen and their customers. The excellent advisor and his clients use a long-term portfolio to build wealth by capturing "many or most of the major themes of modern global capitalism." They increase both income and capital across the generations, even as they "smooth out the peaks and valleys... somewhat."

▶ "An elegant solution." Need we say *that much* more? (Can elegance be "proven"? *Does it need to be?)*

Could I ask you to take a pause, here, and go back and read this script, and the commentary thereon, one more time? Because what you're looking at is nothing more or less than the excellent advisor's whole approach to presenting investments:

The excellent investment advisor knows that the truth is always greater than the sum of all the facts.

I said earlier, and now say again, that no one ever became an Excellent Investment Advisor until he learned to rise above the facts. I hope you can see, now, what your destination is when you *do* transcend fact: you arrive at The Truth. The excellent advisor's presentation flows gently and easily downstream from the headwaters of a few great, conceptual truths. (The journeyman tries desperately to row upstream toward truth through a raging torrent of facts, numbers and ratios, in which he and his poor, benighted prospect ultimately drown.)

The great conceptual truths you've just read are simply **(1)** that the total return of equities is the optimum—if not the only—source of multigenerational accretion of both income and capital, and **(2)** that diversification across many different sizes, types, and geographical locations of great (and potentially great) companies may intuitively be seen to smooth out the journey to multigenerational wealth.

Everything else is details. And not only is the truth not in the details, but no accumulation of the details can be made to add up to The Truth. Conceptual truths are the moral high ground of a presentation; in order to object to those truths, a prospect is forced to fight an almost literally uphill battle.

2 **Who's managing the money, and how I feel about them.** "You can actually get virtually all of the benefits I've described by owning [*Optional, if it's true:* **as I do**] five separate portfolios which my firm and I have selected, and sort of balanced off against each other, to carry out the aims and goals we've just spoken of.

"We're fighting a war for multigenerational wealth, and the five portfolios are the forces that'll do the actual fighting. Think of them as the Army, Navy, Marines, Air Force and the Merchant Marine. Each does something supremely well that the others can't do, and together they form the force we need to win the war.

"Before we examine each of these portfolios in detail, I'd like to tell you something about the overall strength of the forces we've assembled.

"We'll own more than 1000 companies worldwide, selected by people with research staffs in New York, Boston, Los Angeles, London, Tokyo, Paris, and a dozen other business capitals of the world. The five portfolio managers have over 125 years of total investment experience among them.

"Each of the five believes passionately in his approach, so they're all likely to stick to their disciplines. The benefit to you of that discipline is that **it keeps you diversified at all times.** And that's critically important, because when long-term discipline goes out the window, you can wake up one morning and find that you own five portfolios, all with the same nifty fifty growth stocks in 'em. In creating portfolios like yours, give me a choice between five eclectic geniuses and five managers with iron discipline, *and I'll take the managers who stick to their knitting* **every single time.**

"You can see the wisdom of maintaining the discipline of diversification, can't you?"

You could, I guess, also mention some other magnitudes ("The total size of the five portfolios is $18 billion; the five management companies manage a total of $220 billion"), but I'm not sure that's wise. One person reads a big number as strength; another infers from the same big number an elephantine slowness of foot. And the whole thrust of my approach is so personal that big numbers may actually send the wrong signal [*"How can a behemoth managing $100 billion really care about me and my family?"*]. Use your own judgment on this one. Where you think it will give comfort, fire off the big number. Where you think it may **daunt, don't.**

The big people point here, of course, is that you actively want managers who will have the discipline to stay out of favor when their basic approach goes out of favor. In the CNBC/MTV/Internet/*USA Today* world we live in—"Get what's hot, not what's not!" —this is almost countercultural. And yet it is critical to the unifying logic of true diversification. No "eclectic geniuses," please; give us disciplined professionals into which we can forge an unbeatable team!

And once again, here, you see that the excellent advisor does not simply say the same things the journeyman says, only in new and fascinating ways. The excellent advisor talks about, and therefore causes his prospect to think about, entirely different things.

The journeyman would have taken Point #2 literally (who's running the money), and would have fired off a whole clip of specific names which didn't mean anything to the prospect, followed by a 10-minute discourse on "The Fundamental Differences Between Growth and Value Investing, In Monosyllabic Words, For Pre-School Children." And you can be sure that the air would be full of so many "performance" numbers that the prospect would completely shut down any conceptual faculty he might have been trying to use, in order to keep up with the journeyman's data deluge.

The excellent advisor used Point #2 to make the point—which I assure you that few investors have ever thought of—that in a truly diversified portfolio some stuff always appears to be "not working." And that *that's how you know the portfolio is properly diversified.* If everything in a portfolio is "working," i.e. is in sync with the market trends/vogues *du jour*, the plain fact is that you haven't got a portfolio. You've got a bet.

The excellent advisor also says, in effect, "My firm and I know how to identify managers with discipline." This does a couple of important things. It says that the excellent advisor's professional judgment is the primary issue in creating a truly diversified portfolio—as opposed to some highly abstruse, academic modeling that you need a course in theoretical statistics to understand.

It also says that the main thing you want from any individual manager inside a diversified portfolio is discipline—as much or more than his stock-picking prowess—and discipline is a character issue, not an issue that lends itself to four stars/nine moons/three suns kinds of "objective analysis." "Character is fate," the Greeks said, and character is best assessed by grown-ups who are good judges of character, rather than by children playing with their computers all day because the real world frightens them so much.

3 **What the investment does *and* 4. How the investment works.** "Please remember that we're selecting your five portfolios-within-a-portfolio as much for how they interact as for how any one of them acts.

"The manager of your large-company growth portfolio says, 'The aluminum industry is largely at the mercy of the automobile industry cycle, but nothing constrains the creative imaginations of the Disney geniuses who brought you *The Lion King*. Give me growth every time.' The manager of your large-company value portfolio says, 'Paying 30 times earnings for the alleged genius of 29-year-old cartoonists isn't my idea of a good time. I like plant and equipment and bricks and mortar. When I can buy Ford below book value, even when its earnings are actually growing south, that's a good day!'

"Your small-company growth manager says, 'I could acquire my top 50 favorite fast-growing companies **in their entirety** for the same money it would take to buy out McDonald's! And my top 50 entrepreneur/technology teams are going to think of infinitely more exciting things than an Arch Deluxe. Big companies...yuck.'

"And your small-company value manager probably goes into shock when he looks at little high-tech growth companies selling for a jillion times earnings. He'll say the same kinds of things his large-company counterpart does, but he'll say them about a dozen smaller companies to whom Ford is outsourcing a lot of things it used to make in-house.

"Finally, your international manager will say, 'Domestic US? An economy that's growing at 2½% a year whether it needs to or not? Give me a break. I can buy China growing five times as fast, or Malaysia, Thailand and Singapore growing four times as fast. Three-quarters of the world's stocks aren't even **traded** in the US. I've got 10 of the world's 10 largest real estate companies in my portfolio, nine of the world's 10 largest banks, and seven of the world's 10 largest chemical companies... and not a one of 'em is an American outfit. Domestic US? **Bo-ring!**'

"Now, which one of them is right? The genuinely amazing thing to me is that they're **all** right. These are all major investment themes that serious investors like us want very much to own for the long haul. But the real beauty in a portfolio context isn't just that our managers are all right, it's that **they're all right at different times.** All of these themes tend to run on different cycles: they all have both their days in the sun and their days in the doghouse **on different days.**

"I could—and would love to—go into as much detail about these individual management styles, and how they cycle, as you want me to. But for all practical purposes, this is way more than 90% of everything that really matters. You can almost **feel** that that's right, can't you?"

Once again, you see here an effort to communicate very large concepts in ways that would make Andrew Wyeth ("If you can express it by just one thing...") happy.

▶**Big-Cap Growth.** It don't make no never-mind how good you are at extruding aluminum if nobody's buying cars. *The Lion King* leads to *Pocahontas* leads to *The Hunchback of Notre Dame.* Control of one's own destiny = growth. Kentucky Fried Chicken growing slow in Sheboygan? How about let's build 'em in Shanghai? *Growth rules!* And the bigger the company the more powerfully able to grow: happiness is positive cash flow.

▶**Big-Cap Value.** Doesn't matter how fast something's growing if it takes you 30 years to earn back your investment. The joys of major industry cycles: buy 'em for scrap, sell 'em when they're the bee's knees. Then do it again. One thing good about the cycle. It always...*cycles!*

▶**Small-Cap Growth.** All *real* growth comes from a very low base, an insanely great idea, and young, hungry entrepreneurs who can't hear the word "can't." You don't want today's Microsoft, you want *tomorrow's.* And look how many candidates you can buy for the price of one behemoth!

▶**Small-Cap Value.** Oh, the joys of little, under-researched, nuts-and-bolts companies feeding off the megatrends of downsizing and outsourcing, among others. Overlooked value, misperceived change: the meat and potatoes of small-cap value. Don't buy Ford below book value; buy two dozen of its suppliers below book value for the same money. Bigger cyclical downs, *bigger cyclical ups!*

▶**International.** Quite simply: where the action is. Two *billion* people freed from the dungeon of communism since 1989, and they've got a lot of catching up to do. The megatrend of privatization. Miss it at your (and especially your heirs') peril. Don't try to figure out where the Mexican stock market will be in six months; think of where the Mexican economy will be in 10 years. Be there (and in Peru, and Poland, and South Korea, and India) or be square.

▶This is "way more than 90% of everything that really matters." The Truth vs. the facts; try, if at all possible, not to answer questions (a) that nobody's asked you and (b) that don't really matter anyway. *Always listen to what you can leave out!*

And so, finally, to the excellent advisor's favorite point: what you have to give up to get all the wonderful things you get in this portfolio.

5 **Risks/Limitations/What the investment isn't.** "Now, while you're contemplating all of the benefits of a broadly diversified portfolio of great companies, managed for you by five high-quality, disciplined professionals—each a true believer in his or her own approach—let me make sure you're clear on what this portfolio **can't** do.

"First and probably most important, you can't diversify yourself completely out of market risk. It's certainly true that these five excellent portfolios will run on different cycles. But be assured that—in a major, generalized US stock market decline—all your US portfolios are almost certainly going to go down…though some may go down a lot less than others, and the international stuff may not go down much, if at all.

"You have to see that the fundamental reality of equity investing is always true: the sometimes significant temporary downs are the price of the permanent ups **which, as we've long since agreed, are the only way you and your family can get where you need to go.**

"Diversification may meliorate those temporary downs, but neither diversification nor anything else can eliminate them, **nor would you want it to.** Markets are, in the long run, as nearly perfectly efficient as anything man-made can be. And the reason that equity returns are so far above those of the other asset classes is that an efficient market demands those premium returns in exchange for having to sit through significant declines. **It's a package deal.** Diversification smooths out the peaks and valleys, but it can't change the basic terms of the deal.

"The other major caveat of this or any properly diversified equity portfolio is that it'll never (or at least I don't plan for it to ever) be firing on all cylinders at the same time. When growth is shooting the lights out, value may be in hibernation. Small-company stocks will sometimes blow past big-company stocks like they were standing still. And there'll be times when your international portfolio goes on a great run, just when the American economy is treading water.

"At such times, you're going to feel—let me amend that: you wouldn't be human if you didn't feel—a natural urge to sell the laggard and reinvest the proceeds in the 'winner.' And you can do that, if that's what you're bound and determined to do. It is, after all, your money. I'm the Chairman of the Joint Chiefs of Staff, but you're still the Commander-In-Chief.

"But in doing so, you'll defeat the whole purpose of diversification. That is, in the process of increasing your bet on a hot sector—a bet that will either be right or it won't—for sure you'll have increased the volatility of the portfolio...which is, I think, just exactly what you never want to do.

"The fact that different components of your portfolio are running on totally different cycles is, therefore, an integral part of what you're trying to accomplish. And in fact, if anything you'll want to think about investing new money in the laggards. If you're like most people, that's really going to take some getting used to.

"These are just some of the highlights of what a diversified equity portfolio **can't** do. And I don't want to rush you past any of these genuinely cautionary ideas. If your goal is real wealth with a somewhat smoother ride, I'm convinced that this is the way to go. But it really doesn't matter what I think: do the trade-offs involved here seem right to **you?"**

I'm happy [*nay, proud*] to tell you that Point #5 in this script takes the longest time to recite. The actual elapsed times for the different Points as scripted here are:

Point #1:	**The concept/The fit**	**3 minutes**
Point #2:	**Who/Why I like**	**2 minutes**
Point #3 & #4:	**What it does/How it works**	**3 minutes**
Point #5:	**Risks/Limitations/What it isn't**	**4 minutes**

Now, I know the statement I'm about to make will put many jesuitical purists of post-modern portfolio theory into geosynchronous orbit, but: **it looks to me like this script tells any investor about 90% of what he ever needs to know for a lifetime of successful equity investing in *12 minutes flat.***

And only when the excellent advisor has gotten the prospect to sign off on this entire conceptual approach will she go ahead and present the specifics of the five portfolios. If, at the end of Point # 5, the excellent advisor invites questions, and one of them is, "Yes, but...what funds do you want me to buy?" her answer is, of course:

"That can't matter yet."

In fact, it hardly matters at all, but to reveal that—true though it surely is—might send the prospect into shock. And besides, the excellent advisor is, just at the moment, making a more narrowly focused point. It is that the particular funding media for this grand strategy can never determine—nor even much influence—the validity of the strategy itself.

Indeed, from the hour in which this 12-minute exposition takes place until the hour when the prospect's children receive his legacies to them, the determinants of total return will probably stack up as follows:

(a) The decision to go all-equity rather than with "asset allocation":	65%
(b) The decision to diversify among the five particular portfolio types above:	10%
(c) The continuing decision (1) not to sell and (2) not to mess with the portfolio structure, regardless of the fears or fads *du jour:*	20%
(d) The decision about which particular investments to make within each of the five portfolio types:	5%
Total:	100%

Purists will demand to know how I arrived at this breakdown, and will—I hope and expect—be incensed to learn that I made it up. Purists, you see, put 95% of their effort into the 5% of this equation having to do with the selection of individual investments, e.g. will Small-Cap Value Raindrop A get to the bottom of the window before Small-Cap Value Raindrop B? Hence, purists form a particular and peculiar subculture within the larger Journeymen tribe: they are people whose anxiety causes them to spend a hugely disproportionate amount of their time and energy trying to *be right*, rather than trying to *do good*. But I digress.

In the end, it will not matter which general you put in charge of the China-Burma-India theater, nor to which admiral you assign command of the Pacific Fleet. These decisions may affect the course of the war, but not its outcome: the Allies are going to win, and the Axis is going to lose.

Similarly, real wealth always flows downstream from decisions (a), (b) and (c), above; it never flows upstream from (d). Your prospect's daughter's daughter will never be able to go to Duke rather than N.C. State because of which small-cap value fund the prospect bought. She'll be able to go to Duke because he bought *any* small-cap value fund (plus *any* example of the other four equity portfolios in the Five-Pointed Equity Star in this chapter) rather than the very best bond funds on earth.

Thus the excellent investment advisor makes the point that the more committed you are to a lifetime investment strategy based in whole or large part on a diversified equity portfolio, the less important "relative performance" becomes in the great scheme of things.

It should be clear to anyone, after 15 years of this most glorious anomaly, The Mother Of All Bull Markets that began in 1982, that all "performance" numbers are of marginal utility at best. There is absolutely nothing that could more reliably set the newly evangelized equity investor up to fail than extrapolation of these 15 years. As rampantly long-term bullish as I am, I can't even conceive of a second 15 years that could combine the fabulous returns and evanescent volatility of the last 15. But even if it's possible, it doesn't seem probable. And the best investment plans can only be based on reasonable probability.

Well, then, how about "performance" records of more than 15 years? My answer: in the near future, you'll almost certainly be working with (if you don't already have) different portfolio managers than the ones responsible for records going back 20 years and more.

And, of course, to the extent that you try inferring anything from periods much *less* than the last 15 years, you begin to see "performance" as, if anything, a perverse indicator. One of my prized possessions is this delicious chart, which lists the average returns of the top-performing six fund categories (by investment objective) for the five years through February 28, 1989...and then compares them to the *next* five years, through the same date in 1994:

Objective	1989 5-Year Results	1994 5-Year Results
1. International Stock	20.60%	9.37%
2. Equity Income	14.31%	11.21%
3. Growth & Income	14.20%	11.90%
4. Growth	13.30%	13.90%
5. Small Company	10.26%	15.87%
6. Aggressive Growth	8.91%	16.31%

How much do you love it? There's a perfect inverse correlation in the five-year rankings. And need I tell you that the 1989 net sales of international stock funds went up (in percentage terms) twice as much as sales of aggressive growth funds?

"Performance" is a toxic fiction. It almost never says what people think it says, and, in a very real sense, it may not say anything at all. But whatever it says is the smallest piece of the puzzle in the quest for real long-term wealth. And it is the one variable which most readily distinguishes the journeyman from the excellent advisor. The journeyman hides behind "performance;" the excellent advisor rises above it. The journeyman will cry, "But if you don't sell 'performance,' how will you prove to your prospects that yours are superior recommendations?" The excellent advisor knows that when you've trained people to trust you, you don't have to prove anything. And that if they don't trust you, it won't matter what you can "prove;" they still won't trust you.

The excellent investment advisor knows that it is not his primary job to know which investments are going to "outperform" other, similar investments. His primary job is to make sure his clients reach their goals. And it is never necessary to do the former in order to do the latter.

The excellent advisor commits to helping her clients achieve financial independence and/or multigenerational wealth, as the clients define those terms. She never says she's going to make them the richest people on their block. In the process of achieving real wealth, the equity/debt "asset allocation" is the most important issue. How the clients handle the emotional and financial stresses (in that order) of owning equities is second. The particular types of equities in a diversified portfolio are third. And "relative performance" is somewhere between fourth and a total non-starter.

Yes, but...

what about the person who simply can't stand a portfolio that's basically all equities, less a couple of years' living expenses in a money market fund? What if people simply insist on having some of their capital in bonds?

Let me turn the question around, and ask you: why bonds? I'm perfectly willing to listen to reason on this [*I'm zealous, but not doctrinaire*]; so go ahead and make the case for bonds.

1 **You're guaranteed to get your money back; they're safer.** Sorry, no. You're not guaranteed to get your money back; you're promised—by some entity of greater or lesser creditworthiness—to get back the

same number of units of the currency you lent out. But currency isn't money, and the longer your time horizon, the more de-coupled currency and money become. In the long run, the only sane definition of "money" is "purchasing power." That investment is "safer" which more efficiently preserves "money," as newly defined. *Ergo*, equity is "safer" than debt.

2 **Well, at least you're sure of what you're going to get.** Quite right; you're (reasonably) sure that a long-term loaner will get (ballpark) half the return of an owner. You're also reasonably sure—to the extent that postwar history is any guide—that after inflation and taxes, you'll barely tread water. At this writing, the 50-year record, net of inflation and an assumed 28% tax rate, is: stocks 5.50% a year, long-term government bonds 0.8%, T-bills 0.3%. Efficient markets exact a truly terrifying price for "sureness." You can be "sure," or you can build wealth. But in this world you can never do both. (Matthew 25: 14–30)

3 **My clients need income.** No, your customers want income. Clients listen to The Truth (even—and especially—when it's counterintuitive) and invest for total return. Then they systematically withdraw a percentage of their account which is considerably less than their long-term total return. This provides both a rising income stream and a rising capital base, neither of which is available from bonds. See the next chapter, when—as Hercule Poirot always says as he assembles the suspects in the drawing room—all will be revealed.

4 **But...but...my clients are just too scared to own a 100% equity portfolio.** Yes, exactly. Now that we've got all the empty rationalizations out of the way—now that all those dogs that won't hunt are back in their kennels—let's have the guts to look at the real issue, here. J.P. Morgan was fond of reminding his partners, "A man always has two reasons for the things that he does: a good one, and the real one." "Safety" and

"income" are the investor's stated reasons to prefer bonds to stocks; fear is the real reason.

There is, as I've said before, such a thing as a good irrational decision. And even I will admit that the inclusion of *some* bond exposure in a portfolio can be a good irrational decision...up to a point. But past the point where bonds provide near-term emotional comfort at the cost of long-term financial harm, the excellent advisor has to be prepared to take a walk. Respecting fear is one thing; pandering to it is quite another. Letting an investor pay you to disserve him (or to assist him in disserving himself) and his family isn't compatible with the ethic of the excellent advisor. And it's that ethical decision which, I believe, bonds always force you sooner or later to make.

In Summary

☞ A gigantic percentage of your total lifetime return will be driven by what percentage of your capital you allocate to the asset class whose long-term return is 10.5%, rather than to the two whose long-term returns are 5.7% and 3.7%, respectively. Now *there's* a Blinding Glimpse of the Obvious for you.

☞ "Higher returns with lower risk" isn't modern portfolio theory, nor even ancient portfolio theory. It's voodoo portfolio theory. "Asset allocation" (with portfolio rebalancing) *can* provide somewhat lower returns than equities with disproportionately less volatility...if that's what floats your boat. But the fundamental logic of "asset allocation"—give away some of your permanent ups in order to miss some of the temporary downs—ain't rational.

☞ The more you try to minimize "volatility" (through "asset allocation" or whatever), the more you build it up in the investor's mind as being equivalent to risk, which it's simply not. So when—not if—stocks and bonds go into the tank at the same time, the odds are that the loss-averse investor will still panic. "Asset allocation" is a palliative for the symptom rather than a cure for the disease: fear.

Equity diversification, geographically and by
style, can deliver some of the benefit of "asset allo
(i.e. some reduction of overall portfolio volatility) withou
its terrible price in permanently foregone return.

You can construct an extremely well-diversified equity portfolio out of five components: big- and small-cap growth, big- and small-cap value, and international.

Beware overdiversification (which Peter Lynch calls "diworseification"). There is a limit to how thin you can slice a salami. At some point, you diversify your way into a very unwieldy, very expensive index fund.

In presenting a truly diversified portfolio, **The fit**—the way the different components interact, with some "not working" while others are, *deliberately*—is the Megaconcept. If they all soar at the same time, they'll all dive at the same time, which would defeat the purpose.

Different styles give you diversification, but different objectives (growth, growth and income, equity income, etc.) may not. Beware overlap.

The concept of equity diversification is: capture the long-term returns, but with portfolio components that run on different (and often countervailing) cycles, so as to obtain some smoothing of the peaks and valleys.

☞ The thing you want most from the managers in a diversified equity portfolio isn't so much genius as discipline. Enough "style slippage" at the wrong time can do diversification in.

☞ The overriding conceptual truth of equity diversification is greater than the sum of all the facts about the particular components of the portfolio. And no one ever became an Excellent Investment Advisor until he learned to rise above the facts.

☞ Your clients can effortlessly own 1000 or more of the best businesses on the planet. As recently as a generation ago, this would have been all but impossible, even for the world's wealthiest investors. Touch the miracle. There'll be plenty of time for the arithmetic later.

☞ Make huge, complex ideas comprehensible to people through *analogy* and *example.* A portfolio is allowed to be "a major work of art, painted on a big canvas." And small-cap growth vs. big-cap growth is allowed to be as simple as, "I could acquire my 50 favorite fast-growing companies *in their entirety* for the same money it would take to buy out McDonald's!"

☞ Diversification can moderate volatility, but nothing can eliminate it. At the end of the day, you still have to pledge allegiance to the temporary downs as the price of the permanent ups.

☞ "Relative performance" (a) doesn't reliably predict anything and (b) has only a marginal effect on an investor's ultimate success. Going with equity diversification rather than "asset allocation" is two-thirds of the battle. Failing to panic and/or to monkey with the portfolio structure because of the fears or fads *du jour* is most of the rest. And the portfolio structure itself is nearly everything else.

☞ After 15 years of the greatest bull market of all time, *all* performance numbers are a statistical fact that's also a moral lie: the next 15 years probably aren't going to look that much like the last 15, so extrapolation of any kind will probably mislead you. Oh, and the next five years almost certainly won't look *anything* like the last five, so "performance" may actually be a perverse indicator.

☞ It isn't the Excellent Investment Advisor's job to know which investments are going to "outperform" other, similar investments (which may actually be unknowable, anyway). Her job is to make sure her clients achieve their goals. The former is in no way essential to the latter.

☞ The real reason people want to own debt instead of equity isn't economic, it's psychological: *fear.* Up to a point, in the real world, the excellent advisor has to make allowances for that fear. Beyond the point where fear begins to doom long-term economic well-being—even if that's what the investor "wants"—it's time for the excellent advisor to saddle up and ride on out of Dodge.

12

Equities and the genius of time

"Things in life will not always run smoothly. Sometimes we will be rising toward the heights—then all will seem to reverse itself and start downward. The great fact to remember is that the trend of civilization itself is forever upward; that a line drawn through the middle of the peaks and valleys of the centuries always has an upward trend."

—**Rev. Endicott Peabody,** headmaster of Groton, quoted by his former student, Franklin D. Roosevelt, in FDR's last inaugural address, January 20, 1945.

It's always seemed to me very poignant that, even as FDR's life drew rapidly to its close—he died just 82 days after this shortest of his inaugural addresses—his thoughts returned to a boyhood lesson in faith in the future.

Dr. Peabody's permanent uptrend line, "drawn through the middle of the peaks and valleys of the centuries," is mirrored in the long-term behavior of equity prices. And it is the permanent upward bias of the trendline, not the often jagged slopes between peaks and valleys, that most concerns the Excellent Investment Advisor and his clients. For, if one has faith in the trendline, the peaks and valleys can be put to very advantageous use. (While without faith in the trendline, the investor will sooner or later give way to panic, and all will surely be lost.)

This chapter explores the interplay of the trendline, the peaks and the valleys throughout all the seasons of an investor's lifetime. We'll focus on three aspects of "equities and the genius of time":

▶*Dollar-cost averaging*—an auto-pilot "market-timing" system that can help you outperform your own money managers, with the only effort required being the discipline of regular investing

▶*Systematic withdrawal*—an equity strategy for potential growth of income and principal throughout retirement

▶*The myth of "bear markets"*—or, if you prefer (and I certainly do), the reality of "big sales"

Dollar-cost averaging is such a hallowed and time-honored device that it has almost degenerated into something of a cliché. Yet it remains underappreciated by most investment advisors and investors, who either don't give full credit to its real powers or ask it to do something it was never meant to do.

The great strength of dollar-cost averaging is, of course, that it knows exactly when to be an extremely aggressive buyer of equities (i.e. when they are absolutely getting killed) and when to be a terribly timid buyer (i.e. when they're soaring to undreamed-of heights and everybody loves 'em). If that were all dollar-cost averaging could do—get investors to behave exactly the way they should, which is exactly the opposite of the way they usually do—it would have to be regarded as heaven-sent.

But that's not all it does. By racing out into the marketplace and buying barrelsful of shares when prices are low, and then tiptoeing out and buying thimblesful of shares at euphoric peaks, DCA affords its true disciples a below-average cost, and thus an above-average return. So while most investors underperform their own investments (by piling in relatively late in a major market advance), the DCA devotee actually outperforms his own investments, because he bought a hugely disproportionate number of shares at panic prices.

(You'll find in this undeniable truth yet another reason why investment "performance" is such an abstraction, and how little it has to do with what really counts, which is *investor behavior*. When you know that Americans made net investments of $11 billion in equity mutual funds in the first six calendar months after the 1990 lows, and $118 billion in the first six months of 1996, you've got to know that *investor* "performance" is totally—nay, wildly—unrelated to *investment* "performance.")

Finally—as if anyone could possibly ask DCA to do something else—the more volatile the markets, the better DCA works! "Volatility," the bane of most investors' existence, conspires to make the dollar-cost averaging investor even wealthier.

Here's how it works. We all know that DCA lets you buy more shares when prices are low and fewer when prices are high. If the portfolio experiences increased volatility—higher highs and lower lows—around a trendline, you'll buy even more at the lows and less at the highs.

Say you put $1000 a month into shares of a mutual fund. The fund starts at $10 a share at the beginning of the year, then trades as high as $12, as low as $6, and ends the year back at $10.

Alternatively, imagine that you still invest $1000 a month, but prices are more volatile. Let's say the starting and ending value is still $10, as in the earlier case, but the share prices are $1 higher in the months of uptrend and $1 lower in down months.

Look what happens (see chart). You acquire 7% more shares in the high volatility case, at an average cost that's 6.6% lower. No lifestyle changer, by any means. But enough to suggest strongly that DCA makes volatility your friend, instead of a screaming nightmare from which you can't wake up.

Advantage of DCA Increases with Market Volatility

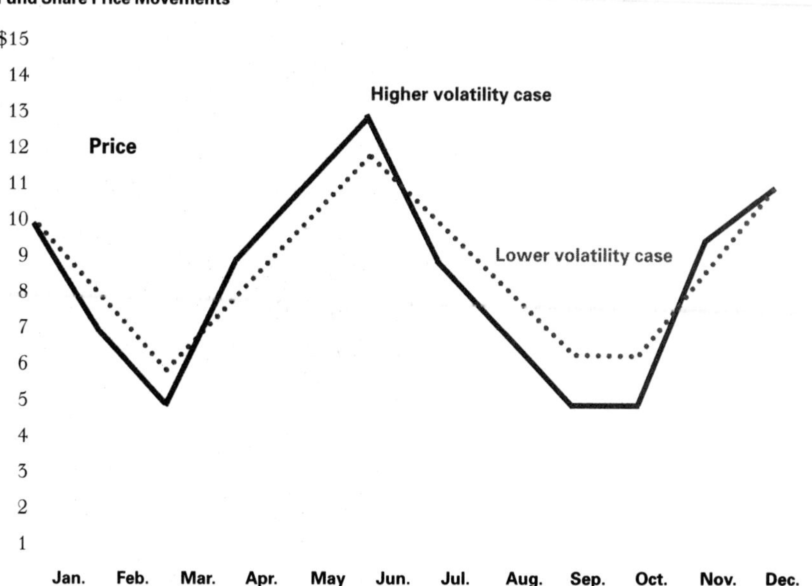

$1000 Systematic Investment Per Month

	Lower Volatility Case		Higher Volatility Case	
Month	Price	Number Of Shares	Price	Number Of Shares
Jan.	$ 10	100	$ 10	100
Feb.	8	125	7	143
Mar.	6	167	5	200
Apr.	8	125	9	111
May	10	100	11	91
Jun.	12	83	13	77
Jul.	10	100	9	111
Aug.	8	125	7	143
Sep.	6	167	5	200
Oct.	6	167	5	200
Nov.	8	125	9	111
Dec.	10	100	10	100
Total shares purchased		1,484		1,587
Average cost per share		$8.09		$7.56

In those elements of your diversified equity portfolio that are inherently most volatile—small-cap and international, to name two—DCA can thus become a major factor in enhancing your return. *The more volatile the style/sector, the higher its built-in return is to begin with, and the more DCA augments that return.*

DCA ♡ VOLATILITY!

Now, suppose you're able to achieve that happiest of circumstances, and select managers who ultimately outperform their indexes in such relatively volatile areas as small-cap growth and emerging markets. Look at the delightful [*and well-nigh inevitable*] chain of outcomes:

1. The indexes in these areas outperform the S&P 500, raising your total portfolio return.

2. The managers outperform their indexes, enhancing total return even more.

3. You outperform your own managers, lifting total portfolio return to new heights.

Most investors ignore the simple beauty of DCA (yet another reason why most investors don't succeed), trying instead to figure out whether Peru is going to outperform Poland, or whether this is the "right time" to get back into Hong Kong, or whether Gronsky's Vietnam Fund is going to outperform Gritsky's. How sophisticated they are; how much smarter than the dumb, happy dollar-cost averager who never got closer to Mexico than a Taco Bell. How distressing, then, that the DCA devotee runs rings around all of 'em. *In his sleep.*

Dollar-cost averaging totally relieves you of the need ever to have a market outlook. You don't have to have any sense of where markets are overvalued or undervalued; you never have to know when they're going to "turn." DCA knows all of those things for you, and always reacts appropriately. "So you and I, Mr. Client, can bask in our ignorance. We'll let people much 'smarter' than we drill themselves into the ground trying to 'time' markets that very few people can understand in the first place. All we know is all we ever need to know:

that we'll automatically become more and more aggressive during panics, and extremely cautious during euphoric booms."

The one situation in which you *don't* want to use DCA is when the client has a relatively large lump sum to invest. Some advisors instinctively look to dollar-cost average such lump sums into the equity markets, feeling that this must be the conservative approach. It isn't. Since US equities go up about 70% of the time, dollar-cost averaging with a lump sum is much more likely to cost you money than to save you money. (As Casey Stengel always said, "You could look it up.")

The probability of your *ever* exacting some kind of a timing advantage from the equity market is virtually nonexistent. I'm sure you've seen the following study done a bunch of different ways, but this is my favorite way of presenting it—and I think the excellent advisor *always* has her favorite way of presenting it near at hand:

> Each and every year from 1960 through 1995, Tom Terrific invested $5000 in the S&P 500 at its low point for the year. John Jerk (probably the brother-in-law of ICA's Louie the Loser) invested $5000 each year at the tippy-top. And Bob Bonus, as his name implies, simply invested his annual bonus in the S&P 500 on July 1 of each year. In other words, Tom had the most perfect timing possible, JJ the worst, and blissful Bob had no timing at all. How'd they end up?
>
> TT: $2,615,866
> BB: $2,476,729
> JJ: $2,197,167

So the difference in return between perfect timing and the most horrific timing imaginable turned out to be a tad more than 1% a year. And if you paid no attention to timing by simply investing at mid-year, you split that difference, *and then some.*

Granted, when a client is sitting there with a $1.1 million rollover—the only seven-figure check with his name on it that he's ever going to see—anxiety may still triumph over arithmetic. There are, as I've said before, such things as good irrational decisions. And feelings are to facts as 19 is to one. Here's one approach:

eia: I want you to be absolutely clear on the fact that, if the entire history of the equity market is any guide, you'll probably be better off investing your lump sum now, rather than trying to scale it in over time. Have I made that clear? Do you need any further demonstration of that?

client: Well...yeah, but...look at the state the world's in...Social Security/the deficit/the balance of payments/Saddam/Boesky/Sheik Yamani/Watergate/Vietnam/Korea/Hitler etc. etc. ...

eia: Wait, please. I'm not arguing with you. ***It always looks like the wrong time to invest.*** I'm simply asking if you can see that, historically, the odds of waiting/scaling in are against you?

client: Yeah, but...

eia: Good. Now—and this isn't the same point at all—have I made it clear to you that ***I personally recommend as strongly as I can that you go ahead and invest now?*** In other words, is it clear to you that I'm not just hiding behind a statistical probability, but that I'm making a personal recommendation to you, based not on numbers but on my own integrity and professionalism?

client: Well, yeah, but...

eia: Good. I just wanted to get those two things on the record. Now, tell me how you feel.

client: I'm just so afraid of making a mistake...

eia: Please, first of all, try to stop being afraid. It's very hard ever to make a good decision about anything when you're afraid. Let's try to narrow the focus of the problem; maybe it'll become a little more manageable. Now, you said you're afraid of making a mistake. How do you define "mistake"?

client: What if I put all the money in, and it goes down?

eia: OK, now we're getting someplace. Do you understand that the values of the great companies can go down, ***but that they can't stay down?***

client: Yes, yes, I do understand that. You've made that clear, and I accept it.

eia: OK, let's keep trying to narrow the definition of "mistake." How about this: I'd feel I'd made a mistake if I invested today, and a year from now my investment had declined X%. What's X, to you?

client: Well, uh, say 20%. Can I say 20%?

eia: It's your money, they're your feelings, and you can say anything you want. I'm here to tell you the absolute, unvarnished truth about investing; I'm not here to edit your feelings. So: down 20% a year from now would feel like a "mistake," yes?

client: [*Visibly breathing easier*] Yes.

eia: OK, that's happened 10 times in the last 50 years. So again, just on the basis of history, there's an 80% chance it's not going to happen. Would you invest 80% of the lump sum today?

client: Gee, I don't know. I'm starting to feel a bit better about this, but 80%...

eia: [*Smiling*] OK, make me an offer.

client: How about...half now, and then we wait and see.

eia: Wait and see what?

client: Well...just...what happens.

eia: With respect, I think that's still a little too vague. How about: 50% now, and the other 50% in equal installments over the next 24 months?

client: [*Really relieved now*] I can live with that.

eia: Sounds to me like we're done, then.

You never, ever, get drawn into a "current events" argument, as we'll see when we get to Q&A/Objections Handling. The larger issue here, of course, is managing anxiety: simply trying to get some reasonable parameters around the investor's unfocused dread, in a therapeutic, non-argumentative way. And getting the investor to do a partially right thing may not be as good as getting him to do the whole right thing. But it sure beats the heck out of arguing with him, to the point where he gets emotionally dug into a commitment to do the wrong thing.

Dollar-cost averaging, as Putnam's Dr. Bob Goodman says in his book *Independently Wealthy*, is "the eighth wonder of the world." It is heaven's own market-timing system for the blissfully clueless, and as nearly effortless a path to the systematic accumulation of wealth as we'll ever have.

As intuitive as dollar-cost averaging may be to you, systematic withdrawal from equities in retirement still seems like a big stretch to most advisors I talk to. Maybe that's because they've never really taken a good hard look at it; maybe it's because they just assume it would be so bitterly counterintuitive to their investors (ah, but won't a real client consider anything you suggest, just because you suggested it?). And maybe this reluctance stems from a fear that systematic withdrawal is potentially DCA in reverse: *selling* barrelsful of shares at panic bottoms, and thimblesful at euphoric tops.

The overriding conceptual problem that most people have with systematic withdrawal is, I suspect, that it involves (at least in the early years) the invasion of principal. And that, to most investors—especially older investors whose financial acculturation is the Depression—is The Mother of All No-Nos.

People have a very visceral instinct to keep their principal intact and to live on their income. The alternative, they fear, is the *de facto* annuitization of their capital: if you spend some of your principal, next year you have even less income, and so have to spend even more principal, and so on, in an awful downward spiral to destitution.

Like most prevailing investment anxieties ("What if I invest now, and the market goes down?"), this one is primarily fueled by an absence of hard numbers. Remember, anxiety is *unfocused* dread; once you reduce it to some kind of objective reality, anxiety tends to evaporate. (At worst, unfocused anxiety may give way to focused fear, but we can deal with fear. You can never really deal with anxiety; it's like boxing with smoke.)

So, for instance, if you're trying to get 6% a year from a portfolio whose total return is 5.7%, you've got genuine cause for fear: the annuitization issue is a very real one. But if you're trying to get 6% a year from a portfolio whose total return is even remotely close to 10.5%... well, now, that's an entirely different—and infinitely tastier—kettle of fish, is it not?

On the psychological level, this is yet another example of the salutary effect of real numbers on unfocused dread. On the financial level, the point is to stop you from arbitrarily bifurcating (principal vs. interest, dividends vs. capital appreciation) money that's essentially fungible. *Think always in terms of total return*, and the picture should instantly become clear. If you're drawing 6% of the water from a well that's replenishing itself at an average rate of 10½% a year, then it really doesn't matter how much of the water came from rain and how much from snow, now does it? (And once again, here, you see that you can ride into town packing all the numbers you want, and I'll meet you at the OK Corral armed only with my analogies—water from the well, rain vs. snow, and the like. I'll even let you draw first. But I guaran-damn-tee you: you're going home in a pine box.)

My friends at MFS were kind enough to run this illustration of a 25-year $60,000-per-year systematic withdrawal plan from a $1 million hypothetical investment in America's first mutual fund, Massachusetts Investors Trust. The assumptions are that the investment was made at the beginning of 1971, and that the $60,000 was withdrawn at the end of that year, and of every year thereafter. (No provision is made for an initial sales charge, but a 0.35% 12b-1 fee is levied.) Taxes are assumed to be paid from another source. Capital gains and income dividends are reinvested. *Please understand that I'm not making any representation about the future performance of MIT or any other investment.*

Period	Invest	Withdrawal	Dividends Income	Dividends Cap Gains	Dividends Reinvest	Market Value
01/01/71	1,000,000	0	0	0	0	1,000,000
12/31/71		60,000	35,619	72,363	107,982	972,171
12/29/72		60,000	34,812	188,979	223,791	1,168,358
12/31/73		60,000	35,611	0	35,611	947,350
12/31/74		60,000	47,809	13,231	61,040	666,059
12/31/75		60,000	32,354	0	32,354	812,105
12/31/76		60,000	31,468	14,256	45,724	940,261
12/30/77		60,000	45,989	18,153	64,142	788,997
12/29/78		60,000	38,756	26,770	65,526	807,691
12/31/79		60,000	43,324	0	43,324	897,161
12/31/80		60,000	60,378	27,254	87,633	1,087,908
12/31/81		60,000	53,709	73,273	126,982	968,126
12/31/82		60,000	56,521	76,139	132,660	1,090,286
12/30/83		60,000	50,577	91,252	141,829	1,228,854
12/31/84		60,000	54,936	132,941	187,877	1,287,368
12/31/85		60,000	57,115	51,985	109,100	1,476,499
12/31/86		60,000	67,305	371,056	438,362	1,838,941
12/31/87		60,000	60,200	208,648	268,848	1,916,311
12/30/88		60,000	67,208	140,925	208,133	2,055,276
12/29/89		60,000	83,917	230,030	313,947	2,737,679
12/31/90		60,000	86,905	170,201	257,106	2,674,976
12/31/91		60,000	85,312	300,988	386,300	3,354,874
12/31/92		60,000	83,025	550,441	633,466	3,542,941
12/31/93		60,000	112,399	487,175	599,574	3,838,433
12/30/94		60,000	82,749	362,465	445,213	3,739,333
12/29/95		60,000	173,935	310,065	484,000	5,150,495

Of course, you could also have taken more than $60,000 a year—and might very well have had to after the inflationary spiral of the '70s. And, as you can see, you had plenty of room to do so.

At your lowest point, after the 1973–74 holocaust—the greatest secular "bear market" of the postwar period—you were down to two-thirds of your original capital. And, given how long it took the market to recover (the Dow was 1003 on November 14, 1972, and 1004 on October 12, 1982), you weren't solidly even again for quite a while. But then you went on to quintuple your principal. (Even if you knock off the *annus mirabilis*—the year of miracles, 1995—you still nearly quadrupled it. And, come to think of it, if you didn't knock off '73–'74, why should you knock off '95?) This is the pure essence of "equities and the genius of time." *And in it, you see that the power of equities is not just creative, but* ***curative.***

I invite you to have this analysis done for you in any or all of the venerable mutual funds which have been around for a comparable length of time, and to which people might very well have committed their life's savings a quarter of a century ago—just before the most nightmarish period in modern times. And just in case you're still afraid you're getting sandbagged in some way, let me tell you that the same exercise—$1,000,000 invested, $60,000 a year withdrawn—in the S&P 500 stock index (if you could have done this, which you couldn't) would have yielded an account value on December 31, 1995, of $6,374,060.

Still, the critical issue remains that, although the well may be replenishing itself at an *average* rate of 10½% a year, there will always be periods of drought. No rain, no snow, no precipitation of any kind. Indeed, at times the water level in the well is actually falling. At such times, your drawing out a fixed percentage of what *used* to be there is really going to put a big dent in the water level. The question is: *does the well ever run dry?* In other words, if you're doing systematic withdrawal in a so-called "bear market," can you run out of money?

The answer is: sure you can, *if* the "bear market" is deep enough, *and* if it's long enough, *and* if you're withdrawing a large enough percentage of your original investment, *and*—most importantly—*if you don't hit the brake before you hit the wall.*

Let's say you put your million smackers in the S&P 500 right at the top in January 1973—the month that the decade-long Night Of The Long Knives began. And let's say further that you took out 7%, or $70,000, every year thereafter. By 1991, you were out of money. (Of course, if you'd bought bonds, you'd lost about two-thirds of your purchasing power in the same period, so there were no really happy outcomes available to you. Again, you just got to pick which caliber bullet you wanted to get shot with.)

This is, however, the worst-case scenario since the unpleasantness of 1929. And I'm constrained to point out that in January 1973 the stock market—especially for the nifty fifty growth stocks—made the Tulip Mania look like a church picnic, with such "one-decision" stocks as Disney, McDonald's and Polaroid sporting p/e multiples between 75 and 90.

At 5% withdrawal, you're historically OK: worst case, over any 20-year period since 1960, you made a little money; best-case you made a lot of money. And a 6% withdrawal rate from the Lipper Growth and Income Fund Index back to 1965 gave you an ending value of $133,869 in the worst period and $914,682 in the best.

This is not to suggest that 5% is "safe," 7% is "risky," and 6% is somewhere in between. It's just that the higher the level of withdrawal, the more you're counting on getting average rain and snowfall most all the time. You're minimizing your margin for error, which isn't something smart people do.

My answer is simply to try not to get either financially or emotionally locked in to any one withdrawal rate. **And above all, when you're doing systematic withdrawal, be sure to have those two years' living expenses in a money market fund.** That way, you never have to hit the wall. Even in the 1973–74 holocaust, if you simply shut off your systematic withdrawal plan once your account value was down 20%, lived on your reserve fund, and didn't start withdrawing again until you were back up to 80% of your original account value, you emerged nearly unscathed, and went on to make a great deal of money. (Have your favorite fund folks gin up this illustration for you. It may take 'em a while, but you—and even they—may be amazed at the results.)

Systematic withdrawal asks the investor to have a fairly high tolerance for ambiguity—higher than most folks instinctively have (which is why most folks ain't rich). So the keys to making it work are [*what else?*] the unflagging faith and patient counsel of the Excellent Investment Advisor. The particular fund, or portfolio of funds, chosen for a systematic withdrawal plan doesn't make the critical difference. Even the percentage rate of withdrawal doesn't make the critical difference. **You make the difference.**

And no matter what your methodology for systematic withdrawal may be, please see that, over a quarter century and more of retirement, it offers the highest probability of *real* (net of inflation and taxes) success. *A totally fixed-income investment strategy in a rising-cost world is suicide.* Trust to equities and the genius of time.

We come now to that most vexing issue in equity investing: the phenomenon which the journeyman thinks of as a "bear market"—a temporary decline in the prices of stocks (though not necessarily in the values of companies) of 20% or more.

The last word on "bear markets," as on so many other major issues of life, is Shakespeare's (in *As You Like It*, II. i. 12–18):

> "Sweet are the uses of adversity,
> Which, like the toad, ugly and venomous,
> Wears yet a precious jewel in his head;
> And this our life exempt from public haunt
> Finds tongues in trees, books in the running brooks,
> Sermons in stones, and good in everything.
> I would not change it."

"Sweet are the uses of adversity," echoes the Excellent Investment Advisor, and above all, "I would not change it." For he is in possession of the supreme secret that lies at the heart of the genius of time:

The excellent investment advisor knows that all "bear markets" are, in actuality, "big sales."

Dr. Peabody's permanent uptrend line, "drawn through the middle of the peaks and valleys of the centuries," is the key concept here. Major declines in stock prices are cyclical, temporary and absolutely necessary. And they always, *always* afford the excellent advisor and her clients the opportunity to add to their holdings in portfolios of great companies *when the values and the yields of those companies are most attractive—i.e. when prices are lowest.* As Sir John Templeton has always said, the best time to be buying stocks is "when others are urgently and anxiously selling them." For it's always necessary to have a bad seller in order to make a good buyer. And, as Wall Street has long observed, "A bear market is a period of time during which common stocks are returned to their rightful owners."

In order to establish a frame of reference for this discussion, let's look at the life cycle of the modern bear: a natural history of the major declines (minimum 20%) since the end of WWII.

A Natural History of the Modern Bear

Beginning		*Ending*			
Date	*DJIA*	*Date*	*DJIA*	*% Decline*	*Days*
05/29/46	212.50	5/17/47	163.21	–23.2	353
04/06/56	521.05	10/22/57	419.79	–19.4	564
12/13/61	734.91	6/26/62	535.76	–27.1	195
02/09/66	995.15	10/07/66	744.32	–25.2	240
12/03/68	985.21	5/26/70	631.16	–35.9	539
01/11/73	1051.70	12/06/74	577.60	–45.1	694
09/21/76	1014.79	2/28/78	742.12	–26.9	525
04/27/81	1024.05	8/12/82	776.92	–24.1	472
08/25/87	2722.42	10/19/87	1738.74	–36.1	55
07/16/90	2999.75	10/11/90	2365.10	–21.2	87

Yes, I know, the 1956–57 event technically doesn't count, because it isn't quite a 20% decline. But let me assure you that, in this CNBC/six o'clock news/short-attention-span era, even a nice, gentle 19.4% sandpapering that went on relentlessly for 18 months would more than do the trick. It's my book, and I say this one counts.

Before we go on to state some general conclusions about the necessity and evanescence of such disturbances, there are a few things implicit in these numbers that need highlighting.

▶The average of these 10 declines is 28.4%, which is no laughing matter. The psychological strains involved in watching upwards of a third of one's capital melt away—and not the temporary financial setback itself—are the undoing of many equity investors. The financial issues are easy to deal with: either buy more, or stop reading the paper, or both. But the financial facts aren't the real problem, since feelings (in this case, of incipient panic) are to facts as 19 is to one.

▶These things seem to happen on an average of·about once every five to six years. [*Or at least that's been they way to bet.*] Over the long investment time horizons we're talking about in this book, then, people are going to see a lot of them. Training equity investors to withstand major declines thus becomes a critical (if not *the* critical) element in the client relationships of the excellent advisor. (And it is in chickening out of doing this that the journeyman sets his customers—and himself—up to fail.)

▶The average duration of the first eight of these occurrences is 448 days, or roughly 15 months. (And even that statistic begs the question of how long the market took to get even.) When you add in the insta-bears of 1987 and 1990, which you just about missed if you blinked, you shorten the average by three months. But you're still looking at an average decline lasting about a year. The message: maybe we've entered a "new era" in which a bear's life cycle is nearly as short as a mayfly's...but maybe we haven't. *These things usually go on much, much longer than they have in the last 15 years.* (They're temporary, but they sure as hell aren't *momentary.*) And since nearly 85% of the net purchases that have ever been made in the 70-year history of equity mutual funds have been made since the October '90 lows, it isn't reasonable to expect that most people know that. Again, training your clients to deal with fairly long periods of negative return is essential to their and your success.

The obvious solution—and what an elegant solution it would be—is simply to get out of the market somewhere near the beginning of one of these declines, and to re-enter the market rather nearer the bottom. The stark reality that no one has ever been able consistently to do anything like this should tell you that it can't be done.

In addition to the fact that tops and bottoms are impossible to "call," you have to realize that a huge percentage of the market's gains come in the big breakaway upsurges immediately following major bottoms. (December '74–January '75 and August-September '82 are classic examples.) In fact, although this statistic is not without its element of hokiness, if you missed the 40 best months of the last 40 years (through '95), your annual (index) return dropped from 11.4 percent to 2.7 percent. The bottom line: *the only way to be sure of catching all of the permanent ups is to resign yourself to riding out all of the temporary downs.*

Which, in the great scheme of things, is a small price to pay for the real financial independence/multigenerational wealth that only equities have historically provided. Yet it is precisely the emotional inability of most people to pay this price which explains why most people have managed, against overwhelming odds (40 to 6000 in the worst six decades of all time), not to become wealthy.

The whole point here is that it's the psychological stress of major market declines—and not the declines themselves—with which the excellent advisor must deal. So, with the cold statistical information on the modern bear as a backdrop, you need to develop a framework of proper attitudinal and behavioral approaches to the cruel necessity of major declines.

The perception that you have to keep uppermost in your mind in counseling investors about major market declines is that *Americans, God bless 'em, are totally unable to distinguish between fluctuation and loss.* Let somebody's NAV decline 21.2%, and he'll call you and say, "I've (BLANK) 21.2% of my money!" The missing verb form is, of course, "lost." In this investor's Depression-ravaged, principal-obsessed unconscious, a couple of really bad things have happened. First, he's forgotten that stocks are shares of ownership in great businesses; they've somehow become chips in a sort of malignant casino game. But more to the point of this inquiry, this investor can't tell a temporary decline from a permanent loss. The former you get all the time, and they never last. The latter you get only when you panic and sell. Once again, the excellent advisor's stress-reducing mantra to anyone who'll listen is: *no panic, no sell; no sell, no lose.* "The secret to making money in stocks," as Peter Lynch wrote, "is not to get scared out of them."

With that in mind, here's a belief/behavior system for Big Sales:

1 **All major price declines represent major rallies in value and yield.** Just as all major price advances diminish them. It is the natural function of a wild bull market to extinguish all value. Bull markets inflate prices to, and then beyond, what companies are really worth. At that point, the equity market becomes an exercise in the bigger fool theory. And when markets enter Mode Musical Chairs, all the excellent advisors I know are in agony. They can't tell people *not* to buy equities (how can you tell people not to buy equities and expect to get into heaven?). But, late in a great bull market, you're always dealing with a crisis of rising expectations. And, second only to panic, unreasonable expectations are the next most common cause of failed investment programs.

The excellent advisor is liberated and energized by major price declines. When mutual funds are in net liquidation and there's a bear on the cover of either *Time* or *Newsweek* (to name just a couple of reliable signs that you're nearing a bottom), there's a song in the hearts of all real professionals in this business.

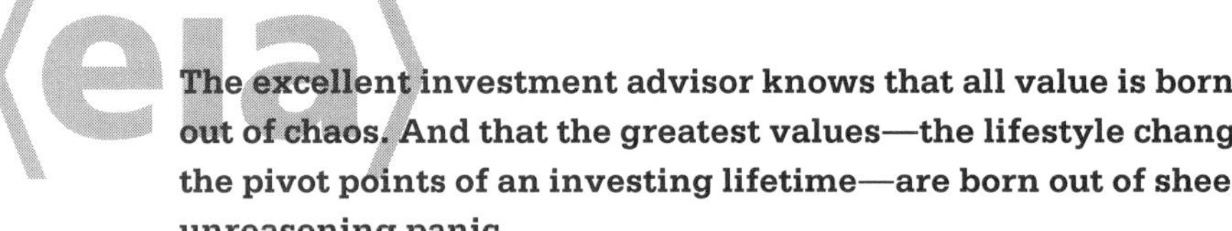

The excellent investment advisor knows that all value is born out of chaos. And that the greatest values—the lifestyle changers, the pivot points of an investing lifetime—are born out of sheer, unreasoning panic.

"I buy," said one of the founders of the Rothschild fortune, "when blood is running in the streets of Paris." But what if they go lower, you may ask? Then you buy some more, and pound the table even more joyously with prospects who said no on the last go-round. The amateur agonizes over identifying the bottom, and always misses it. (The shortest time period measurable by man is the time between when it's "too soon" to buy equities and when it's "too late.") The professional is happy to be operating in a zone of great value, and to let nature take its course. In short, the amateur's bear market is the professional's big sale.

2 **If the declines went away, the returns would go away**. It isn't just that major declines "come with the territory," it's that if those declines didn't happen, there'd *be* no territory as we know it. The returns of equities are purchased at the price of major declines. An efficient market extracts those wonderful returns *as compensation for* the length, depth and frequency of the declines. Reward is always commensurate with risk. And if you want some kind of secular deadening of volatility in the future, you have to see that in the same breath you're asking for returns below the historic norms.

TNSTAAFL [*which my children's mother pronounces "Tinstaffel," with the accent on the first syllable*]: *There's No Such Thing As A Free Lunch.* A six-year period like 1991–96, where the equity market goes up something like 150% without so much as a 10% decline on a closing basis, isn't a norm. It's a miracle. It has literally never happened before in American history. And, if you're interested in building a business as opposed to placing a bet, you'd probably better assume that it's never going to happen again.

If you want the kinds of returns that equities have historically provided, you must accept the kinds of gut-wrenching declines which the equity markets have historically experienced. It's a package deal. And since you can't have it any other way, *you wouldn't want it any other way.*

The journeyman talks about "good markets" and "bad markets." The excellent advisor talks always about *efficient markets,* and teaches his clients to embrace the cycle of temporary downs and permanent ups as an organic whole.

3 **If you're not finished buying yet, why would you want the market to do anything but go down?** Remember the 52-year-old couple we met a few chapters back, who were starting a 10-year capital-accumulation sprint toward retirement? Can you imagine anything in the world dumber than these folks hoping (or having a journeyman advisor encourage them to hope) that the market will go up from here?

I can certainly understand—and even sympathize with—the poor soul who's already got the only $7 million he's ever going to see in this world. He'd a heck of a lot rather that the market go up than down, and who can blame him? But for the great mass of people who are still trying to build wealth a month at a time—and for the excellent advisor who counsels them—wanting the market to go up is counterintuitive.

The journeyman says, "Buy now, market's going up" **(a)** to demonstrate how little he knows about investing, and about the real work of wealth-building, and **(b)** to remind all who have ears to hear what a pandering, transaction-oriented jerk he is. Of course, he doesn't know whether the market's going up or not—he's just trying to stampede his prospect with a false sense of immediacy.

The reason to buy equities is never what the market's going to do next (which is unknowable anyway); it's what the market is *ultimately* going to do. Equities are ultimately going to go up more than most people are capable of imagining. But patient accumulators should always hope the next move is down.

4 **The excellent advisor always gains market share in down markets.** The converse is, of course, also true: real professionals always lose market share in wild bull markets—to amateurs touting the highest returns, and to the malignant fiction of do-it-yourself. "Financial genius," John Kenneth Galbraith said, "is a short memory in a rising market."

Bull markets trivialize the excellent advisor's caution (born of long experience), and reward the recklessness born of inexperience. So, even though the excellent advisor is doing more business in a bull market—how could one not? —I assure you she's losing market share.

But when markets blessedly decline, the newly minted journeyman, who's never actually seen big downticks before, does his deer-in-the-headlights act. He stops calling his clients, which embitters them; needless to say, he's long since stopped prospecting.

The professional knows that periods of great investor distress are precisely the occasions for him to demonstrate his tremendous added value. Experience, calm, encouragement, opportunism, steadiness—those are the values the professional brings to the table in a bear market. And they're exactly the qualities of which the investor suddenly feels most in need.

Put another way, the amateur obsesses about how upset his clients are, and he freezes up. The professional obsesses about how upset *everybody else's clients are.* And he goes after them with renewed vigor. Suddenly he's writing a letter to everybody in his prospect card file—a letter full of warmth, encouragement...and the scent of bargains! (And, of course, he's following each and every letter up with a phone call, because just sending out letters is non-prospecting.)

The excellent advisor is also giving as many seminars as he can, as fast as he can. And he's packing them in, with the topic: "Your Investments: What You Should Do **Now.**" Because the value-added professional knows that the newly chastened investor just wants someone to tell him what to do now.

Just find the energy to tell a whole lot of new people what you believe in times like this. Prospecting is, after all, the ultimate numbers game, and your chances of winning that game are greatest when you have the fewest competitors. That only happens in lousy markets. And the lousier the markets get, the more this wonderful outcome happens. A "bear market" is always played on the excellent advisor's home field, with the obvious attendant advantage.

5 **The accounts you pick up in times of adversity will be with you for a very long time, and will be great referral sources.** Friendships formed in combat often last a lifetime. And the bonds you form with a new account during periods of great adversity [*"Hang on, buddy; we'll get through this together"*] are often the real emotional ties that make for career-long relationships. (Whereas the bonds that are formed in bull markets are usually based on "performance," and are, therefore, no bonds at all.)

Moreover, since you'll have repositioned the account in times of low prices, your recommendations will probably look very good before too long, and that really gets the referral machine rolling. The client's mind-set is, "This is the person who was not only there for me in my hour of darkness, but who got me to buy stuff that subsequently soared." You'll find that he has a hard time keeping this to himself.

You can see from this list of beliefs/behaviors concerning Big Sales that, as in every other aspect of what we do, your own attitudes govern what's going to happen to you and to your clients. Once you've accepted that there's no real way both to enjoy equities' long-term return and to avoid the significant temporary price declines, you're free to choose the way you process the experience of those declines.

You can try to figure out *when* and *why* a decline will end (ceding the agenda to the investor, who asks precisely these unanswerable questions); that way lies anxiety, confusion, anger, fear, and capitulation—right at the bottom. Alternatively, you can profess serene and total ignorance of when and why a decline will end, because you're in possession of something much more valuable: the unshakable faith *that* it will end.

Granted, I'm the product [*and possibly the victim*] of my experience. But I remember a 10-day period in October 1973—right around my 30th birthday, in fact—when **(a)** OPEC tripled the price of oil, and embargoed its sale to the United States, and **(b)** the Vice President of the US pleaded *nolo contendere* to one felony count of tax evasion, and resigned his office. In sum, the country was simultaneously rocked by the greatest economic and constitutional crises of the postwar period.

At the time, no one could say *how* or *when* those crises would be resolved—as you'll see by looking at the free-falling chart of stock prices during those days. But if you just had faith *that* they'd end—that Dr. Peabody's permanent uptrend line had not, in fact, been broken—you were buying when everyone around you was "urgently and anxiously selling." *Knowledge* of the future is always unavailable, most maddeningly so in times of great crisis. *Faith* in the future is limitlessly available—even journalism can't take it away from you if you refuse to give it up—and can be used to purchase great value in equities, just when things look worst.

And, speaking of journalism, perhaps we should take a moment, here, and review its always pernicious effects. Journalism **(a)** always gets it wrong, and **(b)** manifests a relentless bias toward the negative. When unemployment reached 8.9 million in January 1992, journalism shrilly announced that *the number of people out of work* was at its highest since 1983. This was narrowly true, but meaningless: the labor force had grown by about 14 million people in the interim. When the Dow went down 161 points one Friday in March 1996, every newspaper and anchorperson in the country called it "the third biggest one-day decline in market history." Again, this was true only in terms of the raw number of Dow points involved, which, since the market was so much higher than it had ever been, was a big number. In percentage terms—i.e. in the only terms that count—that decline was barely in the top 100 one-day hits.

All through the layoffs and downsizing of 1992–96, even as the unemployment rate kept going lower and lower, all journalism could talk about was the number of jobs, and I quote, "lost." (The nadir of this "story" was *Newsweek's* "Corporate Killers" cover article in February 1996. The "killers" included the CEOs of IBM and AT&T.) The unemployment rate was telling you that the huge preponderance of laid-off people *had* to be getting re-absorbed into the work force (if not at the same salaries). But even the venerable *New York Times* elected to ignore this.

In addition to its inherent negativity, journalism's very short time horizon (day-to-day for newspapers, minute-to-minute for CNBC and its ilk) is the enemy of all truth about investing, which is long-term. The closer you get to the markets, the more facts you're deluged with, and the less truth you can see. And remember: it isn't journalism's job to make people good investors. It's their job to keep people coming back for more journalism. And since bad news is good copy, you'll always see a bear on the cover of *Time* and/or *Newsweek* right at the bottom. (Although, in fairness, I should point out that you'll usually see a bull on their covers at the top.)

I suppose my all-time favorite piece of financial journalism will always be *Business Week*'s classic "The Death of Equities" cover article (subtitled "How inflation is destroying the stock market"). It appeared on August 13, 1979—a day on which the Dow closed at 875.26—and said (among other gems), "For better or worse, then, the US economy probably has to regard the death of equities as a near-permanent condition..." If you didn't know that the biggest bull market of all time was on the horizon *before* August 13, 1979, you certainly could have known it when you'd finished reading this howler.

Suffice it to say that, when you're trying to restore your clients' sense of faith in the future during a major market decline, journalism isn't going to help. And you'd better be prepared for this going in.

The best preparation that you can give clients for future Big Sales is, of course, a review of what their investments have done during previous downdrafts.

If you've ever taken an ocean cruise, you know that the first day you're on a ship, the entire ship's company does a lifeboat drill. You're shown exactly which lifeboat has been assigned to you, and you practice the route you would take to get from your cabin to your lifeboat.

The crew doesn't say the ship is going to sink. [*You'd get off if they did.*] They don't warn you, as you sail out of some tropical port, to be on the lookout for icebergs. They simply say, in effect, "Here is all you need to know in order for you not to panic. And if you don't panic—regardless of what happens—**you'll be OK."**

When you're creating an equity portfolio for a new client, or just reviewing your existing portfolios, please consider the ways in which the record of the last 15 years masks rather than manifests the reality of normal market setbacks. The first eight modern bears averaged 448 days from peak to trough; the '87 decline was over in little more than one-tenth that time, and the '90 selloff had less than 20% of the bear's "normal" life span.

Moreover, these two most recent hits happened in the middle of such otherwise terrific years that, from today's vantage point, they're all but invisible. There are hundreds of thousands of Americans walking around out there, blissfully unaware that they own equity mutual funds that went down 40% and more in the three months that ended on Monday, October 19, 1987. You see, in the first seven months of the year, those funds had gone *up* just about 40%.

So, after the biggest crash in stock prices of modern times, they were about even on the year. And on Tuesday, the funds started back up again, ending the year, just to pick a number off a bus, up 2%. The 1990 affair was a mini-replay: lots of funds that went down 25% in the 90 days through October 11 ended the year down a couple of points. So you've got investors studying, on a calendar year basis, the entire last 15 years—which in this short-attention-span era seems almost like a period of geologic time. And they say, "I see how this works: in a good year, like '95, you're up 37%. In a bad year, like '90, you're down 2%. I can handle that; *sign me up.*"

In other words, calendar-year "performance," statistical fact and moral lie that it is, is virtually guaranteed to create a false sense of security, which sets the investor up to fail. The excellent advisor's antidote: lifeboat drills.

At the very least, show your clients and prospects the actual peak-to-trough declines of their investments in 1987 and 1990. If there are elements of their portfolios that are particularly interest rate-sensitive (REITs and utility funds, to name two obvious examples), make sure you also cover the peak-to-trough hit from October 1993 through March 1994. (This period, which tends to be hidden by the fact that it's divided between *two* otherwise pretty good years, marks a huge interest rate spike—the yield on the long Treasury bond went up 50%—with a concomitant swan-dive in prices.) If you're getting people into emerging markets (in general, and Mexico in particular), see that you elucidate *those* hits in very vivid detail. Finally, your high-tech/NASDAQ-heavy holdings demand close attention to the meltdown that climaxed in July 1996.

The bottom line: *do not allow anyone to get surprised* by the perfectly normal, cyclical, temporary declines which are the price of success in equity investing. Let people touch the savagery *and also the evanescence* of these hits. Let 'em see that, even though the ship may stop once in a while to take on ice, it ultimately sails serenely on to their destination. No surprise, no panic. **No panic, no sell. No sell, no lose.**

And that is well and truly the genius of time.

In Summary

☞ The peaks and valleys don't count. The permanent uptrend line drawn between the peaks and valleys is all that counts. The excellent advisor is always empowered by the uptrend line; the journeyman is always victimized by the peaks and (especially) the valleys.

☞ Dollar-cost averaging is heaven's own "market-timing" system for the blissfully clueless. With it, you can even outperform your own investments. And the only effort required is the discipline of regular investing. Investor behavior, not investment "performance," is the critical variable.

☞ The more volatile the markets, the better DCA works. DCA ♡ VOLATILITY. Just relax, and let "the eighth wonder of the world" do its thing.

☞ Try not to let people dollar-cost average with lump sums; the odds are they'll underperform a one-time investment. On the other hand, don't make a moral issue out of it: better to let people be half right, if that's what it takes to keep 'em from being all wrong.

☞ Systematic withdrawal from equities is usually a better long-term income strategy than investing in debt. As soon as you stop arbitrarily bifurcating "principal" and "income," and start thinking in terms of total return, you see this. A fixed-income investment strategy in a constantly rising-cost world is slow suicide.

☞ Don't even think of doing systematic withdrawal without two years' living expenses in a money market fund. That allows you to shut off your systematic withdrawal plan if the market really gets killed, and to make like a camel and live off your hump until you get to the next oasis.

☞ The Excellent Investment Advisor knows that the phenomenon journeymen call "bear markets" can more appropriately be regarded as "big sales." They afford golden opportunities both to the investor and, in the expansion of her market share, to the excellent advisor.

☞ The average postwar big sale came along on an average of about every six years, took the Dow down over 28%, and went south for more than a year. Training people (at best) to buy more equities during these sales, or (at least) to ignore them, is perhaps the most important function of the excellent advisor. Ignoring this history, and/or telling yourself we're in a "new era," isn't an option.

☞ All major price declines are major rallies in value and yield. Most folks don't see that (which is why most folks aren't rich); they sell harder and harder as prices go lower and lower. All value is born out of just such chaos, and the ultimate values are born out of sheer, mindless panic. Sweet are the uses of adversity.

☞ There are no "good markets" and "bad markets." There are only *efficient markets*, in which the temporary downs are the price you pay for the permanent ups. You wouldn't want it any other way, and that's good, because you can't have it any other way. TNSTAAFL.

☞ If you're not finished buying yet—and the huge preponderance of the people we counsel aren't—why would you want the market to go anywhere *but* down?

☞ "Bear markets" aren't just periods in which stocks are returned to their rightful owners. They're periods when accounts are returned to their rightful advisors. The excellent advisor builds market share precisely when the journeyman is doing his deer-in-the-headlights act. And you almost always overperform in accounts you reposition at panic prices. Now, *why* do you want the market to go up, again?

☞ You'll never know *how* and *why* major declines will end. But the excellent advisor can have perfect faith *that* they will end. And sometimes that's all it takes.

☞ Journalism (a) ain't your friend, (b) always gets it wrong, and (c) has a relentless bias toward the negative. ("The Death of Equities," indeed.) Be prepared for this; there'll be times when yours may be the only positive voice your clients hear for quite a while.

☞ Do lifeboat drills with every single passenger (and prospective passenger) on your ship. The last 15 years have been *so* wonderful—the interruptions *so* brief and evanescent—that a lot of people don't know what a real decline looks like. We have an obligation to make sure they don't find out the hard way.

☞ Gathering assets is only a means to an end; retaining assets is the end. And, in equities especially, insulating the investor from his tendency to panic (because he mistakes temporary decline for permanent loss) is the key to asset retention. "The secret to making money in stocks," said Peter Lynch, "is not to get scared out of them."

13

Zen and the art of Q&A/Objections handling

"(Gertrude Stein) turned to Alice (B. Toklas) and murmured, 'What is the answer?' Alice, unable to answer, remained silent. Gertrude said, 'In that case, what is the question?'"

—**the last words of Gertrude Stein,** as reported by James R. Mellow in his book *Charmed Circle: Gertrude Stein And Company*

• • • • • •

It is somewhere during the Q&A/objections handling process that the investor suddenly makes his decision, one way or the other.

We don't know—and I believe we'll never know—exactly when and why the decision happens. (John F. Kennedy said, "The essence of ultimate decision remains impenetrable to the observer—often indeed to the decider himself.")

By process of elimination, we know that the decision *doesn't* take place during your presentation. Because if it did, there'd *be* no Q&A/objections handling discussion: you'd get to the end of your presentation, and the prospect would say, "Got it. Love it. Makes all the sense in the world. Sign me up." Though this occasionally happens, it doesn't often; at presentation's end, the prospect usually still has a lot on his mind.

Moreover, in the style of presentation I've outlined in the previous chapters—a style that might best be described as minimalist—you'll virtually always leave a lot of questions unanswered. This is not only the outcome *but the intention* of the Universal Five-Point Presentation. Its whole tone and content say, in effect, "I presume you're going to love this as much as I do, and I don't want to bore you with a lot of details."

The excellent advisor actively wants to be asked a lot of questions, because he wants the prospect to see the real depth of his conviction.

I can't imagine that you're too surprised to read that the decision doesn't take place during the presentation. What *may* surprise you is that I don't believe the decision happens during that arbitrary endgame (which exists largely in the fevered imagination of the journeyman) called "closing." Q&A/objections handling is itself a slow, rolling "close," in which—when it's done right—all the prospect's fears dissipate, and are replaced by an act of faith in the excellent advisor and in her elegant portfolio solutions. I say again: *it is during the Q&A/objections handling phase of the interview that the investor suddenly makes his decision, one way or the other.*

So Q&A becomes your one golden opportunity to dispel your prospect's most crippling anxieties and/or fears, *provided you can find out what those anxieties/fears really are.* But that turns out to be far more difficult than it may sound. Because you have to remember, above all else, that people don't make their investment decisions in their intellects. They make those decisions in their emotions, and then use their intellects to gin up a rationale for an essentially non-rational (if not overtly *irrational*) decision.

The same is equally true for Q&A/objections. Someone who is acutely afraid of "losing his money" in an asset class that went up nearly 150 times in five dozen of the worst years in human history—even after you've held up the Ibbotson chart six inches from his nose for an hour—can, I think you'll agree, be safely classified as thinking non-rationally. And not only are most people incapable of expressing their deepest anxieties, they often can't even put their finger on precisely what those anxieties are.

So what you end up getting are proxy objections. People will seize on whatever is roiling the markets lately, and say things like, "I'm not going to do anything right now because of...the plunging value of the dollar; look how it's upset the markets; you can't know where this will all end." This can mean anything from "My dad always used the phrase 'sound as a dollar;' what's happening to the world?" to "I still don't know if I can trust you" to "I'm just so scared, and I don't even know why."

If you take the proxy objection at face value, and answer it with a long, abstruse analysis of the ultimate meaninglessness of short-term currency fluctuations to the long-term value of great companies, **(a)** you're intellectually correct, and **(b)** you end up like Br'er Rabbit, punching and kicking the tar baby until you're totally immobilized. *The stated objection is always the tar baby.* Or, as Gertrude Stein might have said: never mind the answer; you have no reason to believe you even know what the real question is yet.

Thus, the Excellent Investment Advisor's whole approach to the Q&A/objections handling process is based on four essential perceptions:

1 **The question the prospect asks is almost always the wrong question.** No matter how articulately and passionately you present the concept of equities as the mainstay of a retirement income portfolio, I can just about guarantee that you'll sooner or later be asked, "What about the risk of the stock market?" And you know this is a very badly framed question, on at least two counts: it confuses temporary decline with permanent loss, and it falls back on the prospect's life-long equation of risk with principal loss, rather than seeing risk as the extinction of purchasing power. The last thing on earth that the excellent advisor will ever do with as badly framed a question as this is answer it.

2 **The stated objection is virtually never the real objection.** As we've just seen, the prospect may not be able to articulate the real objection, and may not even know what it is. The excellent advisor never punches tar babies and never answers stated objections.

3 **The stated question/objection may not even be a question/objection as such. It may just be covering fire laid down by the prospect as he tries to back away from having to make a decision.** The fear of having to make a decision—fear of commitment, fear of looking foolish, fear of making a mistake—is a very natural emotional phenomenon. Often, prospects aren't really objecting to your plan/portfolio at all; they're trying to re-set the agenda in an unhelpful way, so as to create a set of circumstances under which they can evade a decision. "I want to wait 'til after the election" may very well mean nothing more or less than, "My God, this stranger is asking me to put our family's whole financial future in her hands! How can I be absolutely sure she won't hurt us?" And the better we're doing our jobs—i.e. the more we're trying to get the investor to do pretty much the opposite of what he wants to do—the more predictable this kind of anxiety reaction is. Clearly, the excellent advisor will never respond directly to this smoke.

4 **The stated question/objection may just be a way of testing the depth of the excellent advisor's belief and conviction.** It may, in other words, not be in the least adversarial, but rather a buying signal. The prospect may just be crying out for reassurance—for permission to make the gigantic act of faith that the excellent advisor requires, not least of all because he steadfastly refuses to try to "prove" anything. The excellent advisor's refusal even to engage the stated question/objection may, odd as it sounds, be exactly what the prospect is looking—and hoping—for...even when the prospect doesn't consciously realize that.

The excellent investment advisor simply never cedes the agenda to her prospect. She never, ever directly answers the stated question or objection.

Adherents of Zen Buddhism have a saying: "If you meet the Buddha in the road, kill him." They use this and other startlingly contradictory zingers to short-circuit the linear, "rational" left-brain processes that lead away from, rather than toward, the emptiness of mind that is, to Buddhists, a pre-condition of enlightenment. Since no one would ever dream of harming the Buddha, the admonition to kill him is quite literally unthinkable. Thus, meditation on this saying causes one to stop "thinking" in old, counterproductive ways.

In this same vein, the excellent advisor has a number of potentially startling non-responses to stated questions/objections. These non-responses are designed to **(a)** gently shake the prospect up a little, **(b)** re-set the agenda once again on the advisor's terms (because the last person who re-sets the agenda always wins), **(c)** reinforce the distinct impression that questions/objections don't disturb the advisor's confidence and **(d)** force the prospect to re-think and amplify his own question/objection.

If you want to see a classic example of the excellent advisor's approach to Q&A, and you're not into perusing ancient Buddhist texts, I've got a movie for you to rent. Chances are you may have already seen it, but give it another look. It's *The Fugitive,* starring Harrison Ford as the doctor wrongly convicted of murdering his wife, and Tommy Lee Jones as the Federal marshal hunting him down.

At the end of one great chase scene, Jones has Ford apparently trapped. Ford, believing himself caught, turns around to Jones and blurts out, "I didn't kill my wife." There is a wonderful moment where Jones tries to process this statement, which is probably the last thing he might have expected Ford to say. Then Jones's professionalism—which is to say, his whole identity—recovers, and he delivers the single best line in the movie: **"I don't care."**

Do you see the transcendent beauty of it? Do you see how wonderfully evocative it is of the excellent advisor's response to all stated objections? **"I don't care."** I don't care how many stars some other fund has. I don't care how much money your brother-in-law "lost" in a stock fund in 1987. I don't care that the Dow was off 300 points yesterday. I don't even care if it was *up* 300 points yesterday. Those things are outside my jurisdiction (i.e. they have nothing to do with the marvelous plan/portfolio I've built for you, based on what you've told me about your and your family's needs, hopes, dreams and fears).

I'm a marshal; I catch bad guys. I don't adjudicate guilt or innocence. A guy who was convicted of murder in a court of law has escaped. I've been ordered to bring him in, dead or alive. And I'm gonna bring him in, if it's the last thing I ever do.

Likewise, the excellent advisor: I'm a courageous, ethical, knowledgeable leader (not just a manager) to my clients. No one who doesn't have the same last name as you, Mr./Mrs. Prospect, will ever care about your financial success more than I do. I am the product; the funding media I've recommended to you are good for you *because I recommended them*, period. Financial independence (at the very least) and even multigenerational wealth rain down on those who believe in me. To anyone who, out of heaven-only-knows what crippling emotional disturbance, elects not to believe in me, there's really only one thing I can say (though perhaps not in so many words): **"I don't care."**

The excellent investment advisor is totally impervious to all objections about portfolios, markets, economics and politics...because those things have nothing to do with his product, which is, of course, himself.

By process of elimination, then, let's work our way toward the excellent advisor's non-responses by first looking at what they are not.

The Excellent Investment Advisor never agrees and never argues. Agreeing with an objection, even for the split-second it takes to say the dreaded words "Yes, but..." is certain death. Guy calls and says he has a 4% CD coming due, and he's going to roll it over unless we have something better for him to do with the money. We go racing over to his house with a beautiful, bedrock equity income fund that hasn't had a down year since '74. Guy says, "It isn't guaranteed." And we say "Yes, but..." and we feel ourselves die. Indeed, we always die when we say "Yes, but..." We finish the sentence, but it's essentially a post-mortem reflex.

Fact is, we deserve to die for saying "Yes, but..." First, we're trying to sell better returns to people who aren't primarily (or even secondarily) motivated by returns. If they were motivated by returns they wouldn't be lending money at 4%—would they?

Far more important, we deserve the oblivion which "Yes, but..." surely brings because, in the act of saying those two dreadful words, **we've accepted the client's definitions.** And, in the act of accepting his definitions, we give him permission to roll over the CD—which is what he was really looking for when he called us in the first place. You see, the money won't move until the definitions move. And the definitions won't move until you stop accepting them.

The other absolute no-no during Q&A/objections handling is direct argument, which, as I've already said a number of times in this book, is suicide. The plain fact is that it's an essential part of the human emotional compact that *no one ever has to buy anything from someone who's arguing with him.* Arguments, almost by definition, are therefore unwinnable, no matter how intellectually "right" you are. And argument is the most toxic of all direct responses to a stated objection: it inflates the tar baby to 100,000 times its normal size, like the Sta-Puft Marshmallow Man at the end of *Ghostbusters.*

The excellent advisor's three General Principles of Non-Response are

1. The Non-Answer Answer
2. Answering with a Question
3. "Why?"

Let me give you some examples.

Non-Answer Answer

prospect: We only have 10 years to retirement. The stock market is too volatile.

eia: If anything, over those 10 years, you might actually want it to become even more volatile.

Answering with a Question

prospect: Don't you think that so much exposure to the stock market is too risky for people like us?

eia: How are you defining "risk"?

"Why?"

prospect: I'm afraid the market is going to go down after the election.

eia: Why?

After either of the first two classes of non-response, *always wait five full seconds before you say anything else.* This pause lets the clear understanding sink into your prospect's consciousness that his challenge has not disturbed you in the least, and that your deep confidence in yourself and in your recommendations not only hasn't been, *but cannot be,* shaken. Far from being required to bark answers on cue like a trained seal, you see your mission as *helping the prospect reason out the answers for himself.* (Give him a fish, food for a day. Teach him to fish, food for a lifetime.) Incidentally, if your instinct is to shy away from this approach—to feel that your prospects won't rise to the challenge—then you're prospecting people you don't like. That's not their fault, it's yours. Care for another soggy potato chip?

After the third type of non-response—"Why?"—you'll wait *forever* before you say anything else. Because, of course, you've asked a perfectly reasonable question, and are deserving of an answer. If you blurt out an amplification of your question because the silence that ensues after "Why?" unnerves you, your own anxiety may set off an alarm in the prospect's unconscious. And the fragile bond of incipient trust may be irreparably broken. Remember that though the prospect's conscious mind may think it's looking for an intellectual answer, *his unconscious is watching to see how you react emotionally to a challenge.* Let your serene, imperturbable silence speak volumes for you.

Have you seen Ken Burns's Civil War series on PBS? If you haven't—even if you have—buy the tapes, and watch the way the historical novelist Shelby Foote speaks. He has the ultimate calm, and a gentleness—even when he's speaking about the horrors of war—that takes you over. He never raises his voice or gets excited. Foote radiates great charm, and his fine attitude and quiet humor shine through everything he says. The net effect is that *you would never dream of doubting him.* You take every word he says as if it were God's truth. Because of what he says? No, of course not: because of *the way* he says the things he says. Keep that in mind as we continue to explore the principles of non-response.

Also, please understand that you needn't learn specific non-responses to specific questions/objections. When you get used to this, you'll find that you can apply any of the three non-responses to any circumstance. For instance, if the 52-year-old couple with 10 years to dollar-cost average said "I'm afraid the market is going to go down after the election," instead of saying "Why?" you might just as easily (and appropriately) have said, "I certainly hope so, for your sake." This is, of course, a non-answer answer. And, after the obligatory five-second silence, it would have been followed up with a brief discussion of how the benefits of DCA will be magnified if the folks are lucky enough to catch a couple of Big Sales along the way.

Or, to a lump-sum investor who said, "I'm afraid the market is going to go down," the excellent advisor might have given the non-answer, "Well, it either will or it won't." Then, after five stunned seconds of serene silence, the prospect would hear a gentle, therapeutic, non-argumentative version of the advisor's "short-term-unknowable/long-term-inevitable" riff. Alternatively, the excellent advisor might have answered with a question: "How much would it have to go down in a year before you felt you'd made a mistake?" The rest of that particular dialogue can be found in the last chapter, in the section on DCA. *Any of the three classes of non-response can be used on any question/objection.*

Let's go back, now, and look at how each of the three specific examples we've seen so far might play out:

prospect: We only have 10 years to retirement. The stock market is too volatile.

eia: If anything, over those 10 years, you might actually want it to become even more volatile. [*Five-second silence*]

prospect: [*Blurting into the silence*] What? Why on earth would we want it to be **more** volatile?

eia: I can think of at least two major reasons. First, as I mentioned a moment ago, the ups and downs of the equity market are exactly the reason that the long-term returns are what they are. If you think only in terms of an abstract, scary concept like 'volatility,' you focus only on the cost of equity investing and not at all on the benefits. Remember how we agreed that the temporary declines were the price of the permanent advances?

prospect: Yes, I see that now.

eia: OK, so if equities developed sharper peaks and valleys over time, we know that an efficient market would demand even higher returns from them. Personally, I wouldn't worry about that, if I were you. I'd try to stay focused on the most important thing we've agreed on tonight: that the long-term return of equities—running, as it does, around twice that of bonds—seems to be the only way to get you to your retirement income goals. You still see that that's true, don't you?

prospect: It sure seems to be true.

eia: Fine. Now, of course, the specific reason you might want the market to zig and zag around its permanent uptrend even more than it has in the past is that you're going to be dollar-cost averaging over the next 10 years. And, as we've seen, DCA works even better the more Big Sales you run into. At this early stage of the game, you're not so much trying to pile up **dollars** as you are trying to pile up **a whole lot of fund shares at fire-sale prices,** if you're lucky enough to be able to do so. That's clear to you, isn't it?

prospect: Yes, yes, I remember that now. I guess I didn't really see it before.

eia: That's fine. Sometimes the big concepts about investing in the great companies come slowly, especially if you've been accustomed to worrying more about your principal than your purchasing power.

Now, there's one more thing I need to mention, here. **If there were a compelling, decisive reason for you not to invest in equities for your retirement, I would know what it is, and I would have counseled you not to buy equities.** Take all the time you need to explore all the concerns you have, so we can put those concerns completely to rest. But, as we do that, please remember above everything else that my only function is to maximize your opportunity to find the dignified, independent retirement you deserve. I'm not here to **sell** you dignity and independence; I'm here to help you find the highest-probability way of fulfilling those very real needs.

> If you need to go down to the corner store for a loaf of bread, I recommend you walk. If you need to go over to the next county to see your son and his family, I recommend you drive. And if you need to go to Australia, I very strongly recommend that you fly. That's my job; indeed, I believe that's my calling. You tell me where you need to go, and I'll tell you what reason and logic and history say is the best way for you to get there. Can you see that we're totally on the same side of the table on this?

Let's analyze this response by the excellent advisor, and make sure we know what the critical factors in it are:

▶ First of all, the excellent advisor had taken the time to establish that his solution—in this case, equities—was the only way for the prospect to reach his financial goals. Moreover, he had gotten the client to agree with that conclusion during the presentation. Once again: every time you establish a great conceptual truth and get the prospect to sign off on it during the presentation, you've effectively cut off one of his lines of retreat during Q&A.

▶ The advisor had used the presentation (and particularly Point # 5) to make the points that **(a)** in an efficient market, the large price fluctuations are the price of the large returns and that **(b)** the fluctuations down are temporary while the fluctuations up are permanent. In particular, he had made the point that Big Sales are the great friend of dollar-cost averaging. And, of course, he'd gotten the prospect's assent to all those points. So, in effect, the "volatility" objection was dead before it slapped leather.

▶ Please note that the excellent advisor did not repeat the prospect's phrase "the stock market" back to him. Nor did he say the word "stocks." And he only used the word "volatility" once, in the dismissive phrase "an abstract, scary concept like 'volatility.'" He saw the old inverted communication pyramid start whipping around in the wind like the top of the Sears Tower in March, and steadied it down with phrases like "the ups and downs of the equity market" instead of "the volatility of the stock market." He said "sharper peaks and valleys" instead of "increased volatility;" he also used the phrase "zig and zag around its permanent uptrend" to gently but firmly remind his prospect that the fluctuations aren't what matters. He re-set the agenda once again in terms of "investing in great companies," and got in a quiet reminder about how people are used to worrying about principal, but need to worry more about purchasing power.

▶ Perhaps most importantly, the excellent advisor put his own ethics and professionalism on the table ("...if there were a reason not to invest in equities...I would know what it is, and I would have counseled you not to..."). *And then he moved to the prospect's side of the table.* ("I'm not here to *sell* you dignity and independence; I'm here to help you...") Beware the unconscious but very human tendency for Q&A to become adversarial; don't ever allow it to do so. Keep moving to the prospect's side of the table. Keep reminding him that your solution *must* be a good solution, *because it's your solution.*

▶ Finally, there's a statement that what's being discussed is simply the optimum way to get where the prospect has already acknowledged he needs to go ("walk to the store/drive to the next county/fly to Australia"). I'll signal the use of this whole paragraph in future responses to other objections simply by saying **Australia!** You'll find that there are virtually limitless opportunities to use it, because it's the ultimate truth: "You tell me where you need to go, and I'll tell you what reason and logic and history say is the best way for you to get there." Do you believe in your solution? Then never get bogged down in the minutiae. ("Volatility," indeed.) Raise the focus of your non-response, as often as you can, to the great conceptual truth that you, and not your portfolios, are the ultimate solution to the prospect's problem—and that you're on his side.

Now let's look at the completion of our second example, answering with a question.

prospect: Don't you think that so much exposure to the stock market is too risky for people like us?

eia: How are you defining "risk"? [*Five-second silence, during* *which the advisor gently moves the postage stamps just a tad closer to his listeners*]

prospect: Yes, I see what you're saying, but…uh…

eia: [*Gently*] Please go on. I want to understand your feelings about this.

prospect: Well, this is our retirement money, and we're just terribly afraid of losing it.

eia: [*Approvingly*] You wouldn't be human if you weren't. [*Silence. Just sit there beaming your care and concern at them. Don't break the silence.*]

prospect: Well, what do you have to say about that?

eia: I guess I don't really know what to say…other than what we've already agreed upon. We've agreed that a fixed-income investment strategy over two to three decades of rising living costs in retirement is a non-starter. And that a lot of exposure to a potentially rising stream of dividends is going to be critical to maintaining your dignity and independence in retirement. We did agree on that, didn't we?

prospect: Well, that's for sure.

eia: OK, so we kind of backed into a strategy of investing in managed portfolios of the great companies by process of elimination. No one's asking you to **love** equities—I sure do, but I can respect the fact that you're not there yet—you just have to see that nothing else will really support a long retirement with no compromise in lifestyle. You do see that, don't you?

prospect: Yes, I guess so…

eia: We also agreed that your investing time horizon is a quarter century of retirement for yourselves and decades beyond that for your children. And we've seen how there've never been 15 years of negative returns from equities, even through the 1930s and the 1970s. And we've agreed that, if there were ever a time to be long-term optimistic about capitalism in gene and the future of great companies in particular, this is the time. You still feel that way, don't you?

prospect: Very strongly.

eia: And still you can't help feeling afraid of "losing your money." [*Smiling*] I say again: you wouldn't be human if you didn't. That fear was bred into all of us. Helping you manage that fear until it goes away—in other words, letting you feel your feelings but not **act** on those feelings—is why you're hiring me. I'm not trying to **sell** you dignity and independence: I'm here to help you find the highest-probability way of fulfilling those very real needs. **Australia!** Can you see that we're totally on the same side of the table on this?

prospect: Yes, we do see that, and we appreciate it.

eia: Thank you; that's very important to me. Now, please: don't stop being afraid, if you don't want to stop. [*Tapping the stamps one last time*] Just do one thing for me, and for yourselves: **try to be about 19 times more afraid of outliving your money than of losing it.** OK?

prospect: [*Ruefully*] OK. We promise.

Please note the excellent advisor's delightful proclivity to validate her prospects' fear. *Validating fears* ("you wouldn't be human if you weren't afraid") *is totally different from agreeing with them* ("yes, but..."). In effect, the excellent advisor is saying, "I care deeply about the way you feel, but I care too much about you to let you give in to those feelings." And of course she adds, "*That's* why you're hiring me," as opposed to, say, her deeply nuanced understanding of the difference between variance and semi-variance.

Let your prospects *ventilate* their irrational fears; it's very therapeutic. Then *validate* the fears they've ventilated. But after that, if you've done your job right, you get to do the "We've agreed...and we've agreed...and we've agreed..." recitation. You don't *debate* the "objection;" *you use it as a platform to make the "sale" all over again* (while the journeyman is banging on his optimization software, and moaning things like, "...higher returns...lower risk...*aaarrggghh...*"). **Re-set the agenda; re-start the "sale."**

Finally let's look at the third, perhaps most all-purpose General Principal of Non-Response, "Why?"

prospect: I'm afraid the market is going to go down after the election.

eia: Why? [*Silence*]

prospect: Because I'm afraid the bad guy is gonna win, and then we'll have inflation/deflation/higher taxes/bigger deficits/war in Asia/layoffs and downsizing/the bankruptcy of Medicare/a secret tunnel to the Vatican/whatever the apocalypse **du jour** happens to be.

eia: On a scale of one to 10, how sure are you that your retirement date is coming up in 120 months?

prospect: Like, 14. I mean, that's the date. That's what this is all about.

eia: I couldn't agree more. Now, on a scale of one to 10, how sure are you that the election is going to come out the way you think it is, **and** that all this terrible stuff is going to happen, **and** that it's going to set off a big sale on the prices of the great companies?

prospect: Well, I don't know...better than even, anyway.

eia: So, in a sense, what you may be doing is pitting the uncertainty of some negative market event against the certainty of your needing an adequate retirement income on a known date. As your family's financial advisor, I can't advise you to do that. But let me put it another way. Do you really want to sit in a 4% money market fund for six to 12 months—five percent to 10% of all the time you've got 'til retirement—trying to catch a

20% to 30% sale that historically has only one chance in five of happening?

prospect: Well, of course, when you put it that way...

eia: Heck, never mind, then. I'll put it still another way. How long until you retire?

prospect: Ten years, almost to the day.

eia: And how long, please God, are you going to be retired?

prospect: I'm planning on 20 big ones.

eia: So are we looking at a total investing time horizon of something like 30 years?

prospect: That's a big 10–4.

eia: Terrific. Now: what was happening around 30 years **ago?**

prospect: Ugh. Vietnam. Inflation. Riots in the streets, campuses closing all over the place. Robert Kennedy, Martin Luther King...

eia: Brezhnev and the threat of nuclear winter, the Six-Day War in the Middle East...

prospect: Awful.

eia: Worse than now?

prospect: So much worse...hey, what are you driving at?

eia: Got any idea where the Dow Jones Industrials were 30 years ago?

prospect: Maybe 1000?

eia: Maybe less. Are we just about done on this?

prospect: Aw, but look at the headlines.

eia: I looked at a headline once. My dad had it in a scrapbook. It said "Dewey Defeats Truman." Kind of put me off reading headlines for life. You might want to try it for a while.

prospect: OK, OK, what's the point?

eia: Simply that you can absolutely **never** become a good investor by watching current events, but that **you can almost always become a great investor by watching history.**

prospect: Funny, I've never seen that mentioned on CNBC or in *USA Today*.

eia: *Because if they told you that one simple truth, you'd stop watching and reading 'em. They* **can't** *tell you the truth, so they tell you the news, instead.*

prospect: Two more questions, in no particular order. (A) Where have you been all my life? (B) Where do I sign?

It is a central premise of this book that all fear of equities is irrational, and that fear of having one's long-term investing program materially damaged by a short- to intermediate-term market event is irrationality on a grand scale. So when you hear that pathology begin to surface, the best thing to do is to ask a gentle, therapeutic "Why?" Current-events fears, in particular, are fertile soil for irrationality; they're usually blown way out of proportion and/or are a proxy for something else.

We'll look at how to handle the two-headed monster of proxy fear and real anxiety in just a little while, and also talk more about current events. For the moment, just observe that the excellent advisor re-set the agenda by putting the concern into not one but three different contexts, *never by directly addressing the concern:*

(a) He got the prospect to contrast the certainty of his retirement income need with the relative uncertainty of a negative market event.

(b) He established the potentially terrible cost of waiting—4% return for five to 10 percent of the prospect's time until retirement—and stressed the 80% historical probability that the market won't, in fact, go down 20% to 30% in the next year.

(c) He got the prospect looking about as far *back* into history as he must look *forward* to the rest of his life. And as soon as you do that, current events fears tend to evaporate like the dewdrops of an August morning. Once again: You can never become a good investor by watching current events, but you can almost always become a great investor by watching history.

Let's look at some variations on the theme of confusing temporary decline with permanent loss, and some non-responses thereto. This is a persistent issue with investors whom advisors have been trained to think of as "risk-averse." But, as we've had occasion to observe often in this book, these people aren't really risk-averse, they're *loss-averse,* (a) because they don't actually know what risk is and (b) because they can't distinguish between fluctuation and loss.

So the excellent advisor wants to accomplish two things. First, he seeks to communicate—indeed, to infect his prospect with—his own utter imperturbability. This is almost entirely a non-verbal/paralinguistic exercise: in effect, "I'm not trying to get you to know what I know, I'm trying to get you to feel the way I feel." Second, the excellent advisor is trying to move his prospect from victimization ("My money will be totally at the mercy of savage market declines! I'll be helpless to prevent loss!") to empowerment ("All declines are temporary; I can't suffer permanent loss unless *I* panic and pull the ripcord, and *I'm never gonna do that!").*

prospect: The stock market could go down 500 points tomorrow!

eia: Yes it could. [*Silence*]

or

How would that affect you, over the next 30 years? [*Silence*]

or

Which also means it could go up 500 points tomorrow. [*Silence*]

The first and third non-responses are non-answer answers; the middle one answers with a question. They all say, "I don't care." No one day's market action can possibly have any effect on an investment program that'll be measured in decades. (This is most notably true of October 19, 1987, which was reported by journalism as Quite Possibly The End of Economic Life As We Have Known It, and which was, in reality, either The Mother of All Non-Events or The Greatest One-Day Sale In The History of The Great Companies In America, depending on whether or not you still had money to invest.)

The excellent advisor will, after the obligatory minimum five-second silence, follow up any of the above non-responses with some variation on the "short-term unknowable/long-term inevitable" theme. Once again: we don't know what the market will do tomorrow, which is fine, because it doesn't matter. We have a very clear idea of what the market will ultimately do, which is great, because that's what *does* matter over decades of retirement and the lives of one's heirs.

By imperturbably taking your prospect over this same ground—perhaps many times, in non-response to many questions/objections that all lead back to the same basic fear—you have the opportunity to root out that fear once and for all. Don't let Q&A upset you; it has very genuine therapeutic potential.

Let's look now at the Three General Principles of Non-Response as they apply to all issues regarding your compensation.

You've got one big thing going against you—and one *huge* thing going for you—on this issue. The "headwind" issue is the blind, unreasoning prejudice of most financial journalism against the people in our profession.

This bias isn't just unconscious, it's virtually pre-conscious; I don't think journalists even realize they're displaying it. But a single *Fortune* article on fund families, published in August 1996, used the verbs "peddle," "hawking" and "push" to describe the process of investment professionals recommending mutual funds to prospective investors.

Another article in the same issue (on choosing a financial advisor) cautioned readers to "...beware the greenhorn broker. Eight months ago, he might have been working in a shoe store..." This relentless cheapening of our profession is pandemic in journalism—and journalism is where a lot of people get their preconceptions.

Moreover, excepting only no-help funds themselves, journalists are the leading proponents of the toxic fiction that the primary determinant of investment success is fund selection, and that investors can learn to pick superior funds themselves, so there's no reason to pay a professional. In a book by *Wall Street Journal* reporter Jonathan Clements called *Funding Your Future* (smugly sub-titled "The Only Guide To Mutual Funds You'll Ever Need"), one chapter is headed "Loaded Questions: Why You Should Never Pay A Sales Commission." (The chapter itself is not *quite* so doctrinaire: it allows that paying a sales commission may be OK "for the financially naïve.") The effect of all this is to shame the good people who feel they need—or just want—the professional counsel of an investment advisor.

The "tailwind" aspect of the compensation issue—the thing we have going for us *if we have the courage to claim it*—is that the do-it-yourself argument is quite literally counterintuitive. People may readily believe that they can and should mow their own lawns, paint their own houses and change their own spark plugs. But—as those wonderful Alliance Capital ads suggested—people don't (and are right not to) instinctively think they can cut their own hair, perform surgery on their own brains...or create and maintain their own lifetime investment programs.

So the do-it-yourself argument had a long uphill battle to fight. And I think we must ruefully admit that it fought that battle brilliantly—by setting the agenda in terms of a false premise. To wit: it is the commission/fee that you pay or don't pay, *rather than the professional advice you get or don't get*, which determines your ultimate investment "performance." In short, load vs. no-load (the phony issue) rather than help vs. no-help (the real issue). This wildly wrong-headed argument found an eager champion in financial journalism—which, as previously noted, **(a)** ain't your friend and **(b)** always gets it wrong. And that brings us up to today.

So try to take all questions and objections about your compensation in your stride. If you've qualified your prospects properly—if you haven't just bulled your way in there and tried to pitch 'em the fund *du jour*—people will still want to know what they have to pay you. And they may still need you to spell out why. But they won't usually be so much adversarial as just plain confused.

The problem is something called cognitive dissonance: the folks know what they're hearing from you, but they're having trouble squaring it with what they've been trained to think.

Here comes a calm, quiet, mature, caring professional, pledging to treat the folks (and their capital) as he would his own family. But simultaneously banging around in the folks' heads are various forms of the verbs "to hawk," "to peddle" and "to push"—along with admonitions to beware people who just came from a job in a shoe store, and not to be "naïve" enough to pay for advice. (All that, and the incessant jungle drumbeat, "no-load, no-load, no-load...") The result: not antipathy, in my judgment, just plain old garden-variety confusion.

The excellent advisor takes all questions/objections about her compensation simply as a sign that she has not yet completed her work, which is to cause prospects to see that she is the difference between a family's realizing its financial goals and failing to realize them.

The excellent investment advisor knows that her price is only an issue to the extent that her value is in question.

In other words, the excellent advisor believes that she is both the ultimate object of all questions/objections about compensation, *and that she is the ultimate answer to them.* Gently, therapeutically, non-argumentatively, she offers non-responses that begin to clear away the cobwebs.

prospects: Why shouldn't we just buy no-load funds?

eia: Perhaps you should. [*Five-second silence*]

prospects: Huuunnhh?

eia: Well, let me rephrase that. I don't think the issue is no-load funds vs. funds in which you compensate an advisor. The issue is whether you feel you want to create and maintain a lifetime investment program on your own, or whether you feel you need and want the advice and service of someone like me through the years.

Let's say, for the moment, that the difference in cost to you would work out to about 1% a year. If you thought my counsel and that of my firm would probably improve the results you got over your investing lifetime by more than 1% a year, we're probably a good value. If you didn't think that, we're probably not.

[*Smiling*] I don't suppose I need to tell you what I think, but then again, I'm prejudiced. And anyway, it doesn't matter what I think, the only thing that matters is what you think. So what **do** you think?

prospects: We think you've talked more common sense in a shorter period of time than anyone we've met. We just didn't want to be jerks, and pay something we didn't have to pay.

eia: I completely understand. And thank you.

The incidence of all issues relating to your compensation will, you'll find, pretty much rise and fall inversely with your **N**. The lower your N—the more you're prospecting in the bad old transaction-oriented way—the more you'll hear the compensation issue. The higher your N—the harder you're qualifying for serious relationship potential—the less you'll hear it. Because no serious person expects a professional to say, "No one without your last name will ever care more about your family's financial success than I do, and if you'll stick to the plan we make I'll take the responsibility for getting you where you want to go...and of course there'll be no charge."

When you believe, you'll be believed. So if you believe passionately that your counsel is worth multiples of the pittance you're allowed to charge for it, let that belief shine. The right people will see it, and the wrong people won't. And isn't that exactly what you want?

In Summary

- Sometime during the Q&A/objections handling process, the decision takes place. As gently, therapeutically and non-argumentatively as you can, dispel the fears, and give the act of faith a chance to happen.

- Never respond directly to a stated question or objection. The stated issue is virtually never the real issue.

- Offer a potentially startling non-response that (a) gently shakes the prospect up a little, (b) re-sets the agenda on your terms, (c) reinforces the impression that you're imperturbable, that your faith in your solution is unshakable, and (d) forces the prospect to re-think and amplify what he said.

- The Excellent Investment Advisor is totally impervious to all objections about portfolios, markets, economics and politics, because those things have nothing to do with his product, which is, of course, himself.

- The excellent advisor's three General Principles of Non-Response are:
  1. The Non-Answer Answer
  2. Answering With A Question
  3. "Why?"

☞ After the first two classes of non-response, wait at least five seconds before saying anything. After the third ("Why?"), wait forever.

☞ The excellent advisor's presentation is so honest (particularly with respect to Risks/Limitations/What It Isn't), and he's gotten agreement so many times during the course of the presentation, that most or all of the major objections are dead or dying before Q&A even gets off the ground.

☞ The excellent advisor's whole attitude is: you, Mr./Ms. Prospect, told me where you want to go; I'm not trying to sell you anything, I'm just telling you the optimum way to get there. **Australia!** Keep moving to their side of the table.

☞ *Do not* agree and *do not* argue. *Do* let the prospect ventilate his fears; *do* validate them. ("You wouldn't be human if you didn't feel that way.") But make it clear that you care too much for the prospects to let them *act* on their fears.

☞ Don't argue current events, near-term market risk...or anything else. Contrast the certainty of the prospects' need (for a given number of dollars on a given date) with the uncertainty—and evanescence—of market unpleasantness.

☞ All questions/objections regarding compensation are a sign that you haven't finished your work, which is to cause your prospects to see that you represent the difference between lifetime investment success or failure. *Your price is only an issue to the extent that your value is still in question.*

☞ Once again, it isn't load (or fee, or B-share, or whatever) vs. no-load. *It's help vs. no-help.* You are the focus of the objection, and you are the answer to it.

14

Freeing your prospects to close themselves . . . .

"He that observeth the wind shall not sow; and he that regardeth the clouds shall not reap."

—**Ecclesiastes 11:4**

It always looks like the wrong time to invest in equities.

Just as the author of Ecclesiastes said that one could always find a reason not to put in a crop, and then a reason not to harvest it, our prospects can always find a reason why today is no day to be buying equities.

This arises, as we've seen, from a morbid concern with the direction of the *next* move in stock prices, which **(a)** is unknowable and **(b)** doesn't matter anyway. The goal of the excellent advisor is to free his prospects from that unhealthy obsession, so they can focus instead on the serene sweep of the *ultimate* direction of the values of (and income from) portfolios of the great companies.

Please note that, in the Q&A/objections handling process, the excellent advisor is not so much trying to convince people of anything. Rather, he's trying to set them free from their anxieties and fears. The essential medium through which the excellent advisor dispels anxiety is, of course, his own imperturbable confidence in the future, and in the plan/portfolio that he's crafted for his prospects. But that's an almost entirely non-verbal process. It's an underground message, sent from the advisor's unconscious to the prospects'.

Up at the surface, though, the verbal Q&A dialogue is still going on.

prospect: Can't invest in an equity portfolio now. The Fed raised interest rates again yesterday, and the stock **and** bond markets are still in power dives.

eia: [*As gently as possible*] Why do you let things like that bother you? [*Five-second silence*]

prospect: Huh?

eia: I said: why do you let things like that bother you? This portfolio will be in your estate a quarter of a century and more from now. You'll bless it for providing you with an income you couldn't outlive, and your children will bless you for endowing them. That's how it works. Who'll remember today's and tomorrow's zigs and zags? What will any of it matter in the new century?

prospect: Well, I know you're right, but...well, if I could just be **sure...**

eia: I can't even be sure that the sun will come up tomorrow...or that I'll see it if it does. That doesn't change the way I invest.

prospect: Well, don't **you** worry about Greenspan/mercury in your tuna fish/Japan buying Rockefeller Center/Ike's heart attack/the Smoot-Hawley Tariff/Teapot Dome/Lee and the rebels invading Pennsylvania/whatever the apocalypse *du jour* is?

eia: Haven't got the time or the energy. Besides, the next time I turn around, today's crises will be resolved, and there'll be a new one. No, I worry about what quality nursing home care is going to cost when my wife is 90 years old. And I worry about that burden falling on my kids when they're trying to put **their** kids through college (at $250,000 a pop) **and** plan for their own retirements. And I've resolved **not** to let that burden fall on them. And the only way I know to do that is to invest in equities on any day that ends in a Y. I'll take my **insecurity today** so my family and I can have **security in the future.** Beats the heck out of having it the other way around.

prospect: Tell me that last part again.

eia: Glad to. Look: today is the first day of the rest of my investing lifetime. And the day I journey to the happy hunting ground is the last, right?

prospect: Sure.

eia: OK, I figure I can have blissful security on one end of my investing lifetime and terrific insecurity on the other. I just have to choose: on which end of my life do I want each of those conditions? I can certainly go for total security now: money funds, T-bills, CDs, stuff like that. **Total security on the front end.** And 40 years from now, the only way my wife will be able to go in a nursing home is if the kids bankrupt her and put her on Medicaid...if Medicaid even exists then. **Total insecurity on the back end.** Do you see where this is headed?

prospect: I'm afraid I do.

eia: OK, so what I do is elect to take my insecurity on **this** end. I don't know what the Fed, or OPEC, or NAFTA, or NASDAQ is going to do in the next 90 days. But I keep investing anyway, despite the uncertainty. And I know that, given the power of capitalism over time, my willingness to take my insecurity on this end is what buys me and my family the prospect of future **real** security.

prospect: So you're not really paying any attention to the markets at all?

eia: None. Why bother? No matter how much effort I put into it, I'm still never going to know the direction of the next 500-point move in the Dow. But I know exactly the dates on which my wife and I will turn 65. And I know pretty much exactly what we'll need to retire on. If I focus on the uncertainties of the market, even **I'll** end up paralyzed. If I focus on the relative certainty of my family's future financial needs, I'm energized. Believe me, energized beats paralyzed every single time.

prospect: I never thought about it that way.

eia: Our culture conspires to prevent you from thinking of it that way. Someday, there'll be something like the Surgeon General's cigarette warning: every five minutes, CNBC will be required by law to flash on the TV screen a graphic that says, "Nothing that happens in the markets in the next 30 days will matter in 20 years." [*Grinning*] Until that day, you'll just have to make do with me.

prospect: [*Heaving a sigh of relief*] This is such a tremendous load off my mind. I don't really want to watch markets. The whole point of this exercise is to take care of my retirement and my family.

eia: Then, for what it's worth, I'd like to give you permission to stop watching markets and use that energy to watch your family's lives. And I urge you to accept as much insecurity as you can today, so that you maximize your family's security down the road.

prospect: Got it. Let's get started.

Markets are either going up or going down on any given day that you're interviewing a prospect. But 20 years from now, everybody on earth will wish he'd invested today. *Give people permission to invest today*, not by trying to prove anything, but by encouraging people to let go of unproductive anxieties.

prospect: Can't invest in equities now. We're in a recession.

eia: Why does that bother you? [*Five-second silence*]

prospect: Are you serious? Stocks go down in a recession...don't they? I mean, look: they're down 18% in the last six months.

eia: Beats the heck out of them being **up** 18% in the last six months.

prospect: Huh? Why?

eia: Because you haven't started buying 'em yet. [*Silence*]

prospect: I'm getting totally confused.

eia: [*Gently*] I have to confess, I am too. And I really want to help you. So could we start over again? And would you tell me what you're most worried about?

prospect: I guess I'm worried about putting this plan into effect, and having everything I buy go down the next day.

eia: That may very well happen. [*Silence*]

prospect: That's my point! So why don't we wait until it turns?

eia: I guess because you never know that it's turned until it's too late—until after you've missed the turn.

prospect: So what's the solution?

eia: Well, my solution has always been to stop thinking about turns altogether. In fact, to stop thinking about short-term moves in the markets and the economy altogether. Although I **do** get pretty excited at times like this, when everything's on sale. I love to buy things on sale. [*Silence*]

prospect: OK, let's start over again. What about the recession?

eia: Too late to worry about it. It's probably a lot more than half over, which means that virtually all the damage is done…unless **all** the damage is done.

prospect: Help me understand that.

eia: All right, but I can get pretty boring on this stuff, so stop me if you feel yourself dozing off. [*Sees the prospect smile and loosen up a bit; very few people can resist a little self-deprecating humor*] Since the end of World War II, we've had nine recessions; the average lasted something like 10–11 months. If you care, the longest lasted 17 months and the shortest lasted five. OK so far?

prospect: Didn't know that, but...OK.

eia: Good. Now, as you pointed out, we're in a recession right now. The government announced the other day that we'd had two quarters of negative GDP growth, as of the end of the last quarter...which was two months ago, since it takes the Feds a couple of months to get their numbers crunched. Can you see where we're going with this?

prospect: Wait now...if we've had two quarters of recession...that's six months.

eia: Plus the two-month lag 'til they made the announcement...

prospect: Hey, this recession's already eight months old!

eia: Bingo. And what, if history is any guide, does that tell you?

prospect: That this recession is at least half over...if not more!

eia: One more thing. The equity market doesn't trade on today's headlines. It trades on its best guess about what's going to happen six months out. So it usually starts down before a recession actually begins...and starts back up well before a recession ends.

prospect: So right now...

eia: So right now, if you care about such things—**and, as a long-term investor, let me assure you that I don't**—you're probably a heck of a lot closer to the bottom of this cycle than to the top. In fact, going strictly by the book, you may already have passed the trough.

prospect: Well, what do **you** think?

eia: Don't know, can't know, don't care, doesn't matter. Over and out. This wasn't an exercise in market prognostication. It was an exercise in dispelling journalism-induced anxiety. In the end, I don't care if you and I are in the next 18% downtick, just so long as we catch the next 180% uptick. And I only know one way to do that.

prospect: Invest when you have the money, regardless of market conditions, and stay in for the duration?

eia: I could not have said it better myself.

prospect: And I never have to think about the market again?

eia: Not unless you want to.

prospect: Who ever wanted to? I just wanted to do what's best for my family, and I thought studying the market was part of the job.

eia: I understand. I'll take over from here. Just tell me to set the plan in motion, and then go get on with your life.

prospect: General, you may launch the invasion at dawn.

eia: Roger that, Mr. President.

Remember, parameters are the enemy of anxiety. As soon as the excellent advisor put actual historical time frames around the scary, abstract concept of "recession," you saw the prospect's unfocused dread begin to break up. Being a student of the business and of markets, the excellent advisor was able to show the prospect that a recession-driven equity market decline was almost literally yesterday's news.

Now, how about the opposite anxiety:

prospect: Can't invest in equities now. Market's too high.

eia: Why?

prospect: It's gone from 1000 to 6000 in the last 15 years!

eia: Hey, that's nothing. It's gone from 40 to 6000 in the last 64 years. That's what it does. [*Silence*]

prospect: But...but...it's never been this high before!

eia: In relation to what?

prospect: What? What?

eia: That's what I asked. You said stocks have never been this high before, and I asked: in relation to what?

prospect: Well, I don't know, I just...doesn't it worry you?

eia: Not at all. Of course, that may be because I'm looking forward, and not backward.

prospect: What does **that** mean?

eia: Just that, when you look back at something that's been going up all your life, it'll probably look pretty high from where you're standing. But if you look forward at where that uptrend is going—if you look at all the terrific things that haven't happened yet, and are going to—you tend to feel pretty good.

prospect: Yes, I suppose, but...

eia: The other thing is: you have to relate prices to something. For instance, if you look at the real earnings of the great companies, the market at 1000 in 1973 was much, **much** more expensive than it is today. I guess it's just a question of your perspective. Did I ever tell you my favorite Warren Buffett story?

prospect: I don't think so.

eia: Well, Buffett is one of the richest people in the world, as you know, and the only one who's built that kind of fortune by investing in stocks. When he graduated from Columbia's Business School in 1951, his teacher, the great Ben Graham, told him not to buy stocks yet. Seems the Dow had traded under 200 every year since the end of the war, and it hadn't done so yet in '51. Buffett invested anyway, and the Dow never got under 200 that year—or ever since. "I had about 10 thousand bucks," Buffett says, "and if I listened to that advice I'd probably still have about 10 thousand bucks." Isn't that a great story?

prospect: [*Sighing*] Yes, I guess it is.

eia: Are we OK on this now? Do you see that the big issue for you and your family is not where the values of the great companies have been, but where they're going in a new century of global capitalism?

prospect: Reckon I do.

Are you getting the hang of this? Do you see that the excellent advisor never engages a current-events/current-market-conditions objection, but instead seeks to free her prospect from worrying about it? (How could the excellent advisor debate a market outlook to begin with, since she deliberately never has one?) There's no such thing as a good answer to a bad question. And indeed, successful investing isn't primarily about answers: *it's about making sure you have the questions framed right.* When the basic agenda item is the appropriateness of a lifetime of equity investing for The Great Goals of Life, all current events/market issues are, by definition, badly framed questions. Don't answer them; reframe them. In so doing, you'll free your prospects from their anxiety.

Granted, you'll find this most difficult to do during periods of "event shock." But shocking events tend not to have any lasting effect on markets or on the economy. The single most shocking event in my lifetime was the death of President Kennedy. The Dow Jones Industrials closed that day at 711. The Dow was 25% higher a year later and 33% higher two years later.

In a much larger sense, perhaps the most horrifying event in our national life since World War II was Watergate. But if you started systematically buying stocks the day Vice President Agnew resigned in October 1973 and continued until President Nixon left office 10 months later, you were up about 60% by the end of 1976.

And "waiting to see" how some crisis *du jour* resolves itself is one of the lowest-probability strategies around. The October '90 lows came and went virtually unnoticed, because everyone was fixated on events in the Persian Gulf. We'd given Saddam an ultimatum: get out of Kuwait by January 15 or we're coming in shooting. And he'd said, in effect, take your best shot. So investors waited to see if a war was going to start—convinced that, if it did, the market would crater. Sure enough, right on schedule, the war started. And literally within hours, when it became clear that Saddam's Scud missiles couldn't hit the Saudi oil fields—for this was, in case you'd forgotten, a war about oil—the market started a six-week 25% runup, during which it never left a skid mark. (And I'll bet you dollars to doughnuts there are people *still* waiting to buy "the pullback.")

Once and for all: the key to all issues of current events and current market conditions isn't their outcome. *It's that their outcome won't matter* to the long-term investor. So you can do a very wonderful thing for your prospects—something all the newspapers and TV newscasts in the world not only can't do but refuse to do. *You can give them permission to stop worrying about it*—whatever "it" happens to be. The good ones (and their heirs) will bless you for this; the jerks will just keep arguing. For many are called, but few are chosen.

* * *

Another whole species of questions/objections has to do with the particular funds/managers you've chosen for a prospect. Harried on every side by the "Six Hot Funds To Buy Now" school of journalism, the investor becomes obsessed with "performance." And the excellent advisor often has to spend some time talking him down off that ledge.

prospect: What about Shazam Micro-Cap Incomprehensible Internet Technology Fund? I read an article that said they were the top-performing fund of the last 17⅔ months.

eia: I don't know the manager. [*Five-second silence*]

prospect: What? You don't know him? Well, look, he's written up right here.

eia: [*Waving off the magazine*] Thanks, but that wouldn't help me. If you want to put some money in that fund, by all means go ahead. I can't advise you on that, and of course I couldn't make that fund a part of the core portfolio for which I'm responsible to you and your family. After all, I don't know the manager. [*Silence*]

prospect: But, look: the fund just got a five-star rating.

eia: I don't pay much attention to ratings, in general—too backward-looking for my taste, too much like investing through a rear-view mirror. But if something just recently got its fifth star, that's usually not a good sign. Anyway, my real problem is: I can't recommend—and so I won't be responsible for—the work of someone I don't personally know. Or who isn't at least well-known to, and recommended to me by, the top people in my firm. [*Silence*]

prospect: Let me understand this: you wouldn't recommend a money manager you didn't personally know?

eia: [*With magisterial calm*] Well, I wouldn't, no. Some other financial advisor might, I suppose; I see a lot of people doing very complex computer screening of funds these days. And I think that stuff's OK, as far as it goes—which to me isn't nearly far enough. At the end of the day, I just don't know how I could be responsible to you and your family for the work of people I'd never even met.

The best individual stockbroker I ever knew told me that he had trouble following more than about 15 companies at a time, out of the thousands of stocks on the exchanges and NASDAQ. But he said he felt he knew those 15 companies as well as anybody on the Street. And he did really well for his clients.

I always thought that was a good approach; anyway, it's worked well for me and my clients.

prospect: But what if other funds are doing better?

eia: There are always other funds doing better. But I don't hear about a lot of **investors** doing that much better. And how my investors do is all I really care about. I have to tell you, I'm still not sure—over the multigenerational time frames we're talking about—how much of a difference individual fund selection is really going to make.

I know the most mediocre stock funds are orders of magnitude better than the best bond funds, over time. And I know that a mediocre stock fund that you hold on to through a 30% market decline is infinitely better than a world-class stock fund that you get scared out of.

But will your granddaughter have student loans or not have student loans because of which small-cap growth fund you owned? I don't think so.

I have a high degree of confidence that the plan/portfolio we've looked at here tonight—with five consistent, disciplined managers doing the fighting—will win the war for wealth as you've defined it. Might a different portfolio, **on paper**, have a higher return? Sure...although not, I suspect, without more risk. But will a lot of real investors do that much better than you, if you stick to this plan? I strenuously doubt it. And will **any** investor have a financial advisor who cares more about his success than I care about yours? I can promise you: no. Do you feel that that gives you a basis on which to proceed?

Once again, here, you see that the advisor whose product is the investments he sells will always live in chaos; he'll always have to try to compete with better "performance." The Excellent Investment Advisor, whose product is herself, has no competition. Because she has set her own agenda: "No one who doesn't have your last name, Mr./Ms. Prospect, will ever be more committed to your family's financial success than I am."

Eventually, when all the stated objections the prospect can think of are gone, you'll often hear really sad proxy objections (though you still may not know what they're a proxy for) like:

prospect: I just want to watch it for a while.

eia: What exactly do you want to watch it do?

prospect: [*Spluttering, choking sounds*]

eia: Seriously, in the next 60 days, this portfolio will either go up or down, probably less than 5%. If it's up, that won't make me right; and if it's down, that won't make me wrong.

The only thing we can say conclusively is that, over the next 60 days, two of the 144 months until your boy goes to college [*or:* you retire] will have slipped away.

And for what? Over the last 10 years, this portfolio turned one dollar into four. But if you look at it in two-month clips, you'd probably say: "Nothing happened."

Also, two months from now, you won't know anymore about the managers' expertise—or about my professional and personal commitment to helping you reach your goals—than you do right now.

It's never the wrong time to hire the right people. **Do you believe that we're the right people?**

What all objections like this may come down to is the inability of the prospect to trust you yet. *Ask for the trust*; give the prospect permission to stop worrying.

eia: It's really just the difficulty of making an important decision like this, isn't it? I understand; I struggle with it all the time myself. What the decision comes down to—and there's no way around this—is a matter of trust. You have to find in yourself a belief that I'm as committed to your goals and as careful about choosing investments as I've told you I am. In the meantime, just think: you're retiring in 12 years. Look at what this portfolio has done for people in the last 12 years. And ask yourself: **How would you feel today if you'd passed up the chance to invest in this portfolio 12 years ago?**

In the bad old transaction-oriented days, we were taught to ask for the order. From now on, *ask for the trust.* The order comes with the trust, anyway. And what a far more meaningful thing happens when the prospect consciously gives you not just the order, but the trust.

When you give the prospect permission to trust you, you free him to "close" himself. (And unless and until he trusts you, all the "closing techniques" in the world will just bounce off him.) Indeed, I hope you can see now that the number of times you got the prospect to agree with you, all throughout your presentation and after each question/objection, had the cumulative effect of allowing him to "close" himself—and that you had been "closing" since you began the interview.

You can't educate your way to a "close." There is no quantum of information which, when communicated to a prospective client, will cause him to move in response to its sheer intellectual luminosity. But you can—and you must—empathize your way. Again, this isn't a function of what you know. Still less is it a function of what you say. *The critical issue is how you feel, and how you make your prospect feel.* And the more times he's genuinely agreed with you throughout the interview, the better he feels...and the more he's already "closed" himself. There is, in effect, nothing left to decide.

* * *

And with the "close" of the sales/counseling interview, we come to the close of this book. I leave you with my very best wishes, expressed, far more eloquently than can I, by Andrew Carnegie:

> *"Think of yourself as on the threshold*
> *of unparalleled success.*
> *A whole clear, glorious life lies*
> *before you.*
> *Achieve! Achieve!"*

In Summary

☞ It always looks like the wrong time to invest in equities. And, long-term, it's always the right time to invest in equities. Most people's focus is on the first point; the excellent advisor frees them to focus on the second.

☞ All long-term security is purchased at the price of short-term insecurity. The more insecurity you can get someone to accept on the front end of the rest of his investing lifetime, the more real security he and his family will have on the back end.

☞ Whatever the apocalypse *du jour* is, we've survived—and prospered after—much worse. Does your prospect think the US economy could survive an 86% drop in stock prices and 27% unemployment? Well, it not only can, but—in 1929-32—it did.

☞ Someday all financial journalism will have to carry a warning: "Nothing that happens in the next 30 days will matter in 20 years." Until that day, only the excellent advisor stands between the investor and his fears.

☞ Parameters are the antidote to anxiety. The excellent investment advisor puts real historical brackets around scary, abstract concepts (e.g. "recession"), and breaks up investors' unfocused dread.

☞ The equity market always looks "too high" if you're looking backward. Great investors don't look backward, they look forward, to a new century of global capitalism.

☞ Short-term, the equity market hates uncertainty—so periods of great uncertainty usually offer great opportunity. If you wait until the uncertainty is clearly resolved—the market's already gone.

☞ Give prospects permission to stop worrying about current conditions. They'll either accept that permission or they won't. The good ones will; let the others go in peace. This is a numbers game.

☞ Stand up for your right to work with a finite portfolio of investments that you know really well. How other investments are doing on paper doesn't matter. The only thing that matters is how real clients are doing in real life.

☞ Don't ask for the order, ask for the trust. When you give someone permission to trust you—and he accepts that permission—you've freed him to "close" himself. There's nothing left to decide.

☞ Achieve! Achieve!

Appendix 1
Acknowledgments/Resources

I owe a great debt of gratitude to the many people who helped me create this book.

First, last and always, to the love of my life, the mother of my children, my most severe critic and my very best friend, Joan Carrick Murray: thank you, and thank you, and thank you.

Our daughter Karen, to whom this book is lovingly dedicated, served both as a gently acerbic editor and as an absolutely preternatural proofreader. [*She can spot a misplaced comma from a thousand feet up, like one of those eagles that catch salmon on the* National Geographic *specials.*] Karen's sister Joan was (and is) my role model when it comes to disciplined work habits. And their brother Mark—although he didn't realize he was doing it at the time—gave me the idea, and perhaps the courage, to self-publish. I learn from, and thank God for, these three people every day of my life.

Penny Winters rendered my often indecipherable yellow-legal-pad scribblings into printable form. I couldn't have managed this book—or much else in my business over the last year—without her.

I thank Barry Vinocur, Bob Clark and Angie Finch at *Dow Jones Investment Advisor* magazine for providing me a monthly forum both to develop my ideas and to refine my ability to communicate those ideas. The magazine has helped me immeasurably—and it'll help you, too. Don't think of trying to become an Excellent Investment Advisor without it. Subscription is free to industry professionals; call (908) 389-8700, extension 130.

Three people whose expertise was vitally important to this book, and who can be very helpful to you, are Aaron Hemsley, the premier behavioral psychologist in our industry (714-832-6109); Steve Moeller, a gifted consultant and business coach (714-730-7844); and Michael P. Sullivan, who for my money has the best handle in America on the sales/marketing of investments to the aging (704-554-7863).

Bob Stanger, my publisher for 10 years, was—as always—the perfect gentleman about my decision to graduate to self-publishing. Without him, I would probably still be wondering if I might be able to write a book some day.

The book-design team of Brian Sisco and Susan Evans made the daunting prospect of self-publishing seem not just possible, but (almost) fun. They not only have eyes to see, but ears to hear, and I can't even imagine having gotten the book out so quickly without them.

Jo Dawn Jensen of MFS—who does with hypothetical illustrations what Rodin did with bronze and what Michelangelo did with Carrara marble—effortlessly produced all the information I needed on systematic withdrawal. She is one of those rare people who intuitively sees that mutual funds are a service business, not a product business. I thank MFS's Bob Leo for introducing me to Jo Dawn. I thank Barry Mandinach at Zweig Mutual Funds, who (with a little help from his friends at Ned Davis Research) is my—and ought to be your—source for a complete understanding of the reality of bear markets.

I don't know what I think until I hear what I say. So, in addition to thanking every client and prospect who's asked me a tough question over the last 30 years, I particularly want to express my gratitude to the sponsors of the 100+ speaking engagements I've had every year for the last five years. I hope my audiences have learned from me half as much as I've learned from them.

Appendix 2
Bibliography

Because you must be a constant student of the business, of markets, and of what's going on in your own head, you have to make the time to read well. "The only new thing in the world," said Harry Truman, "is the history you don't know."

The one indispensable book for anyone planning to be in the investment business through all its cycles is *Extraordinary Popular Delusions and the Madness of Crowds*, the 1841 classic by Charles Mackay. Just read—and keep re-reading—the section on financial crazes, like the South Sea Bubble and the Tulip Mania. "This book," said the great speculator Bernard Baruch, "has saved me millions of dollars."

The two most important books of the 1990s for people in our profession are Michael Rothschild's *Bionomics* and Jeremy Siegel's *Stocks for the Long Run*. They form the intellectual underpinnings of everything I believe about equities.

Another favorite of mine is *Once in Golconda*, by John Brooks—a beautifully written history of Wall Street in the 1920s. Brooks is the best writer about business that we have; another book of his, *The Go-Go Years*, will take you back to the first mutual fund mania of the 1960s. I recommend it quite urgently.

I mentioned *The Prize*, by Daniel Yergin, a complete history of oil that's both a great lesson and a great read. Another is David Halberstam's *The Reckoning*, about how Detroit got blindsided by the energy price explosion of the 1970s, and how Japan didn't. For people like us, who have to guard against the perils of consensus thinking, this book is a must.

I've recommended constant reading of Emerson's essay on "Compensation" as the ultimate attitude adjustment hour; his essay "Self-Reliance" is almost as important. Dr. Martin Seligman's *Learned Optimism: How To Change Your Mind And Your Life* is worth more than all the self-help and motivational drivel I've ever seen. It is a wise, practical book by a gifted psychologist.

A constant theme of this book is that belief and decision, followed up by perseverance, yield any goal you care to set for yourself. This is the key to whatever success I've personally had, and it comes from Napoleon Hill's timeless classic *Think And Grow Rich.* Modern readers find Hill hard to read these days, with his archaic writing style; of course, much the same can be said of the Bible.

Finally, read David McCullough's biography of Harry Truman. It doesn't have much to do with economics, markets or investing—it's just good for your soul.

Appendix 3
The No-Load Cardiologist

Gathering Assets, a book that contains 33 of the articles I wrote for *Dow Jones Investment Advisor* magazine between 1990 and 1994, may be out of print by the time you read this [*you can call the publisher at 908-389-3600 to find out*]. One of my favorite pieces from that collection is "The No-Load Cardiologist," a sort of vaudeville "doctor sketch" that appeared in the magazine in October 1993. I'm loath to see it disappear, because I think it still has something to say to us.

The Allmerica Financial companies later produced an award-winning video of the sketch, with a very gifted comic actor as the patient, and yours truly as Dr. Murray Murray. If you do business with them, you may want to ask them to bring the tape to your next meeting. I don't claim to be objective, but I think it's hilarious.

The scene opens in a doctor's office, replete with diploma, the obligatory skeleton hanging in the corner, a blood pressure cuff mounted on the wall, an exam table covered with white paper and the other trappings that signify the practice of medicine.

The lights come up as the office door opens. An extremely worried-looking patient, glancing nervously about, is shown into the office by an intelligent, well-read, intellectually independent nurse.

Nurse: If you'll just have a seat on the examining table, the doctor will be with you in just a moment. [*Exits*]

Doctor: [*Enters stage left, staggers across stage, applies stethoscope to skeleton.*] Ah, good morning! Went a little too far on that liquid diet, did we?

Patient: Doctor, I'm over here.

Doctor: And not looking much better, either! Well, how are you feeling?

Patient: Actually, doctor, I'm feeling very poorly.

Doctor: Ah! What seems to be the trouble?

Patient: Well, I have this terrific tightness in my chest, mostly on the left side. I'm very short of breath. And I have a lot of pain in my left arm. Do you think it's my heart?

Doctor: Sure sounds like it, sonny. So you've come to the right place. I'll give you exactly the treatment you want. And what's much more important, **you'll never pay a load.**

Patient: Well, Doctor, uh...

Doctor: Murray.

Patient: I beg your pardon. Is that your first name or your last name?

Doctor: Precisely!

Patient: Huh?

Doctor: My first name is Murray, and my last name is Murray. I'm Dr. Murray Murray, the no-load cardiologist! And my motto is: maybe you'll get better, maybe you won't. But you always know: **you'll never pay a load!** And these days that's the most important thing, don't you think?

Patient: Well, Doctor, I'm not sure. In fact, I think the most important thing is...not dying!

Doctor: [*Smacking his forehead with delight*] Ah! This is **wonderful,** sonny. I **love** a patient who knows what he wants. It makes a no-load cardiologist's job so much easier.

Patient: Well, uh, thank you, Doctor.

Doctor: My pleasure, sonny! Now, let's get right to work. First of all, what kind of treatment would you like?

Patient: What kind of treatment would I like? Doctor, shouldn't you be telling me?

Doctor: Good heavens, **no!** For that kind of cardiology, you got to pay a **load,** God forbid! In no-load cardiology, the patient picks the treatment...and I give it to him! And the most important thing is: **you never pay a load!**

Patient: Doctor, I'm just not sure I understand. Can't you give me any sort of guidance at all?

Doctor: Of course, sonny! Why didn't you ask sooner? I have this wonderful little questionnaire. I ask you questions about your symptoms, feelings, attitudes, fears, foibles and misconceptions. And when the form is all filled out, we know exactly what kind of treatment you wanted all along. And, best of all, **you never pay a load!**

Patient: Well, all right. I'll try anything. What do you want to ask me?

Doctor: Well, first of all: What's your pain tolerance?

Patient: My what?

Doctor: Your pain tolerance, sonny. How much pain do you like?

Patient: Doctor, for heaven's sake, I **hate** pain!

Doctor: See? Already we're making tremendous progress! [*Makes huge, theatrical check mark on chart.*] You hate pain. So already we can rule out treatments like bypass surgery, or angioplasty. Ho boy, that smarts!

Patient: [*Starting to become desperate*] But, Doctor, what if bypass surgery is actually the best thing for me? What if I **need** angioplasty?

Doctor: [*Beaming*] Sonny, rest assured: you want it, I'll perform it, same day, no questions asked! After all, I'm Dr. Murray Murray, the no-load cardiologist, and my motto is: the treatment you want is the treatment you get—with a smile! And best of all, **you'll never pay a load!**

But, my boy, you're the one who says he hates pain. So how about maybe you try some nice nitroglycerin pills. Tell me, sonny, what's your favorite flavor?

Patient: Why, uh, chocolate.

Doctor: Oh, too bad! We got no chocolate-flavored nitroglycerin pills. Got some very nice chocolate-flavored children's aspirin, though. Here...

Patient: [*Shouting*] Wait a minute! Wait a minute! I may fall over dead of cardiac arrest at any moment, and you're giving me children's aspirin?

Doctor: Hey, sonny, now don't you get testy with me! Look here at your chart. NO PAIN, you said. CHOCOLATE, you said. Me, I've always liked licorice flavor, myself. Got some very nice licorice-flavored angina pills. But you said chocolate, so...

Patient: [*Almost screaming now*] Doctor! Let me make this perfectly clear! I didn't say I want chocolate. **I said I don't want to die!**

Doctor: [*Sagely*] And I couldn't agree with you more, sonny.

Patient: THEN WHAT EXACTLY DO YOU RECOMMEND?

Doctor: Sorry, sonny, I've tried already to explain. Recommend? This is not my field. You got the problem, you pick the treatment. [*Puts arm around patient, comfortingly*] I'll be with you every step of the way. And best of all...

Patient: [*Miserably*] Yes, yes, I know: I'll **never pay a load.** Doctor, now about these nitroglycerin pills.

Doctor: The licorice ones?

Patient: Never mind the flavor! Just tell me: do these pills have a good track record?

Doctor: Sonny! They have a **great** track record! Why, nobody who's taking these pills today is dead! Can you imagine?

Patient: What about people who stopped taking them?

Doctor: Well, sonny, you know, that's human nature.
They decided they wanted 'em, then later I guess they decided they didn't want 'em anymore. May they rest in peace, sonny, but at least I can console myself: live or die, **they never pay a load.**

Patient: Oh no, not that again. Doctor, precisely what is a load?

Doctor: I couldn't really say, sonny. But it must be a terrible thing; everyone says so. Personally, I don't charge one, so I don't really know...

Patient: Didn't you go to medical school?

Doctor: [*Proudly*] Yes, at night. I put myself through medical school, working days as a telemarketer for a no-load mutual fund. Those were the days! We were all 20 years old, the telemarketers; not a care in the world...

Patient: [*Suspiciously*] What medical school did you go to?

Doctor: Dr. Bob's No-Load Cardiology and Transmission Repair Academy.

Patient: How long did you attend?

Doctor: Why, the entire four weeks!

Patient: Oh, my God. And when did you graduate?

Doctor: What day is this?

Patient: Thursday.

Doctor: Then it must have been...Tuesday.

Patient: This **past** Tuesday? The day before yesterday?

Doctor: Well, yes. That's the thing about no-load cardiology. It's kind of an entry-level job. Nobody stays in it for very long, because it doesn't pay much. How could it? It's no-load.

Patient: I think I'm starting to feel faint...

Doctor: Not to worry, sonny. I won't abandon you. I'm Dr. Murray Murray, the no-load cardiologist. And my motto is: I may not know much, but my heart's in the right place. Your heart, on the other hand...

Patient: Doctor, that isn't funny!

Doctor: Oh, excuse me, sonny! I read somewhere that humor is therapeutic.

Patient: In a medical journal?

Doctor: I think it was in ***Reader's Digest.***

Patient: I think this is a case of the blind leading the blind!

Doctor: Maybe so, sonny, but you got to admit: the price is right.

Patient: Actually, I'm starting to wonder.

Doctor: You lost me, sonny.

Patient: Not yet, Doctor, but I'm working on it. What I meant was: I'm starting to realize that I don't just need treatment, **I need sound professional advice.** Even if I have to pay for it.

Doctor: You know, sonny, I could use some professional advice myself.

Patient: Why?

Doctor: Well, I've been getting these pains in my chest.

Patient: You, Doctor? Well, what are you taking for it?

Doctor: Reese's Pieces.

Patient: Reese's Pieces?

Doctor: Yes. They always made E.T. feel better, so...

Patient: Are they working?

Doctor: Well, no...but since I prescribed them for myself...

Patient: Yes, I know: at least you didn't pay a load. Doc, I think you better get your hat, and let's both go see a full-service cardiologist.

Doctor: I don't know, sonny. I read a detailed study that said you're **never** supposed to do that.

Patient: Was that in a medical journal?

Doctor: No, it was in the same issue of ***Reader's Digest.*** It's the only one I own.

Patient: But doctors don't write ***Reader's Digest.***

Doctor: No, journalists do; you think that's part of the problem?

Patient: I don't know; it's not my field. Are you coming, Doc?

Doctor: [*Sadly, putting on his battered porkpie hat.*] I guess so.

[*Doctor and patient exit stage right, past a desk in the outer office, where the nurse is intently reading something.*]

Doctor: My patient and I are going out for the afternoon.

Nurse: Fine, Doctor; where shall I forward your calls?

Doctor: I'd rather not say. Say, is that ***Reader's Digest*** you've got there?

Nurse: Why no, Doctor, it's the ***Journal of the American Medical Association***. I'm studying to be a neurosurgeon.

Doctor: Not a no-load neurosurgeon?

Nurse: Never!

Doctor: [*Forlornly, to patient*] A very bright woman. Smarter than I, in some ways. She'll go far…

[*Doctor and patient exit. The skeleton falls over on its face. The doctor's diploma falls off the wall. The curtain falls.*]

...And One Final Word

Millbrook School in Millbrook, NY, is perhaps the finest small college preparatory school in America today. It is also, I believe, the future of secondary education. And, when you've toured its Trevor Teaching Zoo, or wandered among the treetops on its Forest Canopy Walkway, you know you've been to a genuinely magical place.

A portion of the proceeds from the sale of every copy of *The Excellent Investment Advisor* will be donated to Millbrook. And, if you'd like to help me help the school, it would be my pleasure to send you a personalized, autographed bookplate for your copy of this book. Just write a check for a minimum of $20 [*more if you like; it's tax-deductible*] to MILLBROOK SCHOOL, and send it to me at

The Excellent Investment Advisor
P.O. Box 1415
Southold, N.Y. 11971